THE NEW SECOND GENERATION

ALEJANDRO PORTES

EDITOR

Russell Sage Foundation • New York

The Russell Sage Foundation

The Russell Sage Foundation, one of the oldest of America's general purpose foundations, was established in 1907 by Mrs. Margaret Olivia Sage for ``the improvement of social and living conditions in the United States.'' The Foundation seeks to fulfill this mandate by fostering the development and dissemination of knowledge about the country's political, social, and economic problems. While the Foundation endeavors to assure the accuracy and objectivity of each book it publishes, the conclusions and interpretations in Russell Sage Foundation publications are those of the authors and not of the Foundation, its Trustees, or its staff. Publication by Russell Sage, therefore, does not imply Foundation endorsement.

Library of Congress Cataloging-in-Publication Data
The new second generation / Alejandro Portes, editor.
    p. cm.
    Includes bibliographical references and index.
    ISBN 0-87154-683-3 (hb). — ISBN 0-87154-684-1 (pb).
    1. Children of immigrants—United States—Social conditions. 2. Immigrants— United States—Social conditions. 3. Social adjustment—United States. 4. United States—Emigration and immigration. 5. Ethnicity—United States.   I. Portes, Alejandro, 1944-
    E184.A1N39 1996
    305.23'0973—dc20   95-30639
                                                                                                        CIP

The paper used in this publication meets the minimum requirements of American National Standard for Information Sciences—Permanence of Paper for Printed Library Materials. ANSI Z39.48-1992.

RUSSELL SAGE FOUNDATION
112 East 64th Street, New York, New York 10021

10 9 8 7 6 5 4 3

THE NEW SECOND GENERATION

Contents

Contributors

Carl L. Bankston III is Assistant Professor in the Department of Sociology and Anthropology at the University of Southwestern Louisiana.

Yoshimi Chitose is a doctoral student in the Department of Agricultural Economics and Rural Sociology at Pennsylvania State University.

Patricia Fernández Kelly is Associate Professor and Research Scientist at the Institute for Policy Studies at Johns Hopkins University.

Charles Hirschman is Professor and Chair of the Department of Sociology at the University of Washington in Seattle.

Leif Jensen is Associate Professor in the Department of Agricultural Economics and Rural Sociology at Pennsylvania State University.

Lisandro Perez is Associate Professor and Director of the Cuban Research Institute at Florida International University.

Alejandro Portes is the John Dewey Professor and Chair of the Department of Sociology at Johns Hopkins University.

Rubén G. Rumbaut is Professor in the Department of Sociology at Michigan State University.

Richard Schauffler is a doctoral student in the Department of Sociology at Johns Hopkins University.

Mary C. Waters is Professor in the Department of Sociology at Harvard University.

Min Zhou is Assistant Professor in the Department of Sociology at the University of California in Los Angeles.

Preface

THE CHAPTERS in this book were originally published in a special volume of the *International Migration Review* (volume 28, winter 1994). That volume was dedicated to the adaptation process of the children of America's most recent waves of immigrants, the second generation. The papers were not the result of a joint project, but rather an attempt to bring together early empirical results on an emerging topic of research. For that reason, the data presented by the contributors are disparate, ranging from census files to small surveys in specific cities. The first stage of a project entitled "Children of Immigrants: The Adaptation Process of the Second Generation," conducted in South Florida and Southern California in 1992–93, provided empirical material for four of the chapters. The various data sources and their bearing on the general topic are discussed in the Introduction.

Since publication of the journal volume, the issue of second-generation adaptation has become, if anything, more important for theoretical and policy reasons. In the past, the specific experiences of these children were submerged under the nation's governing panethnic categories: non-Hispanic whites, blacks, Asians, and Hispanics. Yet, this taxonomy does not distinguish immigrants from the native born. In particular, it obscures differences between three distinct categories: immigrant children, children of immigrants, and native-born children of native parentage.

The first category includes youth who are born abroad and come to the United States after early infancy to be raised here. The second includes native-born children of immigrant parents and children born abroad who came at a very early age (sometimes called the 1.5 generation). The third, native-born children of native parentage, represents the vast majority of both the total and adolescent populations. It is not the case, however, that the first two categories are composed exclusively of "minorities" and the third of "nonminorities" (non-Hispanic whites). Instead, all these ethnic categories, on which official and institutional data are currently reported, include cross-sections of immigrant children, children of immigrants, and children born of native parents in unknown proportions. This adds to the confusion about how to study these children and contributes to the frequency with which spurious findings arise from such data.

By focusing on the second generation only (children of immigrants), the studies in this collection seek to overcome these taxonomical blinders and call attention to a clearly defined segment of the American adolescent population whose experiences are both important and problematic. Second-generation children are arguably the fastest growing segment of their age cohort. Moreover, their process of maturation in school and at home cannot be extrapolated from the experiences of their native peers, or from those of children of earlier European immigrants.

Growing up bicultural and bilingual is a trying process, even under the best of circumstances. Doing so in today's America is a still greater challenge. For reasons explained in the coming chapters, serious obstacles now imperil the promise long held out to our country's newcomers: successful adaptation will be rewarded with a middle-class American life. The relative success of different immigrant communities in confronting these challenges and the effects of alternative outcomes on these groups represent a guiding concern in this research. The following studies illustrate and extend this analytic concern.

ALEJANDRO PORTES

1

Introduction: Immigration and Its Aftermath

ALEJANDRO PORTES

THE CHAPTERS in this volume offer the reader a wealth of information on a topic of increasing visibility in the field of immigration. For a variety of reasons, the growth and adaptation of the second generation have not been subjects of great concern for researchers in this field during the recent past. Reasons include the relative youth of the "new" second generation spawned by post-1965 immigration to the United States and the difficulties of studying it on the basis of census and other official data. Scholarly attention in this field has remained focused on adult immigrants, who are more visible and whose progress through the labor market and through the immigration bureaucracy can be traced more easily.

Social scientists whose professional concern is with children, such as sociologists of education, have noted the surge of foreign-origin and, for the most part, nonwhite students in the nation's schools. However, the manner in which data on this new phenomenon have been packaged has hopelessly obscured their character and implications. School records and scholarly surveys most frequently use a classificatory scheme for students based on the panethnic labels Hispanic, Asian, non-Hispanic, black, and white. Such data are nearly useless for the study of the second generation because they mix children of native and foreign parentage as well as those from the most diverse nationalities. The ethnic category Hispanic, for example, combines children whose ancestors were living in the country at the time of the Civil War with those who arrived recently as unauthorized aliens. The category Asian is still more egregious because the children grouped under it

1

do not even share a parental language (Portes and Truelove, 1987; Massey, 1993).

The dearth of accessible census data and the compressing of second-generation youth into a classificatory scheme that obliterates their history have obscured a major phenomenon in the recent evolution of American society. This result is unfortunate because the adaptation of the second generation will be decisive in establishing the long-term outlook for contemporary immigration. It is indeed among the second generation, not the first, where such issues as the continuing dominance of English, the growth of a welfare-dependent population, the resilience of culturally distinct urban enclaves, and the decline or growth of ethnic intermarriages will be decided permanently. For example, the much-debated issue of the loss of English hegemony in certain areas heavily affected by immigration will not be decided by first-generation immigrants but by their descendants. Loyalty to their home language among the foreign born is a time-honored and normal pattern; in the past the key linguistic shift has consistently taken place among their U.S.-born offspring. Whether this is occurring today represents the key question in the future linguistic evolution of these areas (Lieberson, Dalto, and Johnston, 1975; see also chapter 2).

Similarly, the issue of whether immigrants from the West Indies and Africa will succeed in maintaining independent cultural identities or whether they simply will augment the American black population will not be decided by the first generation. As Mary Waters makes clear in chapter 8, most immigrants strive to maintain social distance and a separate identity from native-born blacks. The self-image of second-generation Haitians, Jamaicans, Nigerians, and other African and West Indian–origin youth are another matter and the outcome is far less certain.

Between 1980 and 1990, immigration contributed a full 39 percent of the population growth of the country (Rumbaut, 1994). Rising immigration and the relatively high levels of fertility of many immigrant groups will push the second generation past its former peak of 28 million, reached by the children of earlier European immigrants in the 1940s (Passel and Edmonston, 1992). The new record, which will be reached sometime during this decade, is already adumbrated in results from Charles Hirschman (chapter 4, tables 4.2 and 4.3) that put the total U.S.-born population of Latin American and Asian origin in 1990 at 16.4 million.[1]

Sheer numbers plus the concentration of the second generation in a few states and cities are sufficient reason to assign significance to its study. More important still is that its adaptation and, hence, its long-term effects on society are anything but clear. Borrowing from the historical record of earlier European immigration, scholars and lay writers have commonly settled on the belief in an orderly sequence of assimilation: The struggles and common poverty of first-generation immigrants will be superseded by the gradual entry of their offspring into mainstream social and economic circles. The loss of "ethnic" linguistic and cultural traits, as well as the disappearance of earlier labor market disadvantages, will be complete, for the most part, by the third generation (Sowell, 1981; Alba, 1985).

As the chapters in this volume make abundantly clear, there are serious reasons to question this comfortable expectation. The second generation is the key to establishing the long-term consequences of immigration, but the course of its adaptation is uncertain at present. The questions of shifts in language and ethnic identities, used above as specific examples of uncertainty, are part of a more general puzzle. This puzzle is whether today's children of immigrants will follow their European predecessors and move steadily into the middle-class mainstream or whether, on the contrary, their ascent will be blocked and they will join children of earlier black and Puerto Rican migrants as part of an expanded multiethnic underclass. As the deteriorating conditions of life in American cities suggest, the question is of more than passing significance for the future of American society.

Human Consequences of Immigration

The answer to that key question is related to the long-term role that immigration has played in the structure of the American economy. The countless literary sagas of immigration portray it as the journey of people who struggle to leave political oppression and destitution behind and who seek, and eventually succeed, in rebuilding their lives on freedom's shores. The saga reflects accurately many individual experiences, but it is only part of the story. While individual motivations are undoubtedly important, a political economy analysis shows that what drives the process is not the dreams and needs of immigrants but the interests and plans of their prospective employers. Although geopolitical and other considerations have played roles in granting to certain foreign groups access to American territory, the fundamental reason for sustained immigration, at least since the post–Civil War period, has been the labor needs of the economy (Rosenblum, 1973; Portes, 1978; Piore, 1979).

Employer associations played a decisive role in recruiting European and Asian labor during the nineteenth century. They organized dependable labor flows from Asia, southeastern Europe, and Mexico at the turn of the century and then succeeded in keeping the immigration door open against nativist opposition until World War I. During the interwar period, growers and corporate interests organized the massive recruitment and resettlement of southern blacks and Puerto Rican migrants to replace a dwindling European labor pool. After World War II, the same interests returned to the recruitment and use of foreign labor, this time through the *bracero* program with Mexico and through legal loopholes that preserved a porous border. During the last decade, rising popular opposition to immigration was answered by a massive legalization program for unauthorized immigrants and by a new set of loopholes to the Immigration "Reform and Control" Act of 1986 that allowed the continuation of the clandestine flow. This last outcome attests to the resilient political power of the same economic groups (Bach, 1978; Barrera, 1980; Sassen, 1988).

The overriding interest underlying an open-door immigration policy has been for an abundant source of labor to fuel growing sectors of the economy and restrain the power of domestic labor. Before World War I, railroad construction, mining, and heavy manufacturing were the growth sectors attracting immigrant workers; today, agriculture and urban personal and business services play a similar role. Although skilled and even professional labor has been at times in short supply and has been recruited abroad, immigration has, for the most part, played the role of increasing the pool of unskilled labor. Today, needed skilled and professional immigrants generally arrive through legal entry provisions of the 1990 immigration law, while the bulk of needed unskilled labor arrives through clandestine channels and legal loopholes (Portes and Rumbaut, 1990: chaps. 1–2; Smith, 1992; Zhou, 1992; Margolis, 1994).

Although a political economy analysis clarifies the fundamental underpinnings of the immigration open door, it commonly neglects an equally important fact, namely, that employers hire immigrant workers but assume no responsibility for their offspring. Put differently, the benefits flowing from the abundance and low cost of immigrant labor are privatized by the individuals and firms that hire them, but the potential costs associated with the growth and maturation of the second generation are shifted onto third parties. For example, today's growers and urban service firms employ unskilled Third World workers, many of them unauthorized. The economic benefits of this strategy are self-evident. On the other hand, the employers do not assume the costs related to the potential maladjustment of children of immigrants growing up under such conditions of disadvantage. They are shifted instead onto the immigrant family and, if necessary, onto society at large (Gans, 1992).

In broad strokes, results of this long-term policy can be summarized as follows: The nation takes care of its immediate labor needs, as defined by powerful economic interests, and lets the future take care of itself. A fortunate combination of circumstances, including an expanding economy, a scarcity of labor due to a new global conflict, and other factors, allowed the European second generation to move steadily up in the American economic and social ladders. Their generally successful experience was subsequently captured in academic theories, including the concept of a linear process of assimilation. Children of southern black and Puerto Rican migrants arriving later in the century were less fortunate. A different set of circumstances, including widespread racial discrimination and a changing economy, blocked the mobility of these migrants' children and confined many to the same inferior jobs held by their parents. The perpetuation of these negative conditions eventually led to an interrelated set of urban pathologies. These experiences gave rise to different academic theories, including the concepts of a culture of poverty and the urban underclass (Moynihan, 1969; Wilson, 1987; Gans, 1990; Jencks, 1992).

Today's second generation finds itself somewhere between these extremes. Its members confront the same reduced circumstances in the American labor market affecting domestic minorities. Most second-generation youth are also nonwhite and hence subject to the same discrimination endured by their predecessors (Jensen, 1990; Passel and Edmonston, 1992). On the other hand, immigrant families and communities commonly possess material and moral resources that confer advantages on their young as they seek avenues for successful adaptation. In the new "hourglass" economy shaped by the industrial restructuring of the American labor market, the path toward economic success consists of traversing the narrowing "middle" between dead-end menial jobs at the bottom and the growing pool of managerial and professional occupations requiring advanced degrees at the top (Waldinger, 1992; see also chapter 9).

For mostly nonwhite and poor second-generation youth, the ability to make this journey depends decisively on the resources that their families and ethnic communities can bring to bear. At this specific juncture, the analysis of second-generation adaptation must shift theoretical gears. If political economy clarifies the broad structural framework in which the adaptation process occurs, other less abstract conceptual approaches are necessary to understand how the process unfolds in everyday reality. For this purpose, notions borrowed from economic anthropology and economic sociology are especially relevant. Not surprisingly, the chapters in this volume that focus on questions of ethnic identity, educational attainment, and career prospects make liberal use of concepts such as embeddedness, social networks, and social capital borrowed from the "new" economic sociology (Granovetter, 1985; see also chapter 3).

Data Sources and Results

A profound gap thus exists between the strategic importance of the immigrant second generation and current knowledge about its condition. As seen previously, this is due largely to the dearth of official sources dealing specifically with the topic and to the obscuring of this population into broad statistical categories. Not surprisingly, the information on which the following chapters are based come mostly from original sources.

Five different data sets are brought to address our general topic. Chapter 4 by Charles Hirschman and chapter 5 by Leif Jensen and Yoshimi Chitose scrutinize census sources to find out what they can tell us about the second generation. Jensen and Chitose extract information from the 1990 Census Public Use Microdata Sample to identify households with children of foreign-born parents; Hirschman uses published census tabulations on the foreign born and on the Hispanic and Asian populations to arrive at some preliminary estimates of children of immigrants in 1990. He also uses special tabulations to examine the influence of years of U.S. residence on second-generation school attendance and premarital fertility.

In chapter 8, Mary Waters bases her analysis of second-generation ethnic identities on an intensive observational study and survey of West Indian black immigrants in New York City. In chapter 9, Min Zhou and Carl Bankston draw on their survey of Vietnamese teenagers in New Orleans as well as on their interviews with informants from that immigrant community to examine the self-images and educational attainment of Vietnamese American youth.

Patricia Fernández Kelly and Richard Schauffler, in chapter 3, draw on another original data source based on intensive interviews with 120 immigrant parents to examine similar processes among children of Cuban, Haitian, and Nicaraguan origin in Miami and among Mexican- and Vietnamese-origin youth in San Diego. This parental sample is actually a subset of a much larger survey of second-generation high school students in south Florida and southern California. The survey interviewed a total of 5,266 eighth and ninth graders in forty-two schools in the metropolitan areas of Miami/Fort Lauderdale and San Diego in 1992. Respondents came from seventy-seven different foreign nationalities, although the samples' distribution reflect the dominance of certain immigrant groups in each region. Chapter 6 by Lisandro

Pérez and Chapter 2 by myself and Richard Schauffler make use of the South Florida segment of this survey. Chapter 7 by Rubén Rumbaut analyzes ethnic identities, social relationships, and indicators of psychological well-being in the full sample.

Together these studies contribute to the present knowledge on this subject. They offer broad overviews of the geographical distribution and demographic characteristics of the new second generation and detailed descriptions of the dilemmas that their members face and the social and psychological challenges that they must overcome. In substantive terms, the chapters divide fairly evenly between analyses of sociodemographic traits, linguistic knowledge and preferences, self-identity and self-esteem, and the role of immigrant communities in school performance and career plans.

Still, a great deal remains to be done. The substantive scope of this collection omits a number of significant topics. None of the data sets, for example, including those based on the census, accurately describes the full second-generation universe. The survey of children of immigrants in California and Florida, albeit the largest study of the topic to date, is limited to three metropolitan areas and to a subset of immigrant nationalities. Despite these and other limitations, the combined results of the studies presented in this volume forcefully convey two conclusions: first, the apparent absence of a modal social and economic adaptation among today's second generation; and second, the likelihood that, in some instances at least, the process may lead to downward assimilation. Both conclusions offer a strong stimulus for continuing research and analysis on the topic.

Notes

1. As an estimate of the second generation, this figure is inflated by the presence of Puerto Ricans (2.6 million), who are U.S. citizens of native parentage, Spaniards (an unknown number), and, primarily, third- and higher-generation Mexican Americans and other nationalities. The figure is deflated by the exclusion of the "1.5 generation," that is, foreign-born persons who arrived in the United States as children and whose socialization experience is akin to that of the native born of foreign parentage. Since there is no way to correct for these biases on the basis of the available data, the figure represents a very rough approximation.

2

Language and the Second Generation: Bilingualism Yesterday and Today

ALEJANDRO PORTES AND RICHARD SCHAUFFLER

Where linguistic unity has broken down, our energies and resources flow into tensions, hostilities, prejudices and resentments. These develop and persist. Within a few years, if the breakdown persists, there will be no retreat. It becomes irrevocable, irreversible. Society as we know it can fade into noisy babel and then chaos.—U.S. English policy statement

THIS CHAPTER examines the process of linguistic adaptation and the extent and determinants of bilingualism among children of immigrants, the new second generation spawned by accelerated immigration of the past decade. The setting of the study is South Florida, one of the areas most heavily affected by recent immigration. We review the findings in the context of the history of linguistic conflict and language assimilation that have accompanied U.S.-bound migration over the life of the nation.

The data on which this chapter is based were collected by the project "Children of Immigrants: The Adaptation Process of the Second Generation," supported by the Andrew W. Mellon Foundation, the National Science Foundation (grant no. SES-9022555), the Spencer Foundation, and the Russell Sage Foundation. The chapter was written while the senior author was in residence as a fellow of the Russell Sage Foundation, whose support is gratefully acknowledged. The authors are exclusively responsible for the contents.

The present wave of immigration was triggered by the 1965 Immigration Act as well as by subsequent changes in American asylum and refugee policies. The overall direction of the new policies was toward greater universalism, eliminating previous discriminatory racial barriers and opening the doors of the country on the basis of uniform criteria. Since 1965, occupational skills, family reunification, and fear of political persecution have been the guiding criteria of U.S. immigration policy. As is well known, the result has been a rapid increase in immigration and an equally rapid shift in its origins from Europe to the Third World. Most of today's children of immigrants thus have parents who came from Latin America and Asia, and about half are phenotypically nonwhite (Portes and Zhou, 1993).[1]

The volume of the new immigration has given rise to sizable language enclaves in several U.S. cities and parallel nativistic concerns about these enclaves' resilience. In particular, the growing use of Spanish by Latin American immigrants has triggered gloomy assessments of the future prospects of linguistic unity, as illustrated by the opening quote. Clearly, the decisive issue that would validate or refute the nativists' fears is language use and preferences among the second generation. In the past, almost every first generation's loyalty to their ancestral language has given way to an overwhelming preference for English among their children (Lieberson, Dalto, and Johnston, 1975). The extent to which this process will repeat itself today represents a central question, from both sociological and policy perspectives. South Florida is one of the areas most directly affected by contemporary immigration and the growing use of Spanish. Our sample of second-generation students from this region will allow us to address the current scholarly and public debate about the future of language in America.

Historical Overview

Language Assimilation in Perspective

The current controversy over language is best understood in the context of a cyclical trend in the history of the United States since colonial days. Descendants of earlier immigrants who had "dropped the hyphen" and considered themselves plain Americans often have looked upon later arrivals as the source of potential cultural disintegration. This was true even before the Revolutionary War. Benjamin Franklin complained as early as 1751 that German immigrants in Pennsylvania "will shortly be so numerous as to Germanize us instead of our Anglifying them, and will never adopt our Language or Customs, any more than they can acquire our complexion" (Franklin [1751], 1959:

234). The notion of "one nation, one language" was often idealized as a state of linguistic perfection to which the nation should return. This idea was discussed at length by philosophers of the seventeenth and eighteenth centuries, including President John Adams, who contended that "language influences not only the form of government, but the temper, sentiments, and manners of the people" (Adams [1780], 1856: 249–251).

During the colonial and early independence period, the notion that the country and its citizens were defined by a common language was justified on two grounds. First, along with incipient American nationalism came the idea that American English both reflected and constituted the democratic and rational nature of the country. Second, the acquisition and use of English were seen as the litmus test of citizenship. Lacking a common culture or common history, the use of English became the essential part of "real" Americanism (Baron, 1990). The two rationales were related insofar as people perceived that the ability to think logically, and therefore secure democracy, was made possible only by fluency in English.

The perceived necessity for "Good English" has taken many forms throughout American history. In 1902, for example, New Mexico's statehood was delayed until, in the words of one prominent politician of the time, "the migration of English-speaking people who have been citizens of other States does its modifying work with the Mexican element" (Baron, 1990: 8). Nebraska banned teaching any foreign language to students below the ninth grade in 1919 and organized formal "Good English" campaigns from 1918 to the early 1920s. At the time, language loyalty oaths were commonly extracted from schoolchildren (Marckwardt, 1980; Dillard, 1985).

In this and other ways, in schools and public life, monolingualism was linked to the idea of democracy, national unity, and allegiance to the country. Although many parents of upper- and middle-class backgrounds encouraged their children to learn Latin, French, or German, bilingualism on the part of recent immigrants was frowned upon. As today, that attitude was prompted by the existence of large ethnic communities that lay beyond the pale of the English-speaking population, out of sight but never out of mind.

Shifting Implications of Bilingualism

During the early twentieth century, opposition to bilingualism derived strength from the then-dominant scientific wisdom. Academic studies in the fields of education and psychology argued that bilingualism created failure, mental confusion, and damaged the psychological well-being of immigrant children. Two schools of thought existed at the time: one arguing that lower intelligence caused children to fail at acquiring English and another arguing the opposite causation. The first school (low intelligence: low English) based its conclusions on beliefs about genetic differences between races, arguing that heredity limited the ability of immigrants to learn. The second school (low English: low intelligence) based its conclusions on beliefs about environmental factors, in particular the use of a foreign language at home. This school imputed intellectual failure to the "linguistic confusion" of children exposed to two languages.

It was not until 1962 that these views were convincingly disproved by a methodologically sound study of the effects of bilingualism on cognitive ability. French- and English-speaking children in Canada were studied by Peal and Lambert (1962), who demonstrated that, if social class was taken into account, true bilingualism was associated with higher scores on a variety of intelligence tests (see also Lambert and Tucker, 1972; Cummins, 1981). True bilinguals, defined as those who could communicate competently in two languages, were shown to enjoy a greater degree of cognitive flexibility and an enhanced ability to deal with abstract concepts than their monolingual peers. Instead of creating "confusion," having two symbols for each object enhanced understanding.

Subsequent studies have generally supported the findings of Peal and Lambert's pioneer study. An analysis of a national sample of high school students in the United States, for example, found a positive correlation between academic achievement and bilingualism among Hispanic youth (Fernandez and Nielsen, 1986). More recently, a study of San Diego high school students also showed significant differences in academic performance between true bilinguals and monolinguals, as well as between true bilinguals (defined by the local school system as Fluent English Proficient) and semibilinguals (defined as Limited English Proficient). Again, true bilingualism was shown to have a positive effect on scholastic achievement (Rumbaut and Ima, 1988).

Despite accumulating factual evidence on the advantages of bilingualism, the United States is unique in the rate at which other languages have been abandoned in favor of English. Lieberson, Dalto, and Johnston (1975) provide evidence showing that in no other country have foreign languages been extinguished with such speed. In the past, the typical pattern has been for the first generation to learn enough English to survive economically; the second generation continued to speak the parental tongue at home but English in school, at work, and in public life; by the third generation, the home language shifted to English, which effectively became the mother tongue for subsequent generations.

This pattern has held true for all immigrant groups in the past with the exception of some isolated minorities. As in previous periods of high immigration, nativist groups fear that the pattern is about to be abandoned. Our analysis will address this issue. However, growing research about the cognitive effects of bilingualism indicates that the obverse of that question also should be examined. That is, to the extent that knowledge of two languages has positive effects, what determinants are important in the preservation of foreign languages? We explore both angles—English fluency and bilingualism—in the following sections.

Theory

Possible outcomes of the clash of languages confronted by second-generation youths are fairly clear. They can be arranged in a continuum ranging from full language assimilation (English monolingualism), to fluent bilingualism, to full language retention (monolingualism in the parental language). Recent theoretical developments in the sociology of immigration can be brought to bear on the analysis of these outcomes insofar as they emphasize the significance of social class and social context in the adaptation of immigrant groups. Clearly, newcomers from more advantaged educational and occupational backgrounds tend to do better, but often the utilization of individual resources depends on the social context that receives them. Hence, immigrants who face unfavorable governmental or societal forces may find their human capital seriously devalued, while those in the opposite situation may put their individual resources to full use. In addition, those who arrive into large and economically diversified coethnic communities may advance rapidly through use of the social capital that community networks make available (Portes and Sensenbrenner, 1993; Massey, Goldring, and Durand, 1994).

These general notions translate into certain expectations concerning the linguistic adaptation of second-generation youths. Children growing up in sociocultural contexts where the native English-speaking majority is dominant or where immigrants from other linguistic backgrounds are most numerous will lose their home language faster and convert to English monolingualism more quickly. Conversely, those raised in contexts where a large conational concentration exists will have greater probability of parental language preservation. In such instances, there will be a clear economic incentive to retain proficiency in that language, along with greater facilities for learning and practicing it within the community. The predicted outcome will be widespread bilingualism. Parental socioeconomic background will have contradictory effects on bilingualism because, while educated and wealthier parents may wish to transmit their language, they also will make available more opportunities for their children to enter the cultural mainstream. The prediction, in this case, is of a positive effect of family socioeconomic status on English proficiency along with an insignificant effect on parental language retention.

Finally, the passage of time will lead inexorably toward greater English proficiency and English preference and gradual abandonment of the immigrants' tongues. In this case, we draw on the American historical record to anticipate that, regardless of the size and economic power of the coethnic community, the trend over time will be away from bilingualism. These arguments can be summarized in the following three hypotheses:

1. Language assimilation (English monolingualism) among the second generation will vary directly with demographic dispersion of the immigrant group and with length of U.S. residence.

2. Bilingualism will vary directly with demographic concentration and economic diversification of the immigrant community and inversely with length of U.S. residence.

3. Higher parental status will lead toward greater English proficiency, but not toward greater bilingualism because of its contradictory effects on children's cultural adaptation.

Setting and Method

The site of our study, South Florida, has been so transformed by recent immigration that several commentators actually have placed it as culturally closer to Latin America and the Caribbean than to the rest of the nation (Rieff, 1987). Miami, in particular, is home to more foreign-born residents on a proportional basis than any other American city. Cuban exiles have built a large and diverse ethnic community, which also serves as a cultural resource for other Latin American immigrants. Haitians have sought to do the same in Little Haiti, a neighborhood that lies directly adjacent to Liberty City, Miami's main African American area. Many native-born whites have reacted to the immigrant influx and the emergence of the Cuban enclave by leaving the city or by militantly supporting the English-only movement. The result has been a debate over language more acrimonious than in other American cities (Portes and Stepick, 1993).

In 1973, county commissioners voted to declare Dade County officially bilingual. Seven years later, however, a grassroots-led referendum repealed that ordinance and replaced it with a new one stipulating that public funds could not be used to teach languages other than English or "promote a culture other than the culture of the United States" (Boswell and Curtis, 1984: 121). In early 1993, however, the newly elected Dade County Commission, where Cuban Americans now composed a plurality, rescinded the antibilingual ordinance mandating that public notices and brochures be printed in Spanish and, in certain cases, French Creole, as well as in English. The decision triggered an immediate spate of lawsuits by opponents who argued that the county could not countermand the English-only amendment to the state constitution, passed two years earlier (Stewart, 1993).

There is little doubt that foreign languages, particularly Spanish, are widely spoken by first-generation exiles and immigrants in South Florida. This pattern parallels that followed by large immigrant groups in the past. Italian, Polish, and Jewish communities created by turn-of-the-century immigration also retained their home languages for a long time (Glazer, 1954). The central theoretical and policy question, however, is the language shift in the second generation and the effects of time, differential levels of ethnic clustering, and parental status on that shift. It is possible, as some nativists argue, that the extraordinary concentration of immigrants in this area is changing the historical patterns and creating instead a permanent linguistic enclave where Spanish is the predominant language. Alternatively, South Florida may simply be in the early stages of absorbing a large foreign influx that inevitably will follow the time-honored pattern.

We examine this question on the basis of data from a survey of 2,843 eighth- and ninth-grade students in Miami (Dade County) and adjacent Fort Lauderdale (Broward County) schools. Inclusion of schools in Fort Lauderdale was dictated by the need to compare highly clustered immigrant communities in Miami with a nearby area where immigrants and their children are far more dispersed among the native population. The sample included children from the most diverse national origins, although, reflecting the composition of the immigrant population to the area, the largest contingents come from Cuba, Nicaragua, other Latin American countries, Haiti, and the West Indies. The survey defined "second generation" as either youths born in the United States with at least one foreign-born parent or youths who were born abroad but had lived in the United States for at least five years. The sample is evenly divided between boys and girls, and the average age is 14.8 years. The sampling design used for the survey included both inner-city and suburban schools as well as targeted schools where children of particular immigrant groups were known to concentrate and those where children of diverse immigrant groups were dispersed among a majority native-born population.

The questionnaire included an extensive array of items on family and individual characteristics such as the child's age, sex, national origin, place of residence, length of residence in the United States, education of the father and the mother, occupation of the father and the mother, home ownership, and class self-identification. We explore how these characteristics affect the children's proficiency in English, their knowledge of the parental language, and their overall linguistic preference. The measure of English proficiency is constructed from the students' reported ability to speak, understand, read, and write English. Previous studies have indicated that self-reports of language ability, unlike other individual characteristics, are both reliable and valid (Fishman, 1969; Fishman and Terry, 1969). Students rate their English-language ability using four categories (Not at All, Not Well, Well, and Very Well), which were converted into an overall proficiency score. Knowledge of the parental language is measured with the same four self-reported indicators, coded identically. Other related questions asked about retention of the parental language and language preferences. Language preference is tapped with an attitudinal question asking which language the child mostly prefers to speak.

With a sample size this large, almost every relationship turns out to be statistically significant. To discriminate between substantive and trivial relationships, we use a coefficient of strength of association, Cramer's V^2, selected because of its fixed range between 0 and 1. Only associations where V^2 is greater than .12 (significant at the .001 level) will be considered of empirical import. Multivariate analyses involving determinants and consequences of language proficiency employ both least squares and maximum-likelihood methods, described in the following sections.

Results

Bivariate Relationships

The first question of interest is the extent to which today's children of immigrants become proficient in English. On this point, the evidence is unmistakable. For the sample as a whole, 73 percent report that they are able to speak, understand, read, and write English "very well" and an additional 26 percent "well." This leaves the sum total of those knowing little or no English at just 1 percent. Table 2.1 presents cross-tabulations of English proficiency with ten variables describing individual background. Only age, national origin, and length of U.S. residence are significantly related to English proficiency. It is important to note that such differences exist only between the "well" and "very well" categories, signaling relatively minor variations in English

Table 2.1 Language Knowledge and Preferences Among Second-Generation Youth in South Florida, 1992

| Characteristic | English Proficiency | | | | Foreign Language Proficiency | | | | Language Preference "I generally prefer to speak . . ." | | | Totals[b] |
	Not at All/ Not Well (%)	Well (%)	Very Well (%)	V²ᵃ	Not at All/ Not Well (%)	Well (%)	Very Well (%)	V²ᵃ	English (%)	Other Language (%)	V²ᵃ	(N)
Sex				0.066 (0.010)				0.064 (0.010)			0.022 (0.240)	
Male	1.3	28.8	69.9		36.0	36.9	27.1		81.1	18.9		1,367
Female	1.3	23.1	75.6		33.4	33.6	33.0		79.4	20.6		1,476
Age				0.120 (0.001)				0.038 (0.250)			0.087 (0.001)	
13 or younger	0.7	19.5	79.8		34.2	37.9	27.9		86.1	13.9		549
14	1.2	23.7	75.1		33.0	36.2	3.7		79.9	20.1		1,286
15	0.7	31.1	68.2		36.3	32.5	31.2		78.8	21.2		804
16 or older	5.9	35.8	58.3		39.2	31.9	28.9		72.1	27.9		204
National origin				0.126 (0.001)				0.265 (0.001)			0.132 (0.001)	
Cuban (private school)	1.2	27.3	71.5		11.0	51.2	37.8		93.5	6.5		172
Cuban (public school)	0.6	23.9	75.5		27.5	4.0	32.5		81.0	19.0		991
Nicaraguan	3.1	41.7	55.1		22.1	36.4	41.4		73.9	26.1		321
Other Latin American	1.0	26.6	72.4		27.0	38.2	34.8		74.6	25.4		692
Haitian	4.6	25.7	69.7		67.8	20.4	11.8		85.5	14.5		152
West Indian	0.8	17.9	81.3		63.7	15.6	13.7		83.3	16.7		262
Other nationality	1.2	18.6	80.2		58.1	24.9	17.0		85.5	14.5		253

				η (p)				η (p)			η (p)	N
Length of U.S. residence				0.157 (0.001)				0.120 (0.001)			0.155 (0.001)	
Five to nine years	2.9	4.1	57.0		24.5	32.7	42.7		70.8	29.2		660
10 years or more	0.8	28.3	70.9		35.4	35.2	29.4		77.6	22.4		724
U.S. born	0.8	18.2	81.0		38.9	36.3	24.9		85.8	14.2		1,459
Place of residence				0.063 (0.010)				0.177 (0.001)			0.043 (0.030)	
Miami (Dade County)	1.3	26.9	71.8		31.5	36.9	31.5		80.9	19.1		2,504
Fort Lauderdale (Broward County)	1.5	18.3	80.2		57.5	22.4	20.1		75.5	24.5		339
Father's education				0.061 (0.010)				0.031 (0.300)			0.048 (0.060)	
Not high school graduate	1.7	3.0	68.3		28.9	36.8	32.3		77.6	22.4		634
High school graduate	1.0	25.0	74.0		35.5	35.5	28.9		81.1	18.9		1,010
College graduate	0.7	21.5	77.8		32.9	35.2	31.9		82.6	17.4		767
Mother's education				0.062 (0.001)				0.015 (0.890)			0.066 (0.010)	
Not high school graduate	1.5	3.7	67.8		33.5	35.1	31.4		76.0	24.0		678
High school graduate	1.4	24.3	74.3		34.6	35.7	29.7		82.2	17.8		1,319
College graduate	0.3	22.1	77.6		32.7	36.0	31.3		81.2	18.8		633
Father's occupational Status[c]				0.080 (0.001)				0.057 (0.03)			0.067 (0.020)	
Lower	0.9	30.1	69.0		33.8	35.4	30.8		78.3	21.7		957
Lower middle	0.9	21.6	77.5		36.0	37.3	26.8		82.5	17.5		467
Upper middle	0.7	18.5	80.8		28.3	34.9	36.8		81.4	18.6		421
Higher	0.7	21.1	78.2		34.2	38.8	27.1		85.2	14.8		436

(continued)

Table 2.1 (*continued*)

Mother's occupational Status[c]				0.098 (0.001)				0.071 (0.010)			0.083 (0.001)
Lower	1.1	30.6	68.3		35.0	35.3	29.7		77.3	22.7	836
Lower middle	0.7	26.9	72.4		31.9	38.4	29.7		81.2	18.8	417
Upper middle	0.5	16.5	83.0		44.7	30.7	24.6		84.7	15.3	394
Higher	1.3	19.3	79.5		31.3	38.0	30.8		84.8	15.2	400
Class self-identification				0.079 (0.001)				0.023 (0.550)			0.079 (0.001)
Working class or poor	2.2	33.1	64.7		32.4	35.7	31.9		74.3	25.7	586
Lower middle class	1.5	26.7	71.9		34.1	36.1	29.8		80.3	19.7	963
Upper middle class	0.8	21.9	77.3		36.1	34.2	29.7		82.8	17.2	1,294
Totals	1.3	25.9	72.8		34.6	35.2	30.2		80.2	19.8	2,843

[a]Cramer's V^2 measures the strength of association ranging from 0 to 1. Coefficients above .12 are interpreted as representing at least moderate relationships. Probability levels in parentheses.
[b]Table totals exclude missing data.
[c]SEI occupational prestige scores collapsed as follows: Lowest 40% = "Lower"; next 20% = "Lower middle"; next 20% = "Upper middle"; top 20% = "Higher."

knowledge. In agreement with the first hypothesis, length of U.S. residence has the strongest association with this dependent variable. Slightly over half of foreign-born children with less than ten years in the country report knowing English very well; the figure climbs to more than 80 percent among the native born.

National origin also has a strong correlation with English ability. In this area, the large Cuban-origin group is divided into those attending Latin-oriented bilingual private schools in Miami and those attending public schools. Differences between both groups on English knowledge are minimal. Over 70 percent of each category report knowing English very well. Highest proficiency is associated with children of European and Asian origin, grouped in the "Other nationality" category, and with those of West Indian parentage. The latter result is a natural consequence of the fact that most West Indian parents come from English-speaking countries such as Jamaica, Trinidad, Grenada, and the Bahamas. Second-generation Nicaraguans have the lowest English proficiency. This result is related to the relative recency of Nicaraguan migration. Very few of our Nicaraguan respondents are U.S. born, and most have been in the country less than ten years.

Associations with father's education, mother's education and class self-identification are not significant by our criterion, but they consistently follow the pattern predicted by Hypothesis 3: In every case, the higher the parental position, the better the reported command of English. More counterintuitive is the relationship with age, since older children show less proficiency. This pattern is attributable to the tendency of recently arrived immigrant youths to enter school at grades lower than the respective native-born age cohort. In this sample, older students generally come from non- English-speaking countries and are among the most recent arrivals. Nicaraguan children are heavily represented in this group.

However, the key story in table 2.1 is the overwhelming dominance of English knowledge among children of immigrants and its strong positive association with length of residence in the United States. There is little variance in widespread fluency among the second generation, and whatever variance exists is highly responsive to the passage of time. A very different story emerges when we consider preservation of parental languages. The second panel of table 2.1 presents cross-tabulations of this variable with the same set of individual and parental traits.

The bottom row of the panel indicates that one-third of students in the sample are already English monolinguals. The absolute number of such cases (N = 984) far exceeds the number of children of West Indian and other English-speaking nationalities, indicating a rapid loss of parental language among non–English-speaking groups.[2] Yet a comparable proportion of respondents report knowing parental languages "very well" and, hence, it is worth examining possible determinants of this difference. Among the set of potential predictors in table 2.1, national origin has by far the strongest association with foreign language fluency. There is a clear difference between Latin American nationalities, on the one hand, and Haitian, West Indian, Asian, and European nationalities, on the other. Reported English monolingualism among West Indian–origin students and respondents grouped in the "Other Nationality" category is again a straightforward consequence of many of their parents being English speakers. The same is not the case, however, for Haitian-origin youths whose home language is French or Creole. Almost 70 percent of this group reports little or no knowledge of their parental languages, and only 12 percent declare themselves proficient in either.

The opposite is the case among Latin American groups; foreign language loss affects only about one-fourth of respondents and drops to 11 percent among Cuban students in private schools. Retention of the parental language (Spanish) is in part a consequence of the recency of some migrant flows, such as Nicaraguans. More significantly, however, it reflects the presence of a large and diversified ethnic enclave where Spanish is the language of daily intercourse for all kinds of transactions. Respondents in private bilingual schools are mostly the children of middle-class Cuban exiles who represent the core of this ethnic economy. It is not surprising that they have the lowest propensity to give up Spanish. Combined with the pattern of responses in the first panel of table 2.1, these results indicate that Cuban and other Latin American–origin youth in South Florida are mostly bilingual. These results lend support to Hypotheses 1 and 2 insofar as they predict positive effects of immigrant concentration and a diversified ethnic economy on language preservation.

Because the originally Cuban and now pan-Latin enclave is located in Miami (Dade County), it is possible to predict that the preservation of Spanish will be significantly greater among second-generation youths in this city than in adjacent Fort Lauderdale, where no similar phenomenon exists. This expectation is borne out by the results. Place of residence has the second strongest association with home language retention, with Miami respondents being almost twice as likely to be bilingual (reporting knowing the parental language "well" or "very well") as those living in Fort Lauderdale. The very strong influence of ethnic concentration is counteracted, however, by the passage of time. As shown in the second panel of table 2.1, there is a clear monotonic relationship, so that the longer the child has resided in the United

States, the stronger the tendency toward English monolingualism. Among recent arrivals, 43 percent report full command of a foreign language, a figure that falls to just one-fifth among the native born. This result again supports the first and second hypotheses' prediction of a significant negative effect of time on bilingualism.

Parental education, occupational status, and class self-identification have essentially no association with foreign language fluency. This result supports Hypothesis 3, which attributes it to the contradictory effects of family status on linguistic adaptation. Interviews with some of the immigrant parents of our respondents in Miami indicate that they are consistently in favor of English-language acquisition, but not at the cost of giving up their mother tongue. Those with greater resources are in a better position to implement this bilingual project, but their efforts are frequently neutralized by their children's greater exposure to mainstream culture, which the same parental resources make possible.

Overall, these findings are in close agreement with the theoretical argument outlined previously. Children of relatively isolated immigrants—such as those living in Broward County or Asians and Europeans grouped in the "Other nationality" category—experience a faster language transition toward monolingual English; children of relatively prosperous and highly concentrated immigrants, such as Cubans, are far more likely to retain their parental language. The passage of time significantly increases language proficiency and undermines bilingualism. Education and occupational status of immigrant parents, which reasonably could have been expected to have the opposite effect, fail to do so because of their seemingly contradictory effects on linguistic adaptation.

A final variable of interest is the child's attitude toward speaking English versus speaking the parental or other foreign language, and the evidence on this point is presented in the last panel of table 2.1. Preference for English is overwhelming: 80 percent of the entire sample endorses it. Length of U.S. residence is strongly and positively correlated with English preference, but even among the most recent arrivals, more than 70 percent opt for English over their home languages.

National origin is also associated with language preference, but the trend here differs from those found previously. Children of Haitian and West Indian parents, as well as those grouped in the "Other nationality" category, lean strongly toward English in a fashion congruent with the weak retention of their other languages. Cubans, however, in particular those attending private schools, also have a very strong preference for English. Despite their greater reported knowledge of Spanish, more than 90 percent of Cuban-origin youths prefer communicating in English. This result means that even among youths educated in bilingual schools at the core of an ethnic enclave, linguistic assimilation is proceeding with remarkable speed. Although somewhat lower attachment to English is found among Nicaraguans and other Latin Americans, a probable consequence of their recent arrival in the country, three-fourths of these groups still endorse their new country's language over their native Spanish.

No other predictor has a significant association with language preference, although there is a clear tendency for children of better-educated and higher-status parents to prefer English. Again, however, these differences take place in the context of overwhelming language assimilation. An eloquent indicator of the trend is the absence of significant differences between students in Dade and Broward schools. This finding indicates that whether second-generation children live in an English-only environment or in one where use of Spanish is widespread, their ultimate preference for the language of the land will be the same.

Determinants of Bilingualism

The principal difference observed in our sample pertains to parental language retention rather than English acquisition. In other words, the central difference among immigrant youths is not whether they know and prefer English, but the extent to which they retain some command of their parents' language. As seen previously, past studies have reported benefits of bilingualism in terms of cognitive development and academic achievement.

Because several of the predictors presented above are themselves highly correlated, the preceding bivariate results offer only a preliminary approach to an analysis of determinants of bilingualism. To establish the net effect of each predictor while controlling for the others, we ran multivariate regressions with two different versions of the dependent variable. The first variable is the Foreign Language Proficiency Index, constructed in this case as the logarithm of the sum of responses to the items measuring different aspects of language ability.[3] The effect of this logarithmic transformation is to render unstandardized regression coefficients (when small) interpretable as a proportional increase or decrease in language fluency, excluding other factors. The second is a dichotomous variable where "bilingual" is defined as a respondent who is fully proficient both in English and in a foreign language.[4] This restrictive definition seeks to identify "true" bilinguals, differentiating them from both monolinguals and those with a lesser command of a second language.

Both variables are regressed on the same set of predictors. The first panel of table 2.2 presents results of an ordinary least squares regres-

Table 2.2 Determinants of Foreign Language Proficiency and Fluent Bilingualism, Second-Generation Youth in South Florida

Independent Variable	Foreign Language Proficiency (Logged)				Fluent Bilingualism		
	b	Std. Error	B[a]	p	b	Std. Error	Δp[b]
Intercept	1.600	.216			−1.835	.849	
Age	−.003	.014	−.003	n.s.	−.062	.054	n.s.
Sex[c]	.118	.023	.088	.001	.467	.094	.09
City of residence[d]	−.254	.430	−.108	.001	−.076	.174	n.s.
Father's education	−.007	.010	.014	n.s.	.001	.040	n.s.
Mother's education	−.014	.010	−.029	n.s.	.650	.390	n.s.
Father's occupational status[e]	−.000	.001	−.003	n.s.	−.000	.003	n.s.
Class self-identification	.022	.025	.016	n.s.	.041	.072	n.s.
Length of U.S. residence	−.148	.016	−.180	.001	−.196	.062	−.03
Immigrant nationality							
Cuban (private school)	.741	.072	.219	.001	.966	.167	.21
Cuban (public school)	.532	.045	.381	.001	.526	.096	.11
Nicaraguan	.453	.055	.221	.001	.143	.141	n.s.
Other Latin American	.475	.047	.306	.001	.486	.099	.10
Haitian	.020	.064	.006	n.s.	−.959	.256	−.13
West Indian	−.683	.057	−.272	.001	−.720	.187	−.11
R	.578						
R²	.334						
N	2,840				2,840		
−2 log likelihood					2,837.19		
Model chi square					127.42		
df					13		
p					.001		

NOTE: The abbreviation n.s. stands for not significant.
[a] Standardized regression coefficients. Unlike the unstandardized coefficients (b), Bs are given in a metric free of the measurement scale of the regressed variable. With the present sample size, coefficients with values above ±.08 are significant at the .01 level.
[b] Probability increase or decrease, computed on statistically significant coefficients only at the mean of the dependent variable.
[c] Female = 1; male = 0.
[d] Fort Lauderdale = 1; Miami = 0.
[e] Duncan's socioeconomic index scores.

sion of the logarithmic index. Raw regression coefficients indicate the net proportional gain associated with each predictor. The second panel presents results of a logistic regression of the dichotomous variable of bilingualism on the same array of independent variables. The coefficients represent the net increase or decrease in the logarithm of the odds of being fully bilingual. To clarify the meaning of these results, the column labeled Δp presents the associated probabilities.

Results in the first panel of the table reveal clearly the forces arrayed for and against bilingualism. The most significant factor in the probilingual side is national origin. Latin American nationalities display, without exception, a much greater probability of retaining their parental language. The corresponding coefficients represent the approximate net gain or loss in foreign language proficiency relative to a reference category (not shown) constituted, in this case, by "other nationalities." Cuban-origin students in public schools have, for instance, a significant advantage in foreign language knowledge relative to statistically comparable children of other nationalities. The advantage increases among Cuban American students attending bilingual private schools. Nicaraguan-origin children and those of other Latin nationalities are also strongly inclined to preserve their parents' Spanish. The strong negative effect of West Indian origin is again interpretable as a direct result of their coming from monolingual English households.[5] The factors working against foreign language knowledge are time in the United States and spatial dispersion. Children living outside of Miami are 25 percent less likely to have a foreign language relative to comparable youths residing in Miami's concentrated ethnic communities. The native born are 30 percent less likely when compared with more recent arrivals.[6]

The only unexpected effect in these results is that of gender, which indicates that girls have a significantly greater propensity for retaining the parental language than do boys with similar backgrounds. We may speculate that this result is attributable to the greater seclusion of female youngsters in the home environment, which exposes them to greater contact with parents. That interpretation would represent an extension of the argument about the linguistic effects of ethnic concentration underlying Hypotheses 1 and 2.

Overall, this multivariate analysis shows that the effect of national origin is not a spurious consequence of other individual or family characteristics. There is something unique about specific immigrant communities that leads to different propensities to retain their home language. This influence persists even after controlling for length of U.S. residence and location of household. On the other hand, as predicted, effects of parental education and occupational status are consistently insignificant. These tendencies are buttressed by results in the second panel of table 2.2, which may be interpreted as influences on "true" or fluent bilingualism, defined by speaking both languages very well. Results confirm the overwhelming importance of nationality, which again has the strongest effect on this dependent variable.

In this last analysis, individual nationality effects are not computed relative to the omitted category but relative to the average effect for all categories. Looking at the probability column, we see that Cuban Americans in private schools are 21 percent more likely to be fluent bilinguals, while Haitian and West Indian–origin youths are 13 and 11 percent less likely to be so, relative to the average. The Haitian effect is actually stronger, possibly reflecting less fluency in English. Similarly, Nicaraguan-origin children who, as seen earlier, are significantly more likely to retain their parents' language, are no different from the average in their bilingual skills after we controlled for other factors. As with Haitian Americans, this result reflects their greater difficulties with English. Another major difference in these results is the failure of place of U.S. residence to affect the dependent variable. This finding indicates that while living in a less ethnic environment reduces the likelihood of retaining a foreign language, it does not by itself reduce the probability of becoming fluently bilingual. It is the character of the immigrant community—its internal diversity, history, and cohesiveness—that seems to hold the key to whether second-generation children successfully combine two languages. On the other hand, length of residence in the country again decreases the probability of bilingualism. Jointly, these results lend qualified support to Hypothesis 2.

Finally, there is a resilient gender effect. Among children of similar national origin and length of U.S. residence, girls are significantly more likely than boys to retain their parents' language and to become fully bilingual. This strong and unanticipated effect points to the potential importance of families and differential socialization by sex on the linguistic adaptation of immigrant youth.

Effects of Bilingualism

As seen previously, the past literature on bilingualism and its effects on academic achievement registers considerable debate. While there has been a shift away from predominantly negative views about the effects of parental language retention, the issue has been researched among older immigrant groups or in other countries. So far there is little information about the potential academic effects of bilingualism among the new second generation in the United States. We approach this issue by considering the relationship between fluent bilingualism and four dependent variables. The first two are the individual scores of our respondents on the Stanford mathematics and reading performance tests, drawn from school records. The others are educational and occupational aspirations measured by items in the survey questionnaire.

All variables were measured contemporaneously, and hence it is not possible to speak strictly of effects of bilingualism since the direction of causation is not always clear. However, the key issue in the literature has been the net sign of the relationship, and this can be addressed with the data at hand. We approach the question using a multivariate framework that focuses on the net relationship of each dependent variable with fluent bilingualism, controlling for other predictors, including knowledge of English. Table 2.3 presents the results of this analysis.

The first columns of the table present the relationship between the latest available math scores for each respondent, in Stanford test percentiles, and the independent variables. For this analysis, the English Proficiency Index is allowed to vary through its full untransformed range (1 to 12). Bilingualism is the same dichotomy described previously, with 1 representing fluent bilinguals. Other variables in the equation include age and sex, place and length of U.S. residence, parental education, and paternal occupation measured in Duncan socioeconomic (SEI) prestige scores. Because of its potential significance as a predictor, we also include hours of homework as a control. This is a five-point measure ranging from "less than 1 hour daily" to "five hours or more."

Most predictors have significant effects in the expected direction. In the interest of brevity, we focus exclusively on those of language knowledge. The effect of knowing English is very strong, exceeding four times its standard error. Each point in this index yields a 2.3 percentile gain in math scores. Yet even after controlling for English fluency, bilingualism retains a significant positive relationship. According to these results, bilingual students have a small but significant advantage in math performance over students of similar background who have lost their parental language.

The same is not the case for reading ability. Since the test measures ability to read in English, it is not surprising that the English Proficiency Index has the strongest effect, dwarfing those of other predictors. By itself, this result essentially reflects the validity of the index. It is worth noting, however, that the zero-order relationship between bilingualism and reading performance is positive and significant.

The last two panels of table 2.3 present regressions of educational and occupational aspirations. The first panel is based on responses to

Table 2.3 Determinants of Academic Achievements and Aspirations, Second-Generation Youth in South Florida[a]

Predictors	Math Scores			Reading Scores			Educational Aspirations			Occupational Aspirations		
	b	Std. Error	p	b	Std. Error	p	b	Std. Error	p	b	Std. Error	p
Age	-3.747	.672	.001	-2.000	.583	.001	-.062	.021	.005	-.848	.297	.005
Sex[b]	-.187	1.100	n.s.	-.659	.954	n.s.	.151	.035	.001	3.551	.486	.001
Length of U.S. residence	.174	.701	n.s.	2.077	.608	.001	.021	.022	n.s.	-.317	.309	n.s.
City of residence[c]	-9.809	1.939	.001	3.745	1.681	.030	-.087	.061	n.s.	.295	.856	n.s.
Father's education	1.023	.483	.040	1.308	.419	.002	.066	.015	.001	.334	.213	n.s.
Mother's education	1.914	.478	.001	1.753	.414	.001	.068	.015	.001	.349	.211	n.s.
Father's occupational status	.128	.033	.001	.128	.029	.001	.001	.001	n.s.	.022	.015	n.s.
Hours of homework	2.981	.422	.001	1.799	.366	.001	.129	.013	.001	.891	.186	.001
Knowledge of English	2.341	.468	.001	4.828	.406	.001	.034	.015	.001	.749	.206	.001
Bilingual	3.087	1.347	.030	1.577	1.168	n.s.	.151	.042	.001	1.297	.594	.030
Intercept	60.748	12.824		-23.466	11.124		2.764	.406		51.327	5.660	
R	.345			.414			.373			.252		
R²	.119			.171			.139			.063		
N	2,349			2,349			2,349			2,349		

NOTE: The abbreviation n.s. stands for not significant.
[a]Unstandardized regression coefficients are denoted by b; the associated probability levels are denoted by p.
[b]Female = 1; male = 0.
[c]Fort Lauderdale = 1; Miami = 0.

27

the question: "What is the highest level of education that you realistically expect to get?" Answers were coded on a five-point scale from "less than college" to "graduate degree." The second panel is based on the question, "What occupation do you plan to have as an adult?" Responses were transformed into continuous SEI occupational prestige scores. Results indicate that English knowledge and hours of school homework both have positive and sizable effects on aspirations. Controlling for them, however, we find that bilingualism retains a significant and positive relationship with both dependent variables.

Past research in the sociology of education has found aspirations to be a reliable predictor of subsequent achievement (Sewell and Hauser, 1972; Haller and Portes, 1973; Kerckhoff and Campbell, 1977). To the extent that this continues to be the case, fluent bilingualism is an advantage for immigrant youth since it is associated with both higher current achievement and more ambitious plans for the future. These results lend support to the recent literature that views the ability to speak a foreign language as adding to, not subtracting from, a child's chance for success (Rumbaut and Ima, 1988; Figueroa and Garcia, 1994).

Conclusion

English is alive and well in South Florida. On a proportional basis, Miami is the American city most heavily affected by recent immigration and, hence, the one where the demise of English predicted by nativists should be most evident. Our results indicate that such fears are exaggerated. Children of immigrants not only possess widespread competence in English but also demonstrate an unambiguous preference for it in everyday communication.

Children raised in the core of the Spanish-speaking community in Miami (those attending bilingual private schools) are actually the most enthusiastic in their preference for the language of the land. Moreover, the passage of time strongly influences linguistic assimilation, leading to a steady shift toward English.

These results indicate that, contrary to nativist fears, what is at risk is the preservation of the languages spoken by immigrant parents. Our results support prior research indicating that fluent bilingualism is an intellectual and cultural resource. In this sense, the rapid transition toward monolingualism represents a loss. Even highly educated immigrant parents do not stand much of a chance of transmitting their language to their children. Their hopes of communicating with their children and grandchildren in their native language likely will be disappointed. Our study indicates that only where immigrant groups concentrate physically, thus sustaining an economic and cultural pres-

ence of their own, will their languages survive past the first generation. In the absence of policies promoting bilingualism, even these enclaves will be engulfed, in all probability, in the course of two or three
generations.

Notes

1. This figure is arrived at by adding the percentage of Latin American im-
    migrants estimated to be nonwhite on the basis of the 1990 census figures
    to Asian and black immigrants.

2. The cutoff points for the language categories in this case are slightly
    below those in the first panel of table 2.1, where the strong rightward
    skew of the English Proficiency Index led us to classify into the "well"
    and "very well" categories only those reporting very high proficiency.
    The more balanced Foreign Language Proficiency Index allows less ex-
    treme cutoff points. If the same cutoffs were used, the proportions of
    those reporting themselves as English monolinguals (left-most column of
    the second panel) would increase by 7.4 percent and those declaring full
    command of a foreign language (right-most column) would decline by
    15 percent. The patterns of association with potential predictors in ta-
    ble 2.1 would hold.

3. The untransformed index ranges from 1 to 12 (high).

4. The variable is coded 1 for respondents falling into the "very well" cate-
    gories in the English Proficiency and Foreign Language Proficiency
    panels of table 2.1; all others are coded 0.

5. The nationality coefficients in the first panel of table 2.2 are not inter-
    pretable as the percent change in bilingualism for each group, because
    they are computed relative to a reference category and are excessively
    large. They are appropriately interpreted as indicative of the direction
    and relative strength of the effect associated with each national group.

6. As shown in table 2.1, length of U.S. residence is coded on a three-point
    scale: 1 for foreign-born youths with five to nine years in the United
    States; 2 for foreign-born youths with more than ten years in the United
    States; and 3 for the native born. Each point in this ordinal scale is asso-
    ciated with approximately a 15 percent reduction in knowledge of a
    foreign language.

3

Divided Fates: Immigrant Children and the New Assimilation

M. PATRICIA FERNÁNDEZ KELLY AND RICHARD SCHAUFFLER

ASSIMILATION, perhaps the most enduring theme in the immigration literature, unfolds into descriptive and normative facets. From an empirical standpoint, the concept designates a range of adjustments to receiving environments and points to the manner in which immigrants blend into larger societies. In a normative sense, assimilation is linked to an expectation that foreigners will shed, or at least contain, their native cultures while embracing the mores and language of the host country. Put succinctly, assimilation has always been more than a convenient word to enumerate the ways in which immigrants survive; it has also been a term disclosing hopes about how immigrants "should" behave.

Optimistic accounts of assimilation—captured in the image of the melting pot—can be traced to the early stages of American capitalism, when immigrants were the purveyors of labor for an expanding economy. Tales of weary but resolute arrivals at the shores of opportunity became part of collective self-definitions. Assimilation, conceived as the ideal path toward success, also emerged as the wellspring of national identity. Yet, over the past two decades, economic internationalization has transformed the context in which assimilation takes place. In the Fordist era, workers saw entry-level jobs as the first step toward prosperity. Today, when firms often subcontract services and even product assembly, many of the paths toward socioeconomic improvement have been blocked. Will the new immigrants—mostly from Asia and Latin America—replicate earlier patterns of success or face conditions of arrested progress?

Sketched in the first section is a theoretical framework that assigns priority to interpersonal networks and social capital, a process by which individuals use their membership in a particular group to gain access to valuable resources, including information and jobs. We maintain that the outcomes of assimilation depend on a series of toponomical—that is, socially and physically situated—factors. Immigrants able to draw upon the knowledge of preexisting groups that control desirable economic assets will have a very different experience from those lacking that social nexus.

Collective identity is itself a significant resource in the process of assimilation. Although the fate of immigrants depends on macrostructural changes such as industrial restructuring, it also varies with the recasting of collective self-definitions. The immigrant condition forces individuals to observe themselves even as they are being observed by others. As a consequence, immigrants repeatedly engage in purposeful acts to signify their intended character and the way that character differs from, or converges with, that of other groups. A stigmatized identity can turn assimilation into an injurious transition unless immigrants resort to shared repertoires based on national origin, immigrant status, or religious conviction. Some identities protect immigrants; others weaken them by transforming them into disadvantaged ethnic minorities.

There is an ongoing relationship between migration and ethnicity: Today's ethnics are the immigrants of the past and vice versa; present immigrants are already forging tomorrow's ethnic identities. New arrivals interact empirically and symbolically with their predecessors. At that juncture the African American experience has strategic importance for the study of downward assimilation, a process defined by the incorporation of immigrants into impoverished, generally nonwhite, urban groups whose members display adversarial stances toward mainstream behaviors, including the devaluation of education and diminished expectations.

In defining themselves, immigrants of all nationalities hold the image of the urban underclass as a pivotal referent to delineate their own place in society. Most African Americans were never international migrants in the conventional sense of the word. However, as migrants from the rural South during the first half of the twentieth century, they displayed commonalities in profile and expectations with migrants from other lands. In points of destination, blacks faced barriers that resulted in their arrested socioeconomic advancement. Ironically, current analyses focus not primarily on the migrant past of African Americans but on the distressing behavioral complex surrounding concentrated poverty in the urban ghetto. Yet one way to reframe that phenomenon is to look at it as a product of migration under conditions of extreme hostility over extended periods of time.

In the second section, we pursue the argument through a comparison of five immigrant groups: Mexicans and Vietnamese in southern California; and Nicaraguans, Cubans, and Haitians in South Florida. The data to sustain the comparison is drawn from two complementary sources: a national survey of children of immigrants between the ages of twelve and seventeen conducted in 1992 and a series of ethnographic case studies carried out in the latter part of 1993 and early 1994 with a small subset of 120 families of immigrant children in the original sample. By combining the strengths of quantitative and qualitative analyses, we draw a profile of diverging adaptations, emerging identities, and segmented assimilation.

The concluding section summarizes findings and reconsiders the central questions in light of those findings.

Social Capital and Immigrant Networks

Network analysis became popular in the 1960s and 1970s partly in reaction to the determinism of structural functionalism and the methodological individualism fostered by multivariate statistical inquiries. Studying the relations between real people and organizations reintroduced human agency into sociological discussions. However, what started as ethnographic work in British social anthropology soon devolved into an exercise in mathematical sociology. The warnings of pioneers—such as Boissevain (1974) and Sanjek (1974)—that network analysis might fall prey to technical overelaboration were not heeded. Some current writings on the subject focus on a set of arcane methods, often devoid of sociological meaning, intelligible only to devotees.

Here we take a different approach by grounding our analysis of social networks in the new economic sociology. A central objective of that field is to elucidate the social underpinnings of economic action. The point bears significantly upon immigration research because the character of immigrant assimilation depends largely on social forces leading to differentiated economic outcomes. Indeed, one way to conceptualize immigration is as a phenomenon of labor mobility sustained by interpersonal networks bridging points of origin and points of destination.

Once an immigrant community emerges in a particular location, it achieves a degree of autonomy from market pressures, which serves to reduce the cost and risks of migration and allows for the movement of new immigrants in relatively bounded economic spaces that Sassen (1995) labels transnational labor markets. The concentration of immigrants near global cities depends, to some extent, on the changing nature of labor demand, but also on the existence of networks formed by people who are repeatedly crossing the borders from specific areas of origin to specific areas of arrival. Many of those immigrants appear less interested in blending into the host society than in acquiring the means to maintain status and visibility in their hometowns. International networks, facilitated by the same forces that promote globalization, allow individuals to retain a social proximity to their home communities despite geographical distance.

Perhaps a social network's most important feature is its internal class differentiation, allowing for what Boissevain (1974) calls multiplexity, that is, the presence of miscellaneous links among persons of a dissimilar status, connected in various forms, who move in several fields of social activity. A plurality of linkages and roles facilitates institutional overlap. The integration of groups of various sizes into the larger society takes place via personal connections. Although kinship and camaraderie are the wellspring of trust and reciprocity, even distant contacts with influential members of their network can work to the advantage of individuals. Granovetter's (1990) discussion of strong and weak social ties speaks to that point. A balanced mixture of strong and weak ties reduces isolation and increases the likelihood that persons and groups will gain access to such assets as entrepreneurial know-how, jobs, and information. The opposite is also true: A network's reduced differentiation in terms of class can translate into low levels of multiplexity and, therefore, its separation from vital resources.

The importance of social networks is exemplified by the functioning of the immigrant enclave. In assembling a remarkable business conglomerate in Miami, Cubans relied on social contacts within and outside their group. They avoided discrimination from mainstream financial institutions by obtaining loans to capitalize their firms from banks whose owners and personnel were Latin American and, therefore, Spanish speaking. Beyond their strong feeling of membership in the same community, Cubans benefited from their inclusion in a network characterized by high levels of class heterogeneity; that, in turn, enabled its members to establish multiple connections. The opposite is true about Mexicans and African Americans whose social networks are characterized by low degrees of internal differentiation in terms of class (Portes and Sensenbrenner, 1993).

Those cases also underscore the importance of social capital and its relationship to the quality of resources available. Several major works lead to an understanding of social capital as an incorporeal but vital good accruing to individuals through their membership in particular communities (Coleman, 1988). Social capital is distinct from human capital in that it does not presuppose formal education or skills acquired through organized instruction. Instead, it originates from shared feelings of social belonging, trust, and reciprocity. The concentration of immigrants of various nationalities in particular niches of the labor market occurs via word-of-mouth recommendations. Those, in turn, are made possible by immigrants' membership in social networks whose members vouch for one another.

A dramatic illustration of the workings of social capital is Kasinitz and Rosenberg's (1994) study of business activity in an empowerment zone located in the notoriously destitute ghetto of Red Hook, Brooklyn. Although many businesses in the zone employ multiethnic workforces, including crews of West Indian security guards, they refuse to hire local blacks. Prejudice plays a role in this curious subdivision, but the causes of exclusion and inclusion are more complex. West Indians are joined to the employment structure through personal contacts and endorsements. Thus, although native blacks share the same physical spaces with the businesses, they are socially disconnected and, therefore, bereft of the necessary links to jobs. In that case, the primary reason for ghetto unemployment is not the lack of nearby opportunities but the absence of social networks that provide entry into the labor market.

As important as social capital is the quality of the resources that can be tapped through the network. Interpersonal networks are distinguished as much by their ability to generate a sense of cohesion as by the extent to which they can parlay group membership and mutual assistance into worthwhile jobs and knowledge. What distinguishes the impoverished from the wealthy is not their capacity to deploy social capital—survival of the poor also depends on cooperation—but their poorer access to resources of high quality. Those resources often are embedded in physical locations not available to the impoverished. Similarly, what immigrant children learn about becoming American hinges on what they see around them and the types of contacts they establish. Living quarters, local businesses, places of leisure and entertainment, and, most decisively, schools have a powerful impact on their prospects (Matute-Bianchi, 1986).

To summarize, social networks are complex formations that channel and filter information, confer a sense of identity, allocate resources, and shape behavior. Individual choices depend not only on the availability of material and intangible assets in the society at large but also on the way in which the members of interpersonal networks interpret information and relate to structures of opportunity. Characteristics such as size and composition, location and degree of spatial concentration, and the nature of the transactions among their members invest social networks with distinct profiles. Identities forged within them intercept with others imposed by external groups. In the next section, we compare the experience of several groups swept into the United States by old and new migrations and provide a framework for understanding their options.

Various Meanings of Becoming American

The data for this analysis are drawn from a 1992 survey of 5,266 children of immigrants and from in-depth interviews conducted with a subsample formed by 120 of those children and their parents. For the original survey, eighth- and ninth-grade students in Dade County (Miami), Broward County (Fort Lauderdale), and San Diego schools were randomly selected who met the following definition of second generation: those born in the United States with at least one foreign-born parent or those born abroad but who have resided in this country for at least five years. (See chapter 7.) Questionnaires were administered to these students in both inner-city and suburban schools and to student populations with varying proportions of whites, minorities, and immigrants. In the Miami sample, two predominantly Cuban private schools also were included. The sample is evenly divided between boys and girls; the average age of the youngsters is about fourteen.

The follow-up interviews were conducted with a subset of those originally surveyed. The national-origin groups were stratified on the basis of sex, nativity (U.S. born or foreign born), socioeconomic status based on father's occupation, and family structure (two-parent families consisting of the biological parents of the child or other equivalent care providers). In Miami, the Cuban group also was divided between public and private school students. Names, within the cells thus created, were picked randomly by country of origin for the largest groups in the original sample—Nicaraguans, Cubans, Haitians, and West Indians (mostly Jamaicans and Trinidadians) in Dade and Broward counties; and Mexicans, Vietnamese, Filipinos, Cambodians, and Laotians in San Diego. Our analysis begins with cursory descriptions of five illustrative cases.

An Ethnographic Sampler

Nicaraguan Sliders

On a Wednesday evening, in little Havana, the Angulo family prepares for dinner in their shabby apartment.[1] Originally from Managua,

Nicaragua, Mr. Angulo holds a degree in chemistry and for a time was the manager of a sizable firm in his home country. His wife belongs to a family with connections to the military. They arrived in Miami in 1985 when their son, Ariel, was eight and their daughter, Cristina, was only two years old. Both think of themselves as exiles but are not recognized as such by the authorities. In earnest, Mr. Angulo explains:

> We came with high hopes, escaping the Sandinistas, thinking this was the land of opportunity . . . ready to work and make progress, but we were stopped in our tracks. We haven't been able to legalize our situation. Every so often, we get these notices saying we'll be thrown out of the country; it is nerve-wracking. As a result, we haven't been able to move ahead. Look around; this is the only place we've been able to rent since we came [to Miami]. . . . I work for an hourly wage without benefits, although I perform the duties of a professional for a pharmaceutical company. They know they can abuse my condition because I can't go anywhere; no one will hire me!

Mrs. Angulo, who works as a clerk for a Cuban-owned clinic, worries that Ariel, who is approaching college age, will not be eligible for financial assistance. She does not expect him to go beyond high school, although she and her husband place a premium on education and have typical middle-class aspirations. As it is, Ariel cannot even apply for a legal summer job given his undocumented status. He attends a troubled school, where he mingles primarily with other Central Americans and African Americans. Conflict is rampant and academic standards are low. He complains that other students ridicule Nicaraguans. Ariel feels that his parents are too demanding; they do not understand the pressures at school or give him credit for his effort. Even more distressing is the fact that he cannot speak either English or Spanish fluently. Almost seventeen, he like his mother has a dim view of the future.

Cuban Gainers

Ariel's experience is in stark contrast with that of fifteen-year-old Fernando Gómez, whose family migrated to Miami in 1980 as part of the Mariel boatlift. Originally from Oriente (Manzanillo), Cuba, Fernando's father was employed as a heavy equipment operator and then as a clerk for the same metallurgical firm prior to his migration to the United States. Since his arrival, Mr. Gómez has worked as a mechanic for Dade County. His wife, who used to be a teacher in Cuba, now works providing care for the elderly. Although they hold working-class jobs, the couple's tastes evince an upwardly bound thrust. Their home is part of a Cuban-owned residential development that combines pathways bordered by russet tile and luscious vegetation with pale exteriors, wrought-iron gates, and roofs of an Iberian derivation. The family's living room is embellished with new furnishings.

Proudly, Mr. Gómez states that he has never experienced discrimination; he is not the kind of man who would ever feel inferior to anyone. He expects Fernando, an even better student than his older brother, to go far. There is no doubt that he will finish college, perhaps work toward an advanced degree. Although Fernando wants to become a policeman like his brother, Mr. Gómez dismisses that intent as a passing whim; he would like his son to work with computers because "that is where the future of the world is."

Haitian Strivers

Being admitted into the home of Aristide Maillol in Sweetwater, Miami, transports the visitor into a transfixed space. The location is American but the essence is rural Haiti. Aristide's mother does not speak English. Her eyes drift to the floor when explaining in Creole that her husband is hospitalized and that she had to leave her job as a janitor in a local motel to attend to his needs. There is consternation and reserve in her demeanor.

In the tiny sitting area adjoining the front door, a large bookcase displays the symbols of family identity in an arrangement suitable for a shrine. Framed by paper flowers at the top is the painted portrait of Mrs. Maillol and her husband. Crude forms and radiant colors capture the couple's dignity. Below, on three separate shelves, several photographs show Aristide's brother and three sisters. The boy smiles confidently in the cap and gown of a high school graduate. The girls are displayed individually and in clusters, their eyes beaming, their hair pulled back, their attire fit for a celebration. Interspersed with the photographs are the familiar trinkets that adorn most Haitian homes. Striking, however, is the inclusion of several trophies earned by the Maillol children in academic competitions. At seventeen, Aristide's brother has already been recruited by Yale University. Young Aristide, who is fifteen and wants to be a lawyer, speaks eloquently about the future:

> We are immigrants and immigrants must work hard to overcome hardship. You can't let anything stop you. I know there is discrimination, racism . . . but you can't let that bother you. Everyone has problems, things that hold them back, but if you study . . . [and] do what your mother, what your father, tell you, things will get better . . . God has brought us here and God will lead us farther.

In silence, Mrs. Maillol nods in agreement.

Mexican Toilers

More than 3,000 miles away, in south-central San Diego, Carlos Mendoza's home stands next to a boarded-up crack house. Prior to the police raid that shut it down, the Mendoza family had covered their own windows with planks to avoid witnessing what went on across the alley. The neighborhood is an assortment of vacant lots, abandoned buildings, and small homes protected by fences and dogs. Fourteen years ago, the family illegally entered the United States in the trunk of a car. Their goal was to earn enough money to buy a house in their hometown in Michoacan, and although they succeeded—and purchased the house in San Diego as well—they laughingly note that somehow they never made it back to Mexico. The family has now achieved legal status under the amnesty program promoted by the Immigration Reform and Control Act of 1986.

For the past ten years, Mr. Mendoza has worked as a busboy in a fancy restaurant that caters to tourists, a position he secured through a Mexican friend. He is a hardworking and modest man who wants his son, Carlos, to study so that he can get a good job: "[I want him] to be better than me, not for my sake but for his sake and that of his own family." Mrs. Mendoza irons clothes at a Chinese-owned laundry and complains bitterly that her employers are prejudiced toward her and other Mexicans.

Carlos is doing well in school; he was the only boy at Cabrillo Junior High to be elected to the honor society last year. He wants to become an engineer and go back to Mexico. Life in San Diego has been hard on him; the gold chain his parents gave him as a gift was ripped from around his neck by neighborhood toughs; his bicycle remains locked up inside the house, because riding it would mean losing it to the same local bullies. His younger sister, Amelia, is not doing as well in school and dresses like a *chola* (female gang member), although she insists it is only for the style. Her parents worry but feel helpless.

Vietnamese Bystanders

Forty blocks to the east, in another working-class neighborhood populated by Mexicans, Vietnamese, and blacks, Mrs. Ly and her daughter Hoa sit in their tiny apartment surrounded by several calendars and clocks, a small South Vietnamese flag, two Buddhist shrines, and four academic achievement plaques. Two of Mrs. Ly's daughters have maintained perfect grades for two years in a row. Hoa, her mother explains, is behind; her grade point average is 3.8 rather than 4.0.

Since their arrival in the United States in 1991, neither Mrs. Ly nor her husband have held jobs; they depend on welfare, although Mrs. Ly is unclear about where exactly the money they receive comes from. Back in Vietnam, she and her husband sold American goods on the black market and supplemented their income by sewing clothes. Leaving their country was filled with trauma and they are still dazed. In San Diego, the family is isolated; people in the area resent the new arrivals. More than anything, what keeps the Lys and other Vietnamese families apart is the language barrier: "We can't speak English," says Mrs. Ly, "so the girls don't go out much, they stay home. I raise my children here the same as I raised them in Vietnam: to school and back home."

Hoa's only friend is Vietnamese. Her mother would like her to have more American contacts so that she could learn the language and the culture of their new country. Eventually, she would like her daughter to get an office job or a job in retail sales. Hoa disagrees; she would like to be a doctor.

The cases just sketched provide a glimpse into dissimilar experiences, and the variations are not arbitrary; they are representative of the groups to which the families belong. Nicaraguans expected the treatment afforded to Cubans under what they regarded as similar circumstances. For many, those expectations were dashed as a result of the political complexities surrounding the relationship between the United States and Nicaragua. Bereft of supports in the receiving environment, many of these new immigrants are experiencing a rapid process of downward mobility although many have middle-class backgrounds. Those of humbler provenance are unable to advance. Especially disturbing is the predicament of children who, confined to immigrant neighborhoods but having spent most of their lives in the United States, cannot speak English or Spanish easily. Unable to regularize their immigrant status and facing acute economic need, many of those youngsters are choosing low-paying jobs over education. With an increasing number of high school dropouts and out-of-wedlock pregnancies, many Nicaraguan youth appear to be recapitulating aspects of the African American trajectory (Fernández Kelly, 1994).

Cubans, by contrast, represent an unusual case of immigrant success partly owing to conditions antithetical to those of Nicaraguan migration. The first large cohorts arrived in Miami during the 1960s, prompting the customary response of more established populations: departure to the suburbs. In the beginning, Cubans, too, were perceived as an undesirable minority. Nevertheless, by contrast to other arrivals, they were a highly stratified mass that included professionals and an entrepreneurial elite. As a result, many were able to escape the pressures of the labor market through self-employment and business formation (Portes and Rumbaut, 1990). That, a shared and vehement opposition to the Castro regime, and assistance from the U.S. government allowed Cubans to form a cohesive community. They proceeded to reconstitute the social foundations to which they had been accustomed, including the establishment of a private school system for those who could afford it.

In 1980, the Mariel boatlift jolted Miami with new waves of mostly working-class immigrants, many of whom were of Afro-Caribbean descent. They, too, were received with some hostility that included the ambivalent feelings of older Cubans. Nevertheless, continued support on the part of the U.S. government and the preexisting ethnic enclave allowed the newcomers to adjust rapidly.

Haitians represent a strategic case that contains, alternatively, elements akin to those found in the Cuban experience and those closer to the experience of Nicaraguans. Despite the ordeal of illegal migration and prejudice in the receiving environment, a substantial number of Haitians, like Aristide Maillol and his brother, are doing surprisingly well in the United States. There is evidence that their fledgling success is rooted in deliberate attempts to disassociate themselves from the stigma imposed upon black populations in the United States through an affirmation of their national identity and their religious fervor.

Other Haitians, however, appear to be blending into impoverished black groups living in ghettos such as Miami's Liberty City. A growing number of Haitian youngsters are showing up in alternative schools, detention centers, and penal institutions (Stepick and Dutton-Stepick, 1994). Given their poverty-stricken status and recent arrival, Haitian immigrants were pushed into areas where rental properties were abundant and real estate prices were low. As a result, Little Haiti, a teetering concentration of Haitian homes and businesses, emerged in close proximity to inner-city neighborhoods, and it is from its dwellers that many Haitians are learning their place in American society.

As in the cases of Vietnamese and Mexicans, when Haitian children speak of discrimination, often they are thinking of the verbal and physical abuses they experience at the hands of native black Americans in their neighborhoods and schools. But by contrast to the first two groups, who attend schools characterized by higher levels of ethnic diversity, Haitians do not have a range of referents in their familiar environments. Their choice is clearly bifurcated: either conscious attempts at self-distinction or yielding to the norm through conformity. Insular and destitute environments can rapidly translate conformity into socioeconomic stagnation or decline.

Mexicans represent the longest unbroken migration of major proportions to the United States. Partly as a result of their widespread undocumented status and partly because of geographical proximity, many Mexicans do not see moving to the United States as a long-term decision; instead, they see themselves as sojourners, guided by an economic motive, whose real homes are south of the border. Expectations about the duration of their stay diminish Mexicans' involvement in entrepreneurship and business formation (Roberts, 1995). That attitude also affects their children's prospects because, as Portes (1993: 27) puts it: "It is difficult to reach for the future when you are constantly confronting your past." With little differentiation in terms of social class, Mexicans do not hold enough power to resist the embattled conditions in the neighborhoods where they live.

The Vietnamese experience is marked by paradox. An early wave of exiles in the 1970s—many of whom started small businesses in the United States—was followed by larger groups of peasants and unskilled workers who confronted harsher than usual journeys. In areas of destination they faced hostility, but their rapid legalization entitled them to public assistance and other benefits—up to 50 percent of Vietnamese in California are on welfare (Kitano and Daniels, 1988). Lack of English fluency and the absence of a larger and cohesive community have translated into acute degrees of isolation. However, in this case, isolation added to a widespread faith in education and discipline, and family unity is producing children who are high achievers. The Vietnamese continue to be in, but not of, the United States.

Figure 3.1 summarizes the nonrandom character of the conditions experienced by the immigrant groups studied. Each group has been assigned a label that captures a distinctive experience (Cubans as Gainers; Vietnamese as Bystanders; Haitians as Strivers; Mexicans as Toilers; and Nicaraguans as Sliders). To complete the comparison, we have added a sixth group (native blacks as Survivors). The purpose of the classification is not to create yet another typology of migration but to decouple the characteristics of segmented assimilation from na-

Figure 3.1 Characteristics of Ethnographic Groups

	Gainers	Bystanders	Strivers	Toilers	Sliders	Survivors
Internal differentiation by class	+++	+−	+−	−	+−	−
Type of reception	+++	++	−	−	−	−−−
Quality of resources	+++	+−	−	−	−	−−
Degree of spatial concentration	++	+−	++	++	+−	+++
Length of time in area of destination	+	−−	−−	++	−−	+++
Arrival dates	1960>	1975>	1980>	1930>	1980>	1630>

tional and ethnic referents, thus exposing the outcomes of migration as a function of the factors listed in the figure: internal differentiation by class; type of reception; quality of resources; degree of spatial concentration; and length of time in area of destination. The first four dimensions designate decisive toponomical factors underpinning the aftermath of various kinds of migration.

Although the figure condenses the generalized experiences of the various groups, it does not capture their internal diversity, especially in terms of social class. Its sole purpose is to serve as a heuristic device for understanding the patterns of adaptation. The positions occupied by the groups in the figure should be understood as approximate points along a continuum. Thus, the variable type of reception ranges from highly positive—as indicated by three plus signs—to extremely hostile—as indicated by three minus signs.

Gainers, characterized by high levels of class differentiation, experienced a relatively hospitable reception, including prompt legalization, government support, and low levels of discrimination. For those reasons, they were able to tap resources of high quality, such as effective schools and adequate, affordable housing. Their spatial concentration worked advantageously, facilitating the use of social capital to gain access to information and other desirable assets. Their experience of socioeconomic mobility markedly diverges from that of Survivors, for whom spatial concentration in antagonistic environments translated into diminished connections to the larger society, resources of low quality, and diminished ability to parlay social capital into economic advantage. While Gainers thrive, Survivors endure. The other groups occupy intermediary positions between those two extremes.

The length of time in areas of destination bears a direct relationship to the consolidation of positive or negative behavioral outcomes. Over extended periods of time, low levels of class heterogeneity added to hostile modes of reception, resources of low quality, and high degrees of spatial concentration inevitably lead to a hardening of negative traits among the children and the grandchildren of internal and international migrants. In the case of African Americans, the time line extends beyond the period covered by the Great Black Migration from the rural South (1910–70) to include a longer stretch that is part of that group's historical memory.

Survey Findings

Survey materials contribute additional insights to the picture made vividly real by the testimonies of immigrant children and their families. Table 3.1 condenses information about school performance,

Table 3.1 School Performance, Parental Human Capital, and Childrens' Aspirations[a]

National-Origin Group	School Performance				Parental Human Capital				Child's Aspirations			
	GPA[b]	Std. Math Score[c]	Std. Reading Score[c]	English Index Score[d]	Father College Grad (%)	Mother College Grad (%)	Father Occup. SEI[e]	Mother Occup. SEI[e]	Occupational Aspirations[f]	Less than College (%)	College (%)	Graduate School (%)
Cuban—private school (N = 183)	2.6	80	69	15.3	55	42	50.4	47.3	65.4	3	32	67
Cuban—public school (N = 1044)	2.2	56	45	15.4	24	18	37.5	36.9	62.9	18	37	46
Nicaraguan (N = 344)	2.3	55	38	14.8	45	31	39.2	30.5	62.7	21	34	45
Haitian (N = 178)	2.3	45	30	15.2	16	15	29.1	29.4	65.6	16	34	50
Mexican (N = 757)	2.2	32	27	13.9	9	5	26.3	24.9	58.3	39	32	29
Vietnamese (N = 371)	3.0	60	38	13.4	24	14	34.2	32.4	61.8	23	40	37

[a] All column differences between national-origin groups are significant at the .001 level.
[b] Grade point average as reported by school district.
[c] Stanford Achievement Test, 8th edition, percentile score.
[d] Self-rated proficiency in reading, writing, speaking, and understanding English.
[e] Duncan socioeconomic index score, based respectively on father's and mother's current occupations.
[f] Treiman occupational prestige index score for child's desired occupation.

parental human capital, and children's aspirations. Some differences and similarities are worth noting. Not surprisingly, Cuban children in private schools display high grade point averages and the highest standardized test scores, followed by the Vietnamese whose grades are better but whose scores lag due to lower English proficiency. Cuban students in private schools dramatically exceed the performance of those in public institutions, illustrating the critical effect of social class even within that highly integrated community. Although they are experiencing downward mobility, the scores of Nicaraguan children, many of whom have middle-class backgrounds, are relatively high. Haitians and Mexicans display comparatively low scores, as generally found in predominantly working-class populations.

Even with that in mind, the contrast between Haitians and Mexicans is noteworthy. On the aggregate, the Haitian indicators are consistent with the divided experience sketched earlier, and those of Mexicans confirm their characterization as a highly homogeneous and vulnerable group. Figures on parents' educational achievement, socioeconomic status, and occupational aspirations are compatible with those profiles. And yet, regardless of national origin and social class, most immigrant children voice high educational aspirations, with Haitians second only to Cubans in private schools in their ambition to go beyond college. Again, it comes as no surprise that Mexicans constitute the only group with a large proportion of its members not expecting to achieve a college education.

Table 3.2 provides information about the friendship networks of the various populations. Regardless of national origin, most children associate with members of their own group and a large number of their friends are foreign born. Within that context, nevertheless, Cubans have the highest degree of contact with members of their own group and the lowest proportion of friendships with outsiders. Oddly, Nicaraguans report a higher degree of relations with Cubans than Cubans voice with respect to Nicaraguans. Similar albeit smaller disparities are found in the contrasting testimonies of Haitians with respect to Cubans and of Mexicans with respect to the Vietnamese. Those discrepancies are explained by two tendencies: that of Cubans and Vietnamese to see themselves as enclosed communities and that of Haitians, Mexicans, and Nicaraguans to be more permeable to other groups in their environments. In addition, the relationship among Nicaraguans, Haitians, and Cubans is marked by status differences; often, the latter are reluctant to admit they know Nicaraguans and Haitians. That tendency is mirrored by Nicaraguans' generalized feelings that Cubans discriminate against them.

Table 3.2 Friendship Networks[a] (in Percent)

National-Origin Group	Number of Close Friends from Abroad			Percentage with Friends Who Are[b]				
	None	Some	Many or Most	Cuban	Nicaraguan	Haitian	Mexican	Vietnamese
Cuban—private school (N = 183)	1.1	5.5	93.4	**98.9**	7.3	0	na	na
Cuban—public school (N = 1044)	2.5	23.2	74.2	**93.8**	29.0	3.3	na	na
Nicaraguan (N = 344)	5.1	18.8	76.2	*78.1*	*79.4*	3.9	na	na
Haitian (N = 178)	9.8	43.9	46.2	26.1	4.2	**87.3**	na	na
Mexican (N = 757)	6.6	44.6	48.8	na	na	na	**82.9**	na
Vietnamese (N = 371)	6.5	38.6	54.9	na	na	na	17.2	**83.1**

[a] All column differences between national-origin groups are significant at the .001 level.
[b] Percentage of those who report having close friends from abroad (that is, excludes those with none). Numbers in bold represent the right-to-left axis of conationals. Numbers in italics represent the asymmetrical pairs of nationalities on left-to-right axes.

Most revealing is the information contained in table 3.3 on percep-tions of discrimination and self-identification. Cuban youth report the least discrimination, a fact that is understandable; it is hard for anyone to feel rebuffed when, as table 3.2 indicates, the overwhelming major-ity of his or her contacts are with members of his or her own group. Nevertheless, Cuban children in public schools experience higher lev-els of discrimination from both blacks and whites than those in private schools. In contrast to private institutions, public schools expose chil-dren to a plurality of ethnic and national groups and are, therefore, less able to shield them from friction. With the exception of the Viet-namese, all other groups report higher levels of discrimination from whites than from blacks.

Only Nicaraguans see Cubans as a significant source of discrimi-nation. That may be related to a panethnic effect in Miami, where the Hispanic community is internally diversified in terms of national origin, with the Cubans occupying a preeminent position and, there-fore, becoming easily identifiable as a source of discrimination, particularly toward other Hispanics. On the other hand, the case of Mexicans in San Diego invites reflection because, despite the existence of a large coethnic community, membership in it does not shield Mexicans from discrimination. That, too, may be an effect of localized factors; a continued climate of hostility against Mexican immigration in California recently has been exacerbated by a severe economic downturn following the state's fiscal crisis and deep cuts in military spending. Mexicans have become convenient scapegoats for height-ened rates of joblessness. Finally, the recently arrived Vietnamese report the most discrimination, a reflection of the negative public reception that greeted their arrival. In addition, they tend to live in working-class neighborhoods populated by black Americans, thus without the benefit of a "Little Saigon" that might insulate them from conflict.

The data in table 3.4 summarize selected characteristics of the schools attended by immigrant children in our sample. The patterns are consistent with the descriptions offered earlier. Taken as a whole, Cuban families show a higher degree of class heterogeneity—as re-flected in the proportions of children receiving free or subsidized lunch, a proxy measure for poverty. Mexican children are located in schools that mirror their position at the lower end of the class hierar-chy. Most Haitian children are to be found in predominantly black, inner-city schools, given the proximity of Haitian residential settle-ment to ghettos. Table 3.4 underscores the extent to which schools sort out children internally in terms of social class.

Table 3.3 Perceptions of Discrimination (in Percent)[a]

| National-Origin Group | Experienced Discrimination | Those Discriminated Against Who Attribute It to | | | | |
		Whites	Blacks	Cubans	Residing in U.S. 5–9 Years	Born in U.S.
Cuban—private school (N = 183)	31.7	46.4	28.6	1.8	3.3	91.3
Cuban—public school (N = 1044)	39.1	31.6	28.9	3.7	10.1	67.6
Nicaraguan (N = 344)	50.6	27.8	22.2	25.0	57.8	7.6
Haitian (N = 178)	62.4	35.8	29.4	9.2	28.7	43.3
Mexican (N = 757)	64.3	42.2	34.4	na	28.4	60.2
Vietnamese (N = 371)	66.3	37.9	40.2	na	42.3	15.6

[a] All column differences between national-origin groups are significant at the .001 level.

Table 3.4 Socioeconomic Status of National-Origin Groups (in Percent)[a]

National-Origin Group	Low SES[b]	Middle SES	High SES	Majority Black[c]	Majority Latin	Majority White	>2/3 Poor[d]	1/2–2/3 Poor	<1/3 Poor
Cuban—private school (N = 183)	7.7	49.2	43.1	0	100	0	0	0	100
Cuban—public school (N = 1044)	25.8	60.1	14.1	2.1	84.2	3.9	31.1	28.8	40.0
Nicaraguan (N = 344)	23.8	65.8	10.4	7.3	79.4	1.5	39.4	16.3	44.3
Haitian (N = 178)	31.0	61.9	7.1	66.9	3.4	2.8	66.9	12.9	20.2
Mexican (N = 757)	66.9	30.4	2.7	.4	17.7	.4	51.3	38.0	10.7
Vietnamese (N = 371)	45.3	46.9	7.7	.3	.8	0	39.2	18.8	41.9

[a] All column differences between national-origin groups are significant at the .001 level.
[b] Based on composite index score using father's and mother's occupations, education, and home ownership. Corresponds to working class (such as busboys, janitors, laborers), middle class (small business owners, teachers), and upper middle class (lawyers, architects, executives).
[c] "Majority means greater than 60 percent of students who attend the school. Note that we cannot distinguish within the Latin group between immigrants and U.S.-born students.
[d] "Poor" is measured by the proxy variable of the percentage of the student body eligible for federally funded free or subsidized lunch.

Ethnic Identities

Additional ethnographic chronicles underscore the vital role of collective identities in the process of assimilation. Even under auspicious conditions, migration is a jarring experience that pushes individuals and groups to acquire new knowledge as they negotiate survival and adjustment. Immigrants learn how they fit in the larger society through the contacts they establish in familiar environments. Whether youngsters sink or soar frequently depends on how they see themselves, their families, and their communities. (See chapter 7.) The immigrant life is preeminently an examined life. Iterative processes of symbolic and factual association and detachment shape immigrants' self-definitions. Schools play a major role in that respect (Matute-Bianchi, 1986).

At school, children mingle with groups differentiated by their own self-perceptions and the perceptions of external observers. Especially when children equate success with power attained through conflict and physical force—as in the case of youth gangs—those groups can exert a strong downward pull on immigrant children. The paths that lead youngsters toward specific clusters are complex. However, one of the most effective antidotes against downward mobility is a sense of membership in a group with an undamaged collective identity. The Méndez children illustrate that proposition.

But for the fact that they are illegal aliens from Nicaragua, sixteen-year-old Omar Méndez and his younger sister Fátima could not be closer to the American Dream. They have grown up in Miami since they were five and three years old, respectively. They are superb students full of spirit and ambition. They attend a school where discipline is strict and where teachers are able to communicate with parents in Spanish. Most decisively, they see themselves as immigrants, and that identity protects them from negative stereotypes and from incorporation into more popular but less motivated groups in school. In Fátima's words: "We're immigrants! We can't afford to just sit around and blow it like others who've been in this country longer and take everything for granted." To maintain her independence, she withdraws from her peers and endures being called a "nerd." She does not mind because her center of gravitation lies within her family.

María Ceballos, a Cuban mother, agrees with Fátima. She despairs about her daughter's interest in material trinkets and her low levels of academic motivation. "At Melanie's age," she states, "I was very determined; maybe because I was born in a different country, I wanted to prove that I was as good as real Americans. My daughter was born here and [therefore] she doesn't have the same push."

Among vulnerable groups, the ability to shift ethnic identity often provides a defense from stigma and an incentive to defy leveling pressures. How they define themselves depends on the context. Miguel Hernández, an illegal Mexican alien in San Diego since 1980, explains that he and his wife define themselves "[depending on] who we are talking to. If we are talking to American people and they don't know the difference, we say 'Latinos'; that's easier for them and we avoid hassles." Miguel consciously avoids the label Chicano: "It's a slang word for lower-class types who don't know who they are. They don't want to be Mexicans, but they don't want to just be Americans; they don't even speak English but they don't know Spanish either [and they] fight for and about everything."

In answering questions about who they are, immigrants resort to antinomies, defining other groups in contrast to their own. Others are generally symbolized by the casualties of earlier migrations, especially inner-city blacks. Typically, immigrants see blacks as the victims of their own individual and collective liabilities. Martin López, a Mexican father, explains:

> Blacks in this country . . . don't want to work; [they] feel very American. They know government has to support every child they breed. [As immigrants] we can't afford to slacken the pace; we have to work hard.

Given their phenotypical commonalities with black Americans and the disadvantages of their neighborhoods, the issue of identity is paramount among Haitians. Madeleine Serphy, an ambitious girl of fifteen, has strong feelings about African Americans:

> It may be true that whites discriminate, but I have no complaints [about them] because I don't know many [whites] . . . but blacks, they're trouble; they make fun of the way we [Haitians] speak. . . . They call us stupid and backwards and try to beat us up. I was always scared, so I [tried] to do well in school and that's how I ended [in a magnet school]. There, I don't stand out as much and I can feel good about being Haitian. . . . Haitian is what I am; I don't think about color.

For working-class Cubans, the problem of identity is equally complex, but for different reasons. As members of a successful group, many resent being melded into the broader classification of Hispanic. Such is the case with Doris Delsol, an assertive divorcée who lives on welfare because of a disability. Although her daughter, Elizabeth, experienced some early setbacks in grade school, Mrs. Delsol doggedly sought paths to uplift her. "We Cubans are not used to failure," she explained. She does not like being called Hispanic because:

We all speak [Spanish] but there are differences. [Cubans] always had self-respect, a sense of cleanliness and duty toward children, a work ethic. Miami used to be a clean city until the Nicaraguans came and covered everything with graffiti.

About American blacks, Mrs. Delsol thinks they are adversarial, disruptive, prone to ruin their homes, and lazy. In her view, both Nicaraguans and blacks evince attitudes opposite to those of Cubans.

Ironically, many Nicaraguans think of themselves as Hispanics precisely because they hold perceptions similar to those voiced by Mrs. Delsol. They experience a strong dissociational push away from their own national group. Sixteen-year-old Elsie Rivas avoids discrimination by shifting between a Hispanic and a Nicaraguan self-definition at school and at the supermarket where she works. She doesn't like the way Nicaraguans speak:

They are vulgar, ignorant. . . . When I am with my Cuban friends I can speak to them normally, but some Nicaraguans make me feel ashamed and I am tempted to deny my nationality; they make all of us look bad because of the way they express themselves, with all the bad words and the cussing.

Like the majority of immigrant children, Elsie's younger sister, Alicia, does not care for those distinctions. She feels "Nicaraguan American because my parents came from Nicaragua and I like the food, but I am really American, more American than those born in this country; here is where I grew up and here is where I am going to stay."

The perceptions of immigrants and their children about themselves and other groups are not always accurate. What matters, however, is that as social constructions those perceptions are an integral part of segmented assimilation that will eventually yield what Bellah (1985) calls "communities of memory." In their journey, the immigrant children of today are already forging tomorrow's ethnic identities. Contact, friction, negotiation, and their eventual incorporation into distinct sectors of the larger society will depend, in the final analysis, on the insertion of immigrant children into various niches of the U.S. economy. Collective self-definitions will improve or worsen depending on the structure of opportunity.

Conclusions

Our purpose in this study has been to unfold the various meanings of assimilation for immigrants arriving into locations distinguished by an assortment of physical, social, and economic characteristics. We have argued that a limited number of toponomical features determine the outcomes of migration. Our analysis was based on survey and ethnographic data about a small number of groups. However, we have noted that each group represents an experience associated not so much with cultural or national features but with the type of reception its members receive, the character of resources available to it, its internal differentiation in terms of class, its spatial concentration, and the length of time its coethnics have resided in the United States.

There is no mystery to tales of immigrant success or failure. The fates of immigrant children divide along lines of economic opportunity. Economic globalization has fostered major transformations, including increasing demand for immigrant labor and the formation of transnational markets unlikely to disappear through purely legislative initiatives. Policy cannot aim solely at regulating immigrant streams to the exclusion of facilitating the adjustment of new arrivals and increasing their connection to the institutions of the larger society. The experience of Gainers shows that a welcoming reception—including government initiatives to facilitate immigrant adaptation—can have long-term benefits. The opposite is also true. Over extended periods of time, hostile receptions have had predictable results: isolation, social dismemberment, and the concentration of behavioral pathologies. For policymakers the lesson is clear—the nightmare of an urban underclass need not be repeated among the protagonists of the new migration if we give attention to the lessons of the past.

Once established, immigrant networks acquire a degree of autonomy from market forces, reducing the costs and risks of migration and promoting the flow of information. When they are internally stratified in terms of class, the spatial concentration of immigrants can yield advantages for the group to which they belong and for the larger society. This, too, has importance for immigration policy. In the 1960s, when the Cuban exile first began, millions of dollars were spent needlessly to scatter the banished around the United States in the belief that this promoted their social incorporation. Instead, Cubans gravitated back to Miami where their strength of numbers, connections, and entrepreneurial know-how quickly translated into economic prosperity. Atomization and geographical dispersion could have had very different results.

Finally, we have begun a discussion of the ways in which immigrants shape identities through repeated interaction with other ethnic groups. Our point has been to underscore the salience of collective self-definitions in the process of segmented assimilation. There is an interactive relationship between the opportunity structure and the way individuals and groups perceive themselves and others. The self-image of the immigrant is, ironically, a hopeful image often bolstered by his or her negative definitions of groups that have experienced arrested mobility. Whether those hopeful images survive will depend on whether immigrant children succeed or fail in the new economy.

Notes

1. The names in these narratives are pseudonyms.

4

Studying Immigrant Adaptation from the 1990 Population Census: From Generational Comparisons to the Process of "Becoming American"

CHARLES HIRSCHMAN

Iᴺ 1980, the U.S. Bureau of the Census dropped the question on the birthplace of parents from the decennial census. Although a new question on ancestry was added, the loss of the parental birthplace question meant that it was no longer possible to identify directly the children of immigrants in census data from 1980 and 1990. Ironically, this loss of critical information coincided with a wave of immigration from Latin America and Asia in the 1970s and 1980s. Tracking the progress (or lack of progress) of the children of new immigrants has become a more difficult task without adequate census data on the topic.

This paper was written while the author was a Fellow at the Center for Advanced Study in the Behavioral Sciences. The author is grateful for the financial support from the National Science Foundation (SES-9022192) and the extraordinary quality of colleagueship at the center. In a casual conversation, Frank Furstenberg offered a suggestion that inspired the direction of this paper. Thanks also go to Alejandro Portes and the anonymous reviewers for their very helpful critiques of the first draft.

The hope that survey data, including the Current Population Survey, which continues to collect data on the birthplaces of respondents and their parents, might fill this void is largely illusory. Even the largest national surveys do not contain a sufficient number of cases for any but the largest regional or country-of-origin immigrant streams. The heterogeneity of contemporary immigration (encompassing people from Portugal, Laos, El Salvador, Colombia, and others) and the variations in immigrant communities across places of settlement in the United States cast serious doubts on studies based on highly aggregated data. Local studies in particular cities and neighborhoods can provide deeply textured accounts of those immigrants and their children, but only census data hold the possibility of comparing specific immigrant streams across the country.

This chapter examines alternative methods to measure the status of second-generation immigrants with data from the 1990 Census of Population. The first method tests the assumption that the cross-classification of ethnic and race data with nativity can identify the native-born children of the new immigrants from Asia and Latin America. Applications of this method with 1990 census data are limited, however, because most of the new second generation were still children or adolescents in 1990. The second method is to examine the status of immigrants who arrived in the United States as children. In many important ways, these "child immigrants" probably resemble their younger brothers and sisters who were born in the United States.

This second method uses the school enrollment rates of teenagers and the marriage patterns and nonmarital fertility of young adults across more than forty country-of-origin populations from the published tabulations of the 1990 census. This preliminary analysis shifts the analytical question from intergenerational change to the impact of "becoming American" (length of exposure to American society). Although there is support for the assimilation theory that predicts social and economic gains with longer exposure to American society, there is also substantial variation by country of origin and type of socioeconomic outcome.

Analyses of the Second-Generation Hypothesis in Census Data

The popular image of the United States as a "nation of immigrants" is deeply etched in American political consciousness (Thernstrom, 1980; Fuchs, 1990). This image has a corollary creed that immigrants and their descendants should have the same political and economic prospects as natives. Although these beliefs were not universally adhered to, especially in the treatment of racial minorities, the basic ideology has served to legitimate the gradual social and economic absorption of successive waves of immigrants over the last two hundred years (Handlin, 1973). The standard model of immigrant progress is generally framed as an intergenerational process (Gordon, 1964; Lieberson, 1980). Immigrants—the first generation—are handicapped by their newcomer status and rarely expected to achieve socioeconomic parity with the native population. Learning a new language, the lack of recognition of educational qualifications from a different system, and native prejudice and hostility toward those with foreign accents and cultures are major obstacles for immigrants. The second generation, the children of immigrants, are socialized and educated both in mainstream society (usually the public schools) and in their ethnic homes and neighborhoods. From the former, the children of immigrants gain the skills necessary for equal participation in the American occupational structure; from the latter, many internalize the immigrant belief that America is a land of opportunity for those with perseverance and determination. The children of early twentieth-century European immigrants reached socioeconomic parity with native Americans during the middle decades of this century (Duncan and Duncan, 1968; Lieberson 1980; Neidert and Farley, 1985; Hirschman and Kraly, 1988, 1990).

This body of research on immigrant generations has been shaped largely by the content and availability of census data. From 1850 onward, a question on country of birth has been included in every decennial census. Data on foreign parentage were collected in every census from 1870 through 1970. These data have allowed for the standard comparisons of immigrants, the second generation ("native born of foreign or mixed parentage"), and everybody else ("native born of native parentage"). In this century, these generational comparisons became the hallmark of the field and are exemplified by use of the same title, *Immigrants and Their Children*, for two classic census monographs, one written after the 1920 census (Carpenter, 1927) and one after the 1950 census (Hutchinson, 1956).

The generational perspective was limited, however, because it was impossible to trace the third generation (the grandchildren of immigrants) in census data. The reference population, "native born of native parentage," included third-generation Americans as well as those whose immigrant ancestors arrived in the distant past. The new census data on ancestry provides additional information, but the loss of the question on parental birthplace makes it impossible to continue the tradition of research on immigrant generations (Farley, 1991). It is unfortunate that scholarship based on census data may reveal less about contemporary immigrants and their children than was possible for earlier waves of immigration.

Orthodox and Revisionist Theses of Immigrant Adaptation

As suggested in the preceding section, the classical hypothesis of immigrant adaptation was of "Americanization"—longer residence in the United States led to socioeconomic progress and the narrowing of differentials with the native-born population. Although this hypothesis was typically framed as a process of intergenerational social mobility, the same logic can be applied to the study of intragenerational immigrant adaptation. Indeed, some research has found that duration of residence in the United States leads to the reduction of earnings differentials between immigrants and the native-born American population (Chiswick, 1978; Jasso and Rosenzweig, 1990). The standard model, whether an inter- or intragenerational process, continues to inform much of current scholarship on immigrant progress, even though it has been questioned in recent years.

The doubts about the validity of the classical hypothesis often are phrased in terms of declining prospects for the new second generation—the children of post-1965 immigrants from Asia and Latin America (Daniels, 1990; Reimers, 1992). This revisionist thinking is based largely on the changing character of the American economy over the past two decades and the decline of opportunities for upward mobility among immigrants and their children. Poorly paid dead-end jobs in the service sector are not attractive options for the American-educated children of immigrants who entered the job market in the 1980s and 1990s (Gans, 1992). Another aspect of the problem is the considerable loss of jobs in the well-paid blue-collar sector, which was the bulwark of economic advancement for earlier generations of domestic and international migrants to cities in the Northeast and Midwest.

Another dimension of the revisionist perspective is the declining social environment in inner-city areas where many new immigrants have settled. The claim is that contemporary social institutions and the cultural environment place much less emphasis on education as a path toward social and economic mobility. The deterioration of public schools, the rise in drug use and violence, and the adversarial culture of many minority youth in inner cities all contribute to an environment with fewer incentives and opportunities for second-generation immigrant children to advance. Assimilation under these conditions may be a disadvantage relative to those who remain wedded to the traditional values of the first-generation immigrant community (Portes and Zhou, 1993; see also chapter 9).

These alternative perspectives cannot be evaluated conclusively with available census data. The published tabulations from the 1990 census, however, provide an initial opportunity to explore empirical patterns aligned with these rather different perspectives. To set the stage for this work, it is useful to begin with a survey of available data on immigrants and ethnicity from the 1990 census.

Composition of Immigrant Communities

Almost 20 million immigrants were counted in the 1990 census. As a fraction of the American population, the foreign born were less than 8 percent—a far lower percentage of the total population than that recorded in the peak years of immigration during the early decades of the twentieth century (Passel and Edmonston, 1994: 37). In absolute terms, however, the number of immigrants in 1990 is the highest ever recorded. Moreover, the current wave of immigration is different from earlier streams because of its origins—primarily from Latin America and Asia. A summary portrait of the 1990 immigrant population by country or region of origin is presented in table 4.1. The table shows each immigrant nationality group by recency of arrival (1980–1990 and pre-1980) as a percentage of the total immigrant population and as a percentage of the total U.S. population.

Of the 19.8 million immigrants in 1990, almost half (44 percent) arrived during the 1980s. The most dramatic shift in modern immigration (in addition to the rise in numbers) is the shift from Europe to Asia as a major source. Although this trend began during the late 1960s and 1970s, the basic comparison between pre-1980 and post-1980 arrivals shows the differences between contemporary and historical composition of immigration. Of the four million European immigrants counted in the 1990 census, over 80 percent had arrived prior to 1980. In contrast, more than half (56 percent) of the five million immigrants from Asia arrived since 1980. For most Latin American country-of-origin categories, recent migration has been quite substantial, with about 50 percent arriving in the past ten years. For the countries in Central America where civil wars have spawned a refugee exodus (El Salvador and Nicaragua), upward of 70 percent of immigrants are recent arrivals (since 1980).

The other vantage point from which to examine the country-of-origin composition is as percentages of all immigrants for the recent past (1980–1990) and the more distant past (prior to 1980). Among the older pool of immigrants (pre-1980), about 30 percent were from Europe, 20 percent from Asia, 43 percent from the Americas, and smaller trickles from the former Soviet Union, Africa, and Oceania. For the past ten years, almost 90 percent of immigrants have been from Asia, Latin America, and Africa. Except for Mexico, with a 25 percent share of recent immigrants, there are few countries with a dominant share.

This tremendous range of diversity poses enormous challenges for social scientists who wish to track the social and economic mobility of the new immigrant waves. Even without direct measurement of the new second generation of immigration, there are several analytical possibilities to explore within the confines of the 1990 census.

Cross-Classification of Asian Americans and Nativity

One avenue for tracking the second generation of new immigrants with census data is to cross-classify nativity status with other census variables that identify country-of-origin populations. Three census variables identify ethnic groups with some information on country of origin: race, Hispanic origin, and ancestry. This section illustrates the logic of this approach with data on the Asian and Pacific Islander population gleaned from the race variable. The usefulness of this method for identifying the second generation depends on the assumption that persons in most "Asian race" categories immigrated recently.

The measurement of race in the census is a relic of an earlier era when both popular and scientific beliefs assumed that phenotypical variations in human populations were associated with biological capacities. Although this assumption has long since disappeared, there remain important reasons to continue race measurement. Data classified by race are necessary to measure the degree of inequality and segregation that has persisted from the days of officially sanctioned discrimination. In fact, there has been an expansion of "races" in recent censuses as more minority groups lobby for inclusion as recognized categories (McKenney and Cresce, 1993). In addition to the listed categories, persons can enter responses in the "other race" category. All responses with a sufficient number of cases are coded and included in the census data files and published tabulations.

The subcategories in the Asian and Pacific Islander population, derived from responses to the race question in the 1990 census, are listed in table 4.2. Not all categories mentioned are listed, only the major ones tabulated in the 1993 census publication *The Asians and Pacific Islanders in the United States, 1990*. The listed groups were either categories on the census questionnaire or were mentioned as possible examples for filling in the "other race" category. The meaning of these race categories is not defined in the census beyond the self-identifica-

Table 4.1 Foreign-Born Population by Place of Birth and Year of Entry, United States: 1990

Place of Birth	Thousands By Year of Entry			Percent of Country/Region			Percent of Foreign Born		Percent of U.S. Population		
	Total	1980–90	Pre-1980	Total	1980–90	Pre-1980	1980–90	Pre-1980	Total	1980–90	Pre-1980
All Foreign Born	19,767	8,663	11,104	100	44	56	100	100	7.9	3.5	4.5
Europe	4,017	721	3,296	20	18	82	8	30	1.6	0.3	1.3
France	119	35	84	1	29	71	0	1	0.0	0.0	0.0
Germany	712	80	632	4	11	89	1	6	0.3	0.0	0.3
Greece	177	23	154	1	13	87	0	1	0.1	0.0	0.1
Hungary	110	13	97	1	12	88	0	1	0.0	0.0	0.0
Ireland	170	33	137	1	19	81	0	1	0.1	0.0	0.1
Italy	581	37	544	3	6	94	0	5	0.2	0.0	0.2
Poland	388	166	272	2	30	70	1	2	0.2	0.0	0.1
Portugal	210	45	165	1	21	79	1	1	0.1	0.0	0.1
United Kingdom	640	154	486	3	24	76	2	4	0.3	0.1	0.2
Yugoslavia	142	23	119	1	16	84	0	1	0.1	0.0	0.0
Soviet Union	334	132	202	2	40	60	2	2	0.1	0.1	0.1
Asia	4,979	2,794	2,185	25	56	44	32	20	2.0	1.1	0.9
Cambodia	119	102	17	1	86	14	1	0	0.0	0.0	0.0
China	530	284	246	3	54	46	3	2	0.2	0.1	0.1
Hong Kong	147	65	82	1	44	56	1	1	0.1	0.0	0.0
India	450	250	200	2	56	44	3	2	0.2	0.1	0.1
Iran	210	104	106	1	50	50	1	1	0.1	0.0	0.0
Japan	290	153	137	1	53	47	2	1	0.1	0.1	0.1
Korea	568	319	249	3	56	44	4	2	0.2	0.1	0.1
Laos	172	131	41	1	76	24	2	0	0.1	0.1	0.0

Philippines	913	448	465	5	49	51	5	4	0.4	0.2	0.2
Taiwan	244	160	84	1	66	34	2	1	0.1	0.1	0.0
Thailand	107	60	47	1	56	44	1	0	0.0	0.0	0.0
Vietnam	543	336	207	3	62	38	4	2	0.2	0.1	0.1
North America	8,124	3,819	4,305	41	47	53	44	39	3.3	1.5	1.7
Canada	745	124	621	4	17	83	1	6	0.3	0.0	0.2
Mexico	4,298	2,145	2,153	22	50	50	25	19	1.7	0.9	0.9
Caribbean	1,938	783	1,155	10	40	60	9	10	0.8	0.3	0.5
Cuba	737	188	549	4	26	74	2	5	0.3	0.1	0.2
Dominican Republic	348	185	163	2	53	47	2	1	0.1	0.1	0.1
Haiti	225	132	93	1	59	41	2	1	0.1	0.1	0.0
Jamaica	334	154	180	2	45	54	2	2	0.1	0.1	0.1
Trinidad/Tobago	116	47	69	1	41	59	1	1	0.0	0.0	0.0
Central America	1,134	765	369	6	67	33	9	3	0.5	0.3	0.1
El Salvador	465	350	115	2	75	25	4	1	0.2	0.1	0.0
Guatemala	226	154	72	1	68	32	2	1	0.1	0.1	0.0
Honduras	109	71	38	1	65	35	1	0	0.0	0.0	0.0
Nicaragua	169	125	44	1	74	26	1	0	0.1	0.1	0.0
Panama	86	32	54	0	37	63	0	0	0.0	0.0	0.0
South America	1,037	540	497	5	52	48	6	4	0.4	0.2	0.2
Colombia	286	146	140	1	51	49	2	1	0.1	0.1	0.1
Ecuador	143	62	81	1	43	57	1	1	0.1	0.0	0.0
Guyana	121	73	48	1	60	43	1	0	0.0	0.0	0.0
Peru	144	87	57	1	60	40	1	1	0.1	0.0	0.0
Africa	364	216	148	2	59	41	2	1	0.1	0.1	0.1
Oceania	104	35	69	1	34	66	0	1	0.0	0.0	0.0

SOURCE: U.S. Bureau of the Census (1993a), Table 1. Some discrepancies arise because of rounding.

Table 4.2 Asian and Pacific Islander Population, by Nativity, Year of Entry, and Age, United States: 1990

Population by Race	Population (in Thousands)				Percent of Total Ethnic Population			Median Age			Population Age 15–24 (in Thousands)	
	Total	Native Born	Foreign Born		Native Born	Foreign Born		Native Born	Foreign Born		Native Born	Immigrants
			1980–90	Pre-1990		1980–90	Pre-1980		1980–90	Pre-1980		
Total U.S. population	248,710	228,943	8,664	11,104	92	3	4	32.5	28.0	46.5	33,340	2,959
Non-Asian and Pacific Islander	241,483	226,274	6,042	9,167	94	3	4	32.7	27.1	48.0	32,898	2,205
Asian and Pacific Islander	7,227	2,668	2,662	1,937	37	37	27	15.6	30.5	42.1	442	754
Asian	6,876	2,363	2,597	1,916	34	38	28	14.7	30.5	42.2	385	745
Chinese	1,649	506	649	493	31	39	30	16.3	31.7	43.3	88	166
Filipino	1,420	506	448	465	36	32	33	14.3	32.8	43.9	110	124
Japanese	866	585	153	127	68	18	15	35.3	29.7	53.3	74	31

Asian Indian	786	193	346	248	25	44	32	8.8	30.3	41.6	32	93
Korean	797	218	327	252	27	41	32	9.0	31.9	41.0	40	98
Vietnamese	693	119	293	181	17	42	26	6.7	27.7	34.2	12	121
Cambodian	149	31	104	14	21	70	9	4.7	24.4	34.8	1	26
Hmong	94	32	47	15	34	50	16	5.2	20.1	27.2	<1	15
Laotian	147	31	93	24	21	63	16	5.4	25.2	29.8	1	28
Thai	91	22	29	40	24	32	44	11.7	30.5	41.3	6	9
Indonesian	30	5	16	9	17	53	30	12.0	27.0	42.2	1	5
Pakistani	82	19	42	21	23	51	26	6.7	29.8	39.4	2	10
Pacific Islander	351	305	25	21	87	7	6	23.5	26.9	37.9	57	9
Polynesian	284	256	13	15	90	5	5	23.6	27.5	37.9	47	5
Hawaiian	206	203	1	1	99	0	0	26.1	25.2	36.2	36	<1
Samoan	58	45	5	8	78	9	14	17.2	27.4	38.2	10	2
Tongan	17	7	5	5	41	29	29	7.4	27.9	37.4	1	2
Micronesian	55	45	7	3	82	13	5	23.9	24.9	38.1	9	3
Guamanian	48	42	4	2	88	8	4	24.9	27.4	41.2	8	1
Melanesian	7	2	4	2	29	57	29	6.6	29.2	37.3	<1	1

SOURCE: U.S. Bureau of the Census (1993b), Table 1.

tion of the person (or the household respondent who filled in the census questionnaire on behalf of other persons in the household).

Responses to the birthplace question do not necessarily match the nationality responses to the race question. For example, persons born in the People's Republic of China, Hong Kong, and Taiwan are likely to identify as Chinese on the race question. In addition, a significant number of persons who immigrated from (or are the descendants of persons who immigrated from) Vietnam, the Philippines, Thailand, and Indonesia identify as Chinese. Similarly, peoples from several countries in South Asia or Southeast Asia may identify as Asian Indian or Pakistani, with religion as a potentially important determinant of "racial" identity. This slippage is illustrated with the comparison of the number of immigrants from Asia (4.98 million, see table 4.1) with the number of Asians (by race) who are foreign born (4.51 million, see table 4.2).

Regardless of the exact meaning of the specific Asian and Pacific Islander categories in table 4.2, the overlap between Asian origins and immigration is probably close enough to provide some information on immigrant generations. The published tabulations in report CP-3-5 on the 1990 census (U.S. Bureau of the Census, 1993b) show a wide variety of social and economic characteristics of Asian and Pacific Islanders by nativity status. Table 4.2 presents their absolute numbers (in thousands), their percentage composition by nativity status (native born, foreign born who arrived after 1980, and foreign born who arrived prior to 1980), the median age of these three groups, and the absolute numbers of young adults (ages fifteen to twenty-four). Although most native-born Asian Americans probably are the children of immigrants, all but a few were still too young in 1990 to provide a base for research on the socioeconomic adaptation of the second generation. There are, however, a significant number of immigrants who arrived as children and are probably close proxies for the second generation.

By "race," 7.2 million Asian and Pacific Islanders—almost 3 percent of the total U.S. population—were counted in the 1990 census. Aside from the fact that Asians and Pacific Islanders are both from homelands across the Pacific Ocean from the U.S. mainland, the combination of the two groups makes very little sense. The distinctive characteristics of Pacific Islanders are obscured in a composite category in which they make up less than 5 percent. Moreover, most Pacific Islanders are not immigrants but the indigenous peoples of American territories. The largest group, Hawaiians (206,000 of the 351,000 Pacific Islanders), are largely resident in the state of Hawaii.

Under the Asian category, there is tremendous diversity: Thirteen populations are listed here, but many smaller groups are included in the overall category. There were six Asian populations with more than a half-million persons in the United States in 1990: Chinese (1.6 million), Filipino (1.4 million), Japanese (.9 million), Asian Indian (.8 million), Korean (.8 million), and Vietnamese (.7 million). Within the Pacific Islander category (subdivided into the origin categories of Polynesian, Micronesian, and Melanesian), there is also considerable diversity.

The major value of table 4.2 lies in the comparison of the numbers of native-born and foreign-born persons of Asian and Pacific Islander origin. Almost all of the Pacific Islander population are native born: 99 percent of the Hawaiians, 78 percent of the Samoans, and 88 percent of the Guamanians. These groups are classified as native born because they are indigenous peoples of American territories. Within the Asian American population, only about one-third of the total is native born. The Japanese American population contains a native-born majority, but among the other groups the percentage of native born ranges from a high of 36 percent for Filipino Americans to a low of 17 percent for those of Vietnamese and Indonesian origins.

What can census data tell us about the second-generation Asian Americans? First, it seems that almost all native-born Asian Americans, with the exception of the Japanese American population (and some Chinese and Filipino Americans), are the children of immigrants.[1] This is a simple product of the recency of Asian immigration— there has been too little time for a third generation to be formed. Some indirect evidence for this claim can be read from the substantial share of Asian immigration during the 1980s (relative to the period prior to 1980). Much stronger evidence is given in the third panel of table 4.2, which shows the median age of each group by nativity status. The median age is the fiftieth percentile, with half of the population younger than the median age.

The foreign-born Asian populations have "normal" age structures with median ages in the twenties and thirties. In contrast, most of the native-born Asian populations are "child populations" with very young median ages—often below ten. For these populations, we can safely assume that almost all of the native born are the children of immigrants (and still children at the time of the census). The native-born Japanese population is the major exception, and there are probably nonnegligible fractions of the Chinese and Filipino populations that are third generation or higher.

The conclusion that most native-born Asian Americans are second generation in 1990 does not mean that census data can be used for intergenerational comparisons on most social and economic variables. The relative youth of the native-born samples—which allows us safely to assume their generational status—also means that relatively few have reached the young adult years where completed schooling, family formation, and employment can be analyzed. The census in the year 2000 will contain much larger samples of older native-born Asian Americans, but there also will be less certainty that all are second generation.

To illustrate the potential for research on second-generation Asian Americans, the last two columns in table 4.2 show the actual numbers (in thousands) of the native born of each nationality from ages fifteen to twenty-four with the comparable figure for immigrants in the same age group. The fifteen-to-twenty-four age group embodies the critical years of the school-to-work transition and potential years of early family formation—important segments of the life course to monitor. Any study of the second-generation hypothesis among Asian Americans will have to contend with the very small numbers of native born at this stage of the life course. The largest numbers are actually in the zero to four and five to nine age categories—too young to show much differentiation. One analytical possibility is to aggregate across country-of-origin categories, but this strategy may sacrifice a potentially important explanatory variable.

Another possibility is to focus on the significant number of Asian American immigrants who are "almost" native born—persons who immigrated as children. The last column shows the number of immigrants ages fifteen to twenty-four in 1990. This sample is typically larger than the native born for the same age group (except for the Japanese American population). On many dimensions, the immigrants who arrive as children (or even as teenagers) are probably closer to their American-born siblings than they are to their parents who arrived as adults. Analyses based on this population can be used to explore the impact of "Americanization" (duration of residence) on adaptation processes.

Cross-Classification of Hispanic Americans and Nativity

The same exercise shown for Asian Americans in table 4.2 is repeated in table 4.3 for the 1990 census population of Hispanic Americans. The 1990 census question on Hispanic origin reads: "Is this person of Spanish/Hispanic origin?" If the response was yes, the listed choices included Mexican/Mexican American/Chicano, Puerto Rican, Cuban, and Other Spanish/Hispanic. For the "other" category, respondents were encouraged to write in specific nationality groups, and several examples were provided as possible answers. Table 4.3, based on the published tabulations in the census report, *Persons of Hispanic Origin in the United States, 1990*, includes the three listed groups (Mexicans,

Puerto Ricans, and Cubans), one Caribbean population (Dominicans), six Central American populations, nine South American populations, and three general categories of Spaniard, Spanish, and Spanish American (U.S. Bureau of the Census, 1993c).

With the exclusion of the non-Hispanic groups from the Caribbean and South America, the list of national-origin populations in table 4.3 is somewhat different from the country-of-birth categories in table 4.1. Moreover, the number of foreign-born persons with Latin American heritage (Hispanic identity) from a specific country (table 4.3) may differ from the number of persons reported to have been born in the same country (table 4.1). These numbers differ because country of birth and national heritage are not always the same and because non-Hispanics from Latin America are excluded from table 4.3. For example, 86,000 are reported to be born in Panama (table 4.1), but only 62,000 persons of Hispanic origin from Panama are foreign born (table 4.3). Analysts need to be very cautious and aware of these nuances of census measurement. The distinctions in census data may be somewhat arbitrary, but they reflect the complex conceptual problems of measuring ethnicity.

Of the 22 million Hispanic Americans in 1990, the Mexican-origin population comprises over 13 million (over 60 percent), with the other major groups being Puerto Ricans (2.7 million), Cubans (1 million), Dominicans (.5 million), Central Americans (1.3 million), South Americans (1 million), and the generic categories of Spaniard, Spanish, and Spanish American (1.1 million). Overall, the Hispanic-origin population is much more likely to be native born than the Asian and Pacific Islander population (64 percent versus 34 percent), but there is enormous variation across the spectrum of Hispanic populations.

Almost all of the Puerto Rican population (99 percent) is classified as native born; all those born on the island or the mainland are classified as native born. The composition of Spaniards by birthplace (83 percent native born) is very similar to those who label themselves Spanish (84 percent native born) and Spanish American (99 percent native born). These three categories largely represent persons with historical roots in the American Southwest that predate the region's incorporation into the United States in the mid-nineteenth century.

Although two-thirds of the Mexican-origin population are native born, the overall population is so large that the foreign-born Mexican population (4.5 million) swamps all the other groups in table 4.3. The number of foreign-born Mexican Americans is almost three-fifths of all foreign-born Hispanics and over one-fifth of all immigrants. All other Hispanic populations have only a minority native born (20 to 30 percent in most cases). All of these groups gained substantially from re-

Table 4.3 Hispanic Population by Nativity, Year of Entry, and Age, United States: 1990

	Population (in Thousands)			
		Native	Foreign Born	
Population by Hispanic Origin	Total	Born	1980–90	Pre-1980
Total U.S. population	248,710	228,943	8,664	11,104
Non-Hispanic origin	226,810	214,884	4,689	7,237
Hispanic origin	21,900	14,058	3,975	3,867
Mexican	13,393	8,933	2,248	2,212
Puerto Rican	2,652	2,619	16	17
Cuban	1,053	299	195	559
Other Hispanic	4,802	2,207	1,516	1,078
Dominican	520	153	196	171
Central American	1,324	278	730	316
Costa Rican	57	18	17	23
Guatemalan	269	53	149	67
Honduran	131	30	68	33
Nicaraguan	203	38	122	42
Panamanian	92	30	26	36
Salvadoran	565	106	346	113
South American	1,036	260	397	379
Argentinean	101	23	31	47
Bolivian	38	9	18	11
Chilean	69	18	21	29
Colombian	379	98	146	136
Ecuadorean	191	50	62	80
Paraguayan	7	2	3	2
Peruvian	175	41	83	51
Uruguayan	22	4	8	10
Venezuelan	48	13	24	11
Spaniard	519	429	30	60
Spanish	445	376	30	39
Spanish American	93	92	1	1

Source: U.S. Bureau of the Census (1993c), Table 1.

cent immigration during the 1980s, especially those from Central America and some groups from South America.

How well does the native-born Hispanic population represent the second generation? It depends on the group. Almost all of the Spaniard/Spanish/Spanish American populations and the majority of the Mexican American population have been in the United States for

Table 4.3 (*continued*)

Native Born	Foreign Born 1980–90	Pre-1980	Native Born	Foreign Born 1980–90	Pre-1980	Native Born	Immigrants
	Percent of Total Ethnic Population			Median Age		Population Age 15–24 (in Thousands)	
92	3	4	32.5	28.0	46.5	33,340	2,959
95	2	3	33.3	30.4	50.5	30,753	1,365
64	18	18	19.6	25.7	40.1	2,586	1,594
67	17	17	18.3	24.2	37.6	1,621	1,074
99	1	1	25.4	26.7	40.3	485	6
28	19	53	15.9	38.8	52.7	74	52
46	32	22	18.9	27.7	41.9	406	464
29	38	33	9.6	27.9	40.0	31	60
21	55	24	8.4	26.7	39.6	44	233
32	30	40	14.3	27.6	42.2	5	6
20	55	25	8.2	26.7	38.9	9	49
23	52	25	9.6	27.2	40.7	5	20
19	60	21	10.4	26.5	40.6	7	34
33	28	39	16.3	27.7	44.2	7	9
19	61	20	6.0	26.6	38.0	11	114
25	38	37	12.3	29.7	43.5	66	103
23	31	47	16.9	31.0	46.6	8	8
24	47	29	12.2	29.0	43.0	3	4
26	30	42	11.4	31.2	43.5	4	7
26	39	36	11.6	30.0	43.1	24	35
26	32	42	12.5	28.3	43.1	13	17
29	43	29	6.4	29.7	43.7	<1	1
23	47	29	11.5	30.4	43.6	9	20
18	36	45	13.9	31.6	44.7	1	2
27	50	23	13.8	28.1	37.4	2	6
83	6	12	28.6	28.9	51.4	74	11
84	7	9	27.4	27.1	45.3	63	11
99	1	1	26.8	16.5	46.4	14	<1

many generations, and inferences about generational change from comparisons between the native born and the foreign born would not be warranted. For the Puerto Rican population, data on nativity really do not speak to the question of birthplace in the island or the mainland. For most of the other Hispanic groups from the Caribbean (Dominicans), Central America, and South America, the majority of the native born are probably second-generation Americans. This seems evident from the significant share of recent (post-1980) immigration and the median age of the native-born segment of each group (less than age fifteen in most cases and less than age ten for several groups).

The last two columns in table 4.3 show the numbers of native-born and foreign-born Hispanics between the ages of fifteen and twenty-four. As with table 4.2, these figures are meant to illustrate the potential samples for an analysis of early socioeconomic attainment and family formation. Except for the groups for which the native born do not represent the second generation (Mexicans, Puerto Ricans, and Spaniards/Spanish/Spanish Americans), the numbers of native born are very small (because the native-born populations are few and very young). In general, the numbers of young immigrants (many of whom arrived as children) represent much more sizable samples for analysis of immigrant adaptation to American society.

Concept and Measurement of "Becoming American"

The concepts of immigrant generations and the socioeconomic life course have not been well integrated. The standard image of immigrants (and the conventional assumption in most immigration research) is of young adults who were socialized and educated in their country of origin. The parallel image of their children is that they are the first members of their community to be educated and socialized in American institutions. The problem with this logic is that a significant fraction of historical and contemporary immigration has been of families who brought children with them. These child immigrants—often labeled the 1.5 generation—were classified as immigrants, but were largely educated and socialized in the United States. Because census tabulations rarely provide sufficient information on year of immigration, most analyses rely on the standard generational comparisons. An unexplored hypothesis is whether country-of-origin differences may be explained by the age composition of immigrant streams.

The critical variable of timing is not simply the duration of residence in the United States but also the age at arrival. The potential influence of the home, neighborhood, schools, peers, and the mass media are sharply differentiated by the ages of children and teenagers. Immigrants who learn English in their teenage years often will retain an accent, while their younger siblings will speak like "natives." Youthful immigrants who are entirely educated in American schools may face fewer problems of adjustment than those who enter at older ages, but the youngest immigrants also may be more susceptible to peer pressures that are at odds with influences from the home. Age at arrival and years of duration in the United States provide benchmarks to test the impact of "becoming American." This framework does not replace the idea of immigrant generations but enriches it by taking into account variations in the age composition of immigrants.

A recently released census report (U.S. Bureau of the Census, 1993a), *The Foreign-Born Population in the United States, 1990*, tabulates a variety of social characteristics of immigrants by the year of arrival in the United States (before 1980, 1980–81, 1982–84, 1985–86, 1987–90). The cross-classification of current age (in 1990) and year of arrival also identifies age at immigration. Among the important socioeconomic variables in these tabulations are school enrollment and children ever born. School enrollment at the older teenage years (fifteen to seventeen and eighteen to nineteen) is a critical indicator for graduation from high school and the transition to college. The data allow for the comparison of current enrollment rates of teenage immigrants who arrived ten (or more) years earlier (almost native born) with those who arrived less than three years before the census.

A comparable analysis can be conducted comparing the marital status and early fertility of women immigrants, age fifteen to twenty-four, in 1990. The data allow for the measurement of nonmarital fertility, an indicator of nonconformity to middle-class aspirations. This variable is particularly important in light of the segmented-assimilation thesis that greater exposure (and assimilation) to American culture may be associated with mixed prospects for socioeconomic attainment.

The classical assimilation model implies that teenage immigrants who have been in the United States longer are more likely to be enrolled in high school and to have lower nonmarital fertility than those who just arrived. The segmented-assimilation model questions this expectation. If greater exposure to American society has primarily been to inner-city environments, which are not conducive for upward social mobility (educationally or economically), then immigrant children with longer U.S. residence (and a younger age at arrival) may not be doing better than recent arrivals.

A satisfactory test of these competing hypotheses would require data on the socioeconomic status of immigrant families and the character of their residential locations. Some aspects of these data are available in the Public Use Microdata Sample census files. In this preliminary investigation, the associations between national origins, duration of residence, and adaptation in the United States are explored. Descriptive patterns across more than forty country-of-origin immigrant populations should provide some important initial insights on the process of assimilation.

Patterns of Educational Enrollment

Table 4.4 shows the percentage of immigrant teenagers enrolled in school for two age groups (fifteen to seventeen and eighteen to nineteen) by year of immigration (five categories from pre-1980 to 1987–90). The younger age group would be enrolled in high school, and the older age group would be enrolled in a mixture of high school and college. The older group's enrollment rates, therefor, should provide a fairly good indicator of continuation to postsecondary schooling. All country- or region-of-origin groups are included in table 4.4. In most cases, the numbers of teenagers in each age group by year of entry and country of origin numbered in the hundreds or thousands, but in a few cells the number of observations dropped below one hundred. Consequently, attention is focused on the broad patterns, not on individual cells.[2]

The overall pattern for all immigrants is one of school enrollment rising with duration of residence (or younger age at arrival) in the United States. The time series shows a modest disadvantage for the most recent arrivals—those who arrived in the last five years—but little variation among those with longer residence. For the high school age group (fifteen to seventeen), enrollments hover around 90 percent, dropping to the 70 to 80 percent range for recent arrivals in some groups. For the sample of older teenagers (ages eighteen to nineteen), about 70 percent of earlier (1984 or before) immigrants were enrolled, but only about 50 percent of the recent immigrants.

A close examination of the country/region populations reveals two distinct patterns. The first is high and constant enrollment, regardless of duration of residence in the United States. The second pattern is an initial handicap—indicated by lower enrollment—for the most recent arrivals followed by higher enrollment for those with five or more years of residence. The first pattern of consistent high enrollments is evident for the younger age group among immigrants from almost all Asian countries, some European countries, the former Soviet Union, several Caribbean and South American countries, Canada, and Africa. The same pattern (at somewhat lower rates) is evident for many immigrant populations in the older age group. For example, among African immigrants, high school enrollment rates are always above 90 percent and college enrollment rates (ages eighteen to nineteen) are always 80 percent or higher.

The pattern of rising enrollment with longer residence in the United States is exemplified by the case of Mexican immigrants for whom high school enrollment (ages fifteen to seventeen) rose from 52 percent for recent arrivals to 88 percent for those who arrived prior to 1980.

(College-age enrollments rose from 22 to 57 percent across the same categories.) This pattern, which is evident for many other countries, especially for immigrants from Central America, provides support for the thesis of immigrant adaptation. Time in the system, and possible socialization at a younger age, leads to increasing opportunities or incentives for continued enrollment. For the older group, the most recent arrivals are less likely to be enrolled than those who arrived some years earlier. Perhaps those who arrived at younger ages were more likely to have graduated from a U.S. high school and were able to continue to college.

Some mixed patterns are consistent with the possibility that greater exposure to American culture leads to poorer prospects for educational mobility. For example, the younger Caribbean immigrants (Cubans, Dominicans, Haitians, and so on) do not always display higher enrollments among the groups that have been here the longest. This is an important finding, because Caribbean immigrants are more likely to be black and to live in neighborhoods with an African American majority. Note that this pattern does not hold for the older Caribbean immigrants. The other groups with inconsistent patterns are some European immigrant groups, particularly at the college-age range. The interpretation would be that greater exposure to American society has dulled the ambitions for higher education that remain strongest among the newest immigrants.

There are many threats to all of the preceding interpretations. The census enumeration is inclusive of all residents, whether temporary or permanent and whatever their reasons for being in the United States. For some nationality groups, including many from Asia, foreign students are included with permanent immigrants. For other groups, temporary laborers (perhaps Mexicans) and temporary refugees (Central Americans) are included with immigrants. Although census data allow for differentiation of citizens and noncitizens, there is no measure of visa status. Moreover, cross-sectional data do not permit independent assessment of selectivity of immigration during particular years of arrival and duration of residence. Small cell sizes, especially for many of the European groups, also reinforce caution.

In spite of these measurement problems, my reading of table 4.4 suggests modest (but not overwhelming) evidence for the thesis of immigrant adaptation. Longer exposure to American society (or younger age at arrival) generally has a positive effect on the enrollments of teenaged immigrants. Some groups, especially those from Asia and Africa, have very high enrollments regardless of duration of residence. Among recent arrivals, Caribbean groups resemble Asians (very high enrollment ratios), but they also show patterns of lowered education

Table 4.4 Percent Enrolled in School of Foreign-Born Youth, by Age and Year of Entry, United States; 1990

Place of Birth	Persons Age 15–17					Persons Age 18–19				
	1987–90	1985–86	1982–84	1980–81	Pre-1980	1987–90	1985–86	1982–84	1980–81	Pre-1980
All foreign born	75	87	91	92	91	48	57	70	71	72
Europe	92	94	95	95	88	73	74	81	77	68
France	94	83	100	90	81	84	88	100	67	73
Germany	96	93	91	95	84	67	77	72	86	61
Greece	81	94	82	82	86	74	83	100	81	68
Hungary	97	82	94	100	75	65	87	88	90	52
Ireland	90	87	100	81	77	39	69	61	39	66
Italy	84	87	92	100	81	67	55	57	76	61
Poland	88	98	97	97	84	71	80	80	83	70
Portugal	83	87	82	90	89	64	48	64	62	54
United Kingdom	91	97	97	98	94	67	79	82	77	78
Yugoslavia	79	96	96	100	97	55	36	91	68	68
Soviet Union	86	92	100	97	93	63	77	84	84	83
Asia	91	95	95	96	96	79	85	86	86	88
Cambodia	91	91	92	95	94	74	79	83	84	83
China	93	94	96	95	94	86	90	93	93	92
Hong Kong	96	98	96	98	98	95	92	88	95	94
India	92	95	95	98	97	82	88	90	92	94
Iran	91	97	97	96	97	82	89	84	80	87
Japan	95	95	100	96	95	92	92	85	96	76
Korea	93	92	95	97	96	86	87	89	88	90
Laos	89	95	91	94	95	68	80	80	76	80

Philippines	89	95	95	95	95	56	79	80	82	85
Taiwan	95	98	96	97	96	90	92	94	99	95
Thailand	93	91	97	98	99	92	89	79	79	72
Vietnam	91	96	96	96	97	77	88	83	89	91
North America	63	80	87	89	88	31	42	56	59	61
Canada	91	97	96	97	95	86	86	79	83	76
Mexico	52	70	81	86	88	22	30	43	53	57
Caribbean	88	92	92	92	88	67	72	74	69	73
Cuba	83	90	91	92	75	67	66	75	67	67
Dominican Republic	85	92	94	93	88	57	65	69	61	62
Haiti	91	93	94	92	89	81	83	74	77	82
Jamaica	93	93	89	95	92	70	76	75	73	76
Trinidad/Tobago	91	92	89	90	87	63	56	85	53	80
Central America	74	89	92	92	90	44	58	65	62	65
El Salvador	70	86	91	91	89	37	51	61	60	66
Guatemala	62	88	92	92	92	38	51	58	48	67
Honduras	85	90	94	92	91	48	60	72	60	55
Nicaragua	84	93	95	93	94	57	72	74	87	67
Panama	87	100	79	100	83	80	76	69	68	61
South America	89	91	94	94	94	64	74	72	75	77
Colombia	89	92	96	94	91	65	67	66	72	72
Ecuador	81	85	92	94	94	58	66	73	78	74
Guyana	89	90	89	93	94	59	75	74	78	79
Peru	91	93	96	98	96	66	82	64	69	82
Africa	92	94	92	94	95	83	84	83	80	87
Oceania	96	93	97	96	96	74	63	61	59	73

SOURCE: U.S. Bureau of the Census, Subject Summary Tape File One (SSTF1): The Foreign-Born Population in the United States, 1990.

for those with longest American residence, as do some Central American immigrants in the older age range.

Early Marriage and Nonmarital Fertility

Table 4.5 shows 1990 census data on young immigrant women, ages fifteen to twenty-four—one panel shows the percent who are married and the other shows the mean fertility of those who are unmarried—for all immigrant populations (the same list as in table 4.4) by year of entry into the United States. The question guiding this analysis is the impact of additional years of American residence on "adaptation" during the formative ages of adolescence and young adulthood, but the expectations are a bit different from those in the previous table. A younger age at marriage is considered "traditional" behavior, with greater exposure to American society leading to marital postponement. On the other hand, nonmarital fertility would be a sign of acculturation to the culture of those American youth least likely to experience upward social mobility. Nonmarital fertility is measured by subtracting the cumulative fertility (children ever born, CEB) of ever-married women, ages fifteen to twenty-four from the cumulative fertility of all women, ages fifteen to twenty-four. The nonmarital fertility rate (mean nonmarital CEB) of this age group is computed by dividing the cumulative fertility of never-married women by the number of never-married women in 1990.

For the total foreign-born population, there is modest support for the hypothesis that greater exposure to American society (earlier immigration) leads to a greater marital postponement. About one-third of young women who are recent immigrants (after 1985) are married (in 1990), but only about one-fourth of young women who immigrated earlier are married. It is possible that selectivity based on immigration law, not differential exposure (or socialization) to American society, explains this pattern. For example, being married (especially to an American resident) may be correlated with eligibility for admission to the United States for young immigrant women in their late teens or early twenties. For young women of the same age who arrived in the United States as teenagers or earlier, the only link between the timing of immigration and the timing of marriage would be the hypothesis of acculturation to the United States. Variations in the relationship across national-origin populations suggest, however, that there is more than selectivity at work.

The hypothesized relationship (more U.S. exposure leads to more marital postponement) is evident for immigrants from some, but not all, countries in Europe, Latin America, and Asia. In particular, the association is strong and consistent for immigrants from India, the Philip-

pines, Cambodia, Mexico, Peru, and Africa. For many other countries—
Vietnam, Thailand, and Taiwan in Asia and most of the Caribbean and
Central American countries—there is no clear relationship.

There are also major differences in age at marriage across countries
of origin. In general, immigrants from Asia, some Caribbean countries
(Haiti and Jamaica), and Africa seem much more likely to postpone
marriage than immigrants from Europe, Mexico, and Central America.
Whether these national variations might be explained as class differences, as opposed to some cultural preferences, cannot be addressed
within the limits of published data.

The data on nonmarital fertility also reveal more variation by national origin than by duration of residence in the United States. In general, nonmarital fertility is much lower for immigrants from Europe
and Asia than for immigrants from Mexico, the Caribbean, and Central America. Levels of nonmarital fertility for immigrants from South
America and Africa are intermediate. There are exceptions to these regional patterns, however. The refugee populations from Asia (Cambodia, Laos, and, to a lesser extent, Vietnam) had higher levels of nonmarital fertility that are comparable to the Caribbean pattern, but not
as high as Central American levels.

Again, there is some support for the thesis that greater exposure to
American society leads to higher rates of nonmarital fertility, especially among the Caribbean-origin populations. The patterns are, however, not monotonic across year-of-arrival groupings. Although the evidence is a bit shaky, nonmarital fertility appears a bit lower among
the longer duration categories (younger age at arrival) within the Central American populations and the Southeast Asian refugee populations. Perhaps this is a sign of immigrant adaptation—adjustment to
the "successful path" for upward mobility for immigrants.

Conclusions

The incorporation of the new wave of post-1965 immigrants and their
children is one of the most important challenges facing American society. Its importance is reflected in the great debates over immigration
policy and the several national commissions charged over the past two
decades with reviewing the progress of immigrants and their impact
on American society (Briggs, 1984; U.S. Department of Labor, 1989;
Bean, Edmonston, and Passel, 1990).

What has not happened, however, is any comparable national effort
to collect new data that might allow for serious scientific research on
the topic. Collection of immigration and emigration statistics is so poor
as to be a national scandal (Levine, Hill, and Warren, 1985). There have

Table 4.5 Marital Status and Nonmarital Fertility of Foreign-Born Women, Age 15–24, by Year of Entry, United States: 1990

	Percent Married					Mean CEB per Nonmarried Woman				
Place of Birth	1987–90	1985–86	1982–84	1980–81	Pre-1980	1987–90	1985–86	1982–84	1980–81	Pre-1980
All foreign born	33	35	28	26	24	0.12	0.18	0.15	0.15	0.12
Europe										
France	17	40	22	17	27	0.02	0.03	0.04	0.05	0.05
Germany	51	35	11	20	28	0.00	0.00	0.04	0.10	0.10
Greece	39	58	42	23	39	0.05	0.06	0.08	0.08	0.10
Hungary	38	59	59	24	26	0.00	0.11	0.00	0.00	0.02
Ireland	20	47	6	19	32	0.03	0.01	0.00	0.00	0.08
Italy	40	27	25	15	20	0.02	0.05	0.06	0.00	0.04
Poland	31	31	20	22	26	0.02	0.05	0.05	0.03	0.04
Portugal	41	36	20	17	23	0.09	0.03	0.01	0.03	0.03
United Kingdom	39	47	15	26	21	0.02	0.01	0.03	0.07	0.04
Yugoslavia	55	66	41	27	37	0.05	0.00	0.05	0.00	0.06
Soviet Union	26	16	20	22	22	0.01	0.00	0.00	0.01	0.02
Asia	27	21	17	16	14	0.03	0.05	0.05	0.06	0.03
Cambodia	25	21	23	18	11	0.14	0.25	0.24	0.14	0.07
China	26	12	7	7	16	0.01	0.04	0.01	0.01	0.03
Hong Kong	10	10	9	9	6	0.00	0.00	0.03	0.03	0.00
India	49	31	28	17	12	0.02	0.02	0.01	0.01	0.01
Iran	30	21	17	10	15	0.02	0.02	0.05	0.00	0.01
Japan	10	10	9	17	20	0.01	0.00	0.01	0.06	0.10
Korea	28	16	9	9	9	0.01	0.01	0.01	0.02	0.02
Laos	50	30	29	30	29	0.14	0.16	0.19	0.21	0.08

Philippines	28	24	20	18	15	0.05	0.05	0.05	0.05	0.06
Taiwan	11	5	4	6	6	0.00	0.01	0.02	0.01	0.01
Thailand	16	32	14	13	26	0.01	0.00	0.04	0.07	0.07
Vietnam	13	13	15	12	11	0.04	0.12	0.06	0.04	0.04
North America	37	41	37	32	30	0.20	0.28	0.27	0.24	0.21
Canada	29	29	19	17	22	0.03	0.06	0.04	0.03	0.04
Mexico	44	50	48	39	32	0.19	0.31	0.33	0.28	0.22
Caribbean	19	22	18	20	26	0.15	0.19	0.19	0.16	0.21
Cuba	24	29	27	28	45	0.04	0.03	0.04	0.08	0.08
Dominican Republic	29	30	23	21	32	0.17	0.22	0.24	0.38	0.32
Haiti	12	18	18	16	16	0.09	0.15	0.22	0.22	0.15
Jamaica	12	14	10	10	13	0.19	0.20	0.19	0.17	0.24
Trinidad/Tobago	19	27	25	25	18	0.14	0.30	0.16	0.17	0.21
Central America	27	34	33	27	28	0.28	0.35	0.29	0.26	0.19
El Salvador	24	36	34	30	30	0.33	0.41	0.34	0.29	0.22
Guatemala	31	36	32	23	29	0.33	0.43	0.27	0.27	0.23
Honduras	29	31	30	36	26	0.30	0.33	0.29	0.21	0.24
Nicaragua	28	27	32	21	27	0.21	0.21	0.16	0.13	0.10
Panama	35	27	27	15	27	0.08	0.15	0.28	0.10	0.21
South America	30	32	27	22	21	0.08	0.12	0.09	0.10	0.10
Colombia	27	34	35	28	24	0.12	0.24	0.12	0.17	0.11
Ecuador	33	34	28	34	28	0.11	0.09	0.11	0.08	0.15
Guyana	21	19	18	14	16	0.07	0.08	0.15	0.09	0.14
Peru	23	34	30	22	17	0.07	0.07	0.06	0.13	0.09
Africa	28	22	15	11	14	0.07	0.07	0.05	0.07	0.08
Oceania	28	32	34	26	24	0.03	0.31	0.04	0.04	0.09

SOURCE: U.S. Bureau of the Census (1990a), Table 1.

been no innovative efforts to collect survey data on a scale comparable to those launched to study other national issues, such as aging and retirement, youth employment, crime victimization, or drug use. This leaves the census as the major, and often only, source of data for the study of contemporary immigration.

During the 1980s, more than twenty countries sent a hundred thousand or more immigrants to the United States. The resulting immigrant and ethnic communities in Los Angeles, Miami, and New York are very different from each other and from almost every other metropolitan area in the country. With such great diversity and weak data resources, knowledge about the social, economic, and cultural mobility of the post-1965 wave of immigrants often seems to rest more on impressionistic information than on solid evidence. For immigration researchers and policymakers, the census appears like the tired old horse to farmers at spring plowing season. The census, like the workhorse, will do the basics, but it could be done much better if modern machinery were available for the task.

The classical model (and method) of studying immigrant adaptation by intergenerational comparisons was dealt a mortal blow with the loss of the census question on the nativity of parents in the 1980 and 1990 censuses. This chapter has explored prospects for using other features of recent census data to investigate the adaptation of immigrants and their children. One potential method is to consider the native-born members of certain race and ethnic communities as equivalent to the second generation. This assumption seems to be justified for most Asian nationality groups (with a few exceptions) and for some groups from the Caribbean and Central America. The only problem is that most of the second generation of these new immigrant groups were still children (below age fifteen) in 1990. The numbers of each national-origin population in the age categories of greatest interest (for example, ages fifteen to twenty-four) typically number a few thousand. For the larger groups (Filipinos and Chinese), the assumption that the native born represent the second generation is open to question.

An alternative research strategy is to examine the impact of duration of residence (or age at arrival) on the socioeconomic outcomes of immigrants. If this technique is applied to teenagers or young adults, duration of residence can span the period from childhood to the years immediately before the census. Although problems of the selectivity of immigration cloud the picture, the impact of "becoming American" (meaning longer exposure to American society and arriving at a younger age) may have a positive, negative, or neutral influence on socioeconomic outcomes.

The second half of this chapter explored this question, in a preliminary fashion, with data from the published tabulations of the 1990 census for two outcomes: educational enrollment and early marriage and nonmarital fertility. Although the results were mixed, the most common pattern seems to be that greater exposure to American society during childhood is positive. There were hints of a different pattern, however. In a few instances, especially for Caribbean immigrants, those with longest U.S. residence had slightly lower high school enrollment rates and slightly higher levels of nonmarital childbearing. Caribbeans are one of the most likely of immigrant populations to be closest to inner-city minority populations. It may be that the classical and revisionist hypotheses of immigrant adaptation describe different aspects of important contemporary trends. These variations may become clearer when the analysis is broadened to include the differential economic status of immigrant families and their communities of settlement.

Notes

1. There is a substantial literature on the descendants of the Japanese immigrants who immigrated to the U.S. mainland and Hawaii around the turn of the century (Kitano, 1976; Bonacich and Modell, 1980; Montero, 1980). Most Japanese Americans are third- or fourth-generation Americans. There is an even earlier history of large-scale Chinese immigration in the late nineteenth century, but the large influx of contemporary Chinese immigration has tipped the balance toward a majority foreign-born population.

2. The published tabulations did not permit the separate computation of enrollment ratios for those age fifteen to seventeen and those age eighteen to nineteen. I am very grateful to Jorge del Pinal, chief of the Ethnic and Hispanic Statistics Branch of the U.S. Bureau of the Census, for his kind assistance in producing this table from the summary file SSTF1.

5

Today's Second Generation: Evidence from the 1990 Census

LEIF JENSEN AND YOSHIMI CHITOSE

C ITIZENS of the United States have long been sensitive to the economic and social consequences of large-scale immigration. During the early 1900s, when southern and eastern Europeans were populating the ghettos of eastern U.S. cities, public outcry led to the enactment of quotas that virtually excluded all but northwestern Europeans (Bouvier and Gardner, 1986). As a result of the 1965 amendments to the Immigration and Nationality Act, recent decades have witnessed another great wave of immigration. This legislation raised the ceiling on immigration, shuffled preference categories to give primacy to those entering to be reunited with kin over those with important job skills, and instituted a more equitable worldwide distribution of visas (Bouvier and Gardner, 1986). Predictably, the pace of legal immigration doubled from about a quarter million annually during the 1950s to roughly a half million annually in recent decades (U.S. Immigration and Naturalization Service, 1991). Also, the percent

Support for this research was provided by the Population Research Institute at the Pennsylvania State University, which has core support from the National Institute on Child Health and Human Development (P30 HD28263-01). The invaluable programming assistance of Nikos George is gratefully acknowledged, as is the clerical assistance of Robbie Swanger. An earlier version of this chapter was presented at the 1993 meeting of the American Sociological Association in Miami. The authors remain solely responsible for errors that remain.

arriving from Asia and Latin America increased from about 30 percent during the 1950s to about 85 percent today (U.S. Immigration and Naturalization Service, 1991).

These trends have sparked a resurgence of old worries about the potentially negative economic and social consequences of immigration (Lamm and Imhoff, 1985). Among immigration scholars, this concern has fostered empirical studies of the labor force characteristics of the new immigrants (Keely, 1975; De Jong, 1990), of their propensity to be poor and to receive public assistance benefits (Jensen, 1988, 1989; Borjas and Trejo, 1991), of their earnings over time (Chiswick, 1979; Borjas, 1985), and of their net effect on public coffers (Simon, 1984; Rothman and Espenshade, 1992). For reviews of the economic consequences of immigration, see Borjas and Tienda (1987), Papademetriou and others (1989), and Borjas (1990).

Compared with the new immigrants themselves, however, much less is known about the status of their offspring—the second generation. As will be described, this neglect is not surprising when it is considered that the 1970 U.S. census is the last large and nationally representative data set that allows researchers to straightforwardly identify the children of immigrants and to conduct reliable analyses of this subpopulation. Nonetheless, the lack of data on the second generation is lamentable in view of longstanding scholarly interest in processes of assimilation and integration of immigrants, both within and between generations (Gordon, 1964). An analysis of today's second generation would seem a natural extension to research on the progress of the children of turn-of-the-century immigrants (Lieberson, 1980). Preliminary work by Portes and his associates (Portes and Rumbaut, 1990; Portes and Zhou, 1993) indicates that the current second generation may be characterized by a new "segmented assimilation" in which different groups experience either traditional assimilation and upward mobility, downward mobility by unsuccessfully competing in the mainstream economy, or upward mobility by living and working in ethnically homogeneous immigrant communities (Portes and Zhou, 1993: 82).

From a policy perspective, the lopsided interest in immigrants to the neglect of their children is unfortunate in view of the obvious importance of the second generation to the long-term consequences of the new immigration (Jasso and Rosenzweig, 1990). If children of the new immigration are as successful, in the aggregate, as those of previous generations (Lieberson, 1980), then they should prove to be a net benefit to the economy and society. Unfortunately, several factors are working against them. First, as a result of industrial restructuring, the new second generation is facing an economy that is neither growing as fast nor is as full of good jobs with opportunities for advancement as that during the early part of this century (Gans, 1992; Portes and Zhou, 1993). Second, compared with previous cohorts, a much higher proportion of today's second generation is nonwhite, which can only exacerbate problems of prejudice and discrimination in already tight labor markets (Gans, 1992). To these liabilities, Portes and Zhou (1993) add the concentration of many second-generation children in the inner city where poverty rates are high and job opportunities are declining (Wilson, 1991).

Prior to speculating about the adaptation of the second generation or their long-term effects on U.S. society, it is important to understand their current circumstances. This chapter analyzes data from the 1990 U.S. Census of Population and Housing to provide a broad statistical portrait of the children of immigrants today. Using children in families as the unit of analysis, we compare native-born children of native-born parents to children with at least one foreign-born parent. The latter are further differentiated by the year of immigration of parents and by whether the children were foreign or native born. These children are compared along a wide range of social, economic, and demographic variables that describe the place of residence, the family and house-hold, the household head, and the children themselves.

Data

The Public Use Microdata Samples (PUMS) of the decennial U.S. Censuses of Population and Housing are based on a random subset of households that receive the so-called census long-form questionnaire. The long form contains a lengthy list of supplementary questions that concern the socioeconomic and demographic characteristics of the household and its members. In general, these data sets are so large that they can provide reliable analyses of even relatively small populations, such as the children of immigrants. Indeed, the 1960 and 1970 PUMS contain information on the nativity of the parents for all individuals in the sample, allowing researchers to identify unambiguously the children of immigrants. Unfortunately, under pressure to constrain the length of the long-form questionnaire, the Census Bureau dropped questions about parental nativity from the 1980 long form. These questions continued to be absent from the 1990 census questionnaire. The lack of information about parental nativity in the 1990 PUMS seriously undermines our ability to provide a contemporary assessment of the circumstances of today's second generation. The best that researchers can do is restrict their analysis to children still residing with their parents. While this is an inferior alternative, it is one we reluctantly follow in this analysis.

We base this study on the PUMS 5 percent Sample A of the 1990 census (U.S. Bureau of the Census, 1992a), which is based on the 15.9 percent of U.S. households that received the 1990 census long-form questionnaire (U.S. Bureau of the Census, 1992b). From this hierarchical file, we constructed two parallel rectangular files with children as the units of analysis. First, we selected own children (natural or adopted) under age eighteen of household heads in households headed by a foreign-born head or of a foreign-born spouse of the head (if present). To these children's data records, we appended selected variables from the person records of their parent(s) and from their household records. Second, for comparison, a parallel data file was constructed consisting of native-born children of native-born parents. Since children of natives constitute a much larger percentage of the U.S. population, these children were sampled at 10 percent from the PUMS. For convenience, we refer to them as "native children." In all, we analyzed 258,875 native children and 381,221 children of immigrants. Since the PUMS is a stratified sample, the descriptive statistics presented have been weighted.

All of the tables in the analysis show means or relative distributions of key variables using the same breakdown. To wit, native children are compared with all second-generation children—broadly defined as children with at least one immigrant parent. The latter are broken down by the year of immigration of the parent(s): 1985 to 1990, 1975 to 1984, 1965 to 1974, and before 1965.[1] A more conservative definition of the second generation would restrict attention to children of immigrants who were born in the United States. Accordingly, second-generation children are further subdivided into foreign-born and native-born categories. All cell entries in the tables are percents, except where indicated.

We emphasize that the lack of information on parental nativity, and the corresponding focus only on those children still residing with their parents, imposes an inevitable selectivity problem. To the extent that there are systematic differences between second- and higher-generation children in the rate at which and reasons for which they leave their families of orientation, these comparisons are biased. We neither assess the magnitude nor attempt to correct for this bias, but raise this caveat both to caution the reader and to underscore the need to complement our analysis with primary data that would provide a more complete picture of the status of the second generation.

Today's Second Generation: A Descriptive Portrait

Places of Residence

Table 5.1 shows percentage distributions for place-of-residence variables. Several measures highlight the propensity for the new second

Table 5.1 Characteristics of Children's Place of Residence (in Percent)[a]

Characteristic	Nonimmigrant	Total	85–90	75–84	65–74	<1965
		Total				
		Parent's Year of Immigration				
Metropolitan residence						
Metropolitan	79.9	94.6	95.1	95.1	94.6	92.3
Nonmetropolitan	20.1	5.4	4.9	4.9	5.4	7.7
Urban residence						
Urban	72.1	92.0	94.7	93.7	92.0	86.7
Rural	27.9	8.0	5.3	6.3	8.0	13.3
Rural farm	1.8	0.3	0.2	0.3	0.4	0.5
State of Residence[b]						
California	8.3	33.9	34.9	37.7	32.6	24.3
New York	5.7	11.7	11.2	10.3	13.4	12.7
Texas	7.0	11.1	9.5	12.7	10.7	9.0
Florida	4.1	6.5	6.8	6.3	6.3	7.2
Illinois	4.6	5.1	3.8	4.9	5.8	5.4
New Jersey	2.6	4.3	4.6	3.6	4.7	5.1
Massachusetts	2.2	2.5	2.7	2.0	2.9	3.0
Arizona	1.5	1.8	2.0	1.6	1.8	2.3
Michigan	4.2	1.7	1.4	1.3	1.9	3.1
Washington	2.1	1.7	2.0	1.7	1.3	2.2
Moved residence in last five years (among those aged 5+)	46.9	53.3	83.3	54.1	49.2	50.8

SOURCE: Public Use Microdata (PUMS) Sample A of the 1990 U.S. Census of Population and Housing. Sample includes children with at least one immigrant parent.
[a] Cell entries are percents except where indicated.
[b] Top ten when rank ordered by percent of total second generation.

generation to reside in urban locales. In 1990, about 95 percent of children of immigrants were living in metropolitan areas (basically counties with at least one city of 50,000 or more and any economically tied surrounding counties). This compares to only 80 percent of native children. Aside from the slightly lower propensity to live in metropolitan areas among children of pre-1965 arrivals, little difference is seen across year-of-arrival groups or nativity categories. An alternative residential distinction is that between urban and rural areas. About 72 percent of native children were living in urban areas (basically minor civil divi-

Table 5.1 (*continued*)

| | Native-Born Children | | | | | Foreign-Born Children | | | |
| | Parent's Year of Immigration | | | | | Parent's Year of Immigration | | | |
Total	85–90	75–84	65–74	<1965	Total	85–90	75–84	65–74	<1965
94.0	93.4	94.5	94.6	92.3	96.4	96.2	96.8	95.8	92.3
6.0	6.6	5.5	5.4	7.7	3.6	3.8	3.2	4.2	7.7
91.4	93.1	93.0	91.9	86.7	95.4	95.8	95.6	93.6	89.3
8.6	6.9	7.0	8.1	13.3	4.6	4.2	4.4	6.4	10.7
0.4	0.3	0.3	0.4	0.5	0.2	0.2	0.2	0.4	0.1
32.3	31.7	36.5	32.0	24.1	39.7	37.7	40.9	40.6	31.8
11.4	10.4	9.5	13.2	12.6	12.5	11.9	12.4	16.6	14.9
11.6	12.2	13.5	10.7	8.9	9.5	7.6	10.6	10.9	14.4
6.3	6.2	5.9	6.3	7.2	7.1	7.3	7.1	6.0	8.7
5.3	4.0	5.2	5.8	5.5	4.1	3.7	4.2	5.7	4.2
4.3	4.1	3.5	4.8	5.1	4.3	4.9	3.9	4.2	3.4
2.6	2.6	2.0	2.9	3.1	2.5	2.8	2.3	2.1	1.5
1.9	2.3	1.7	1.8	2.2	1.7	1.8	1.5	1.9	3.8
1.9	1.5	1.4	1.9	3.2	1.1	1.3	1.9	1.1	0.7
1.7	2.2	1.8	1.3	2.2	1.6	1.9	1.4	0.7	1.8
47.0	75.7	57.2	41.3	37.5	72.5	92.1	63.0	50.4	53.0

sions of at least 2,500 population), compared with 92 percent among the second generation. Here, however, there are important differences by parent's year of immigration and children's nativity. Children of more recent immigrants are much more likely than those of earlier arrivals to reside in urban areas. Urban residence also is more typical of the foreign-born second generation when compared with their native-born counterparts. Finally, rural residence is sometimes erroneously equated with farming. Although 8 percent of the second generation lives in rural areas, only 0.3 percent lives on farms in rural areas.

Table 5.1 shows the distribution of children across ten states that are rank-ordered by the proportion of the second generation residing in each. Not surprisingly, the second generation is concentrated in those states known to be popular destinations for the new immigrants

(Portes and Rumbaut, 1990). For example, while only 8 percent of all native children live in California, over a third (34 percent) of all second-generation children reside there. For the foreign-born second generation, the proportion in California is closer to 40 percent. Looking across year-of-immigration categories, California appears to be a less predominant state of residence among children of the most recent immigrants. That immigrants prefer urban locales explains the high proportion of the second generation in states taking in the New York City and Chicago metropolitan areas (New Jersey, New York, and Illinois). The high proportion of immigrants in states more proximate to Latin America also is seen (Arizona, Florida, and Texas). The final row of table 5.1 presents the percent of children who resided in a different place in 1985 (five years before the census). On the whole, second-generation children appear to be more geographically mobile than native children. Even those second-generation children who arrived before 1985 (whose mobility rates would not necessarily be inflated by the act of migration itself) have higher rates of mobility than do native children.

Households

Social and Demographic Characteristics.   Table 5.2 presents selected social and demographic characteristics of children's households. The first rows indicate that in terms of household size, second-generation children live in households that are slightly larger and have more related children than do native children. The average household size for second-generation children (5.2) is almost an entire person greater than that for native children (4.4). Among the second generation, foreign-born children live in larger households with more children present than do their native-born counterparts.

Being a child in a large household with many siblings is not inherently a liability, as long as the family has the resources necessary to provide for them. The findings in this and other tables suggest that second-generation children may be at a disadvantage in this regard. For example, while their households have more members on average, they have fewer rooms and more total persons per bedroom (table 5.2). Children of more recent arrivals and foreign-born children are especially cramped.

The remaining rows of table 5.2 pertain to language spoken at home. Not surprisingly, children of immigrants are far less likely (17 percent) to speak only English at home than are children of natives (89 percent). The foreign-born second generation is especially unlikely (8 percent) to speak only English. Consistent with the current country-of-origin composition of the post-1965 immigration, the modal foreign language spoken in second-generation households is Spanish (46 per-cent), while the next most popular are Asian and Pacific Island languages (18 per-cent). The pattern across post-1965 parental year-of-immigration cohorts reflects the changing country-of-origin composition of immigrants. The percent reporting Spanish declines from 50 percent (for 1965–74 arrivals) to 43 percent (for 1985–90 arrivals), while the percent speaking Asian and Pacific Island languages at home rises from 13 to 25 percent. Finally, a linguistically isolated household is one in which no one over age four-teen speaks English "very well" (U.S. Bureau of the Census, 1992b).[2] Fully one-quarter of all second-generation children are in such house-holds, compared with less than 1 percent of native children. Among the second generation, children of more recent immigrants and foreign-born children are more likely to be found within linguistically isolated households.

Economic Characteristics.   Table 5.3 reveals stark economic disadvan-tages among second-generation children, which are of concern given the strong empirical links between economic deprivation in childhood and ultimate socioeconomic attainment. The first panel shows poverty rates for children according to three absolute definitions. The first of these is the official Census Bureau definition, which basically defines a child as poor if he or she lives in a family whose annual income is less than three times the cost of a minimal diet for a family of that size (Ruggles, 1990). For example, in 1989 the official threshold for a fam-ily of four with two children was $12,575 (U.S. Bureau of the Census, 1992b). The official poverty rate for native children was 17 percent, while that for children of immigrants was closer to 22 percent, or one-third higher in relative terms. However, this gross comparison fails to capture the tremendous variation in poverty status among the second generation by parental year of immigration and child's nativity. Na-tive-born children of pre-1974 immigrants have poverty rates that are below those of native children. The children of more recent arrivals are much more likely to be living in poverty. About one-third of all sec-ond-generation children whose parents arrived in the five years before the 1990 census were living in poverty; among foreign-born children of recent arrivals, the poverty rate nears 38 percent.

While not unanimous, there is broad sentiment that the official poverty thresholds are too austere, and many means-tested govern-ment programs define as income-eligible those whose annualized in-comes are somewhat above official poverty thresholds (Levitan, 1990). We define as "near poor" all those households bringing in up to one-

Table 5.2 Size and Language Characteristics of Children's Households

Household Variable	Nonimmigrant	Total	85–90	75–84	65–74	<1965
		Total				
			Parent's Year of Immigration			
Total persons in household (mean)	4.4	5.2	5.2	5.4	5.1	4.8
Number of related children (mean)	2.4	2.7	2.6	2.8	2.7	2.4
Number of rooms in household (mean)	6.1	5.0	4.2	4.6	5.4	6.3
Total persons (total bed-rooms + 1) (mean)	2.1	2.7	3.0	2.9	2.5	2.2
Language spoken at home (in percent)						
English only	88.6	16.5	9.4	10.1	16.8	41.3
Spanish	7.2	46.2	43.4	49.3	50.2	33.0
Indo-European	3.4	16.0	17.3	13.6	16.6	20.0
Asian-Pacific Island	0.3	17.9	25.4	23.4	13.4	3.5
Other	0.5	3.4	4.6	3.6	3.1	2.2
Household linguistically isolated (in percent)	0.8	25.7	48.1	33.6	12.9	3.9

SOURCE: Public Use Microdata (PUMS) Sample A of the 1990 U.S. Census of Population and Housing. Sample includes children with at least one immigrant parent.

and-a-half times the income marking the official poverty line. The near-poverty rates are correspondingly higher than the official rates and show the same pattern of disadvantage for the second generation generally and for children of more recent arrivals and foreign-born

Table 5.2 (*continued*)

	Native-Born Children					Foreign-Born Children			
	Parent's Year of Immigration					Parent's Year of Immigration			
Total	85–90	75–84	65–74	<1965	Total	85–90	75–84	65–74	<1965
5.0	4.7	5.2	5.1	4.7	5.7	5.5	5.8	6.1	5.7
2.6	2.3	2.8	2.7	2.4	3.0	2.8	3.1	3.1	2.8
5.2	4.3	4.7	5.5	6.4	4.3	4.1	4.4	4.7	5.0
2.6	2.8	2.8	2.5	2.2	3.1	3.1	3.1	3.1	2.8
19.1	11.9	11.1	17.3	42.1	7.7	7.6	7.5	8.8	12.5
45.8	46.8	49.3	49.2	32.2	47.3	40.9	49.2	64.7	60.6
16.2	15.8	13.8	16.8	20.1	15.3	18.4	13.3	12.7	16.6
15.5	20.4	21.9	13.5	3.4	26.3	29.0	27.2	11.3	7.7
3.4	5.1	3.9	3.2	2.2	3.4	4.2	2.9	2.5	2.6
21.1	37.4	33.4	12.4	3.5	41.4	55.9	34.1	20.7	16.3

children in particular. If anything, they dramatize these differences, suggesting that children of recent arrivals are much more likely than native children to have family incomes that hover just above the official poverty thresholds.

The third definition measures deep poverty—children in families with incomes below one-half the official thresholds. While the pattern

Table 5.3 Economic Characteristics of Children's Households

Household Variable	Nonimmigrant	Total	Parent's Year of Immigration 85–90	75–84	65–74	<1965
Poverty status (in percent)						
Official poverty (100% threshold)	16.5	21.8	33.7	24.9	16.9	9.8
Near poverty (150% threshold)	26.3	35.6	51.1	41.0	29.0	17.6
Deep poverty (50% threshold)	7.8	8.4	14.8	9.1	6.4	4.0
Household income ($1,000s) (mean)	40.9	40.7	29.8	36.8	45.3	53.8
Number of workers (mean)	2.7	2.7	2.5	2.7	2.8	2.9
Number of workers per person (mean)	0.7	0.6	0.5	0.5	0.6	0.6
Housing tenure status (in percent)						
Owned with mortgage	58.5	46.6	20.2	41.3	57.9	67.7
Owned free and clear	8.3	6.2	2.8	5.1	8.0	9.7
Rented	30.7	45.4	74.3	51.8	32.5	21.4
No cash rent	2.5	1.8	2.7	1.9	1.6	1.3

SOURCE: Public Use Microdata (PUMS) Sample A of the 1990 U.S. Census of Population and Housing. Sample includes children with at least one immigrant parent.

of results is the same, the differences are less stark. For example, 8.4 percent of second-generation children are in deep poverty, which compares with 7.8 percent of native children. Still, the fact that about 15 percent of children of recent arrivals (and 17 percent of recent foreign-born children) are this severely deprived is alarming.

In view of the higher poverty risks faced by second-generation children, it is somewhat surprising that when economic status is measured as mean annual household income, the two groups are at parity—both around $41,000. This suggests that income inequality is substantially greater among the second generation than among native

Table 5.3 *(continued)*

	Native-Born Children					Foreign-Born Children			
	Parent's Year of Immigration					Parent's Year of Immigration			
Total	85–90	75–84	65–74	<1965	Total	85–90	75–84	65–74	<1965
18.7	28.0	23.3	16.2	9.3	32.2	37.9	28.9	26.1	26.8
31.6	45.9	38.8	28.1	17.0	49.5	55.0	46.6	42.7	42.1
7.1	11.4	8.6	6.2	3.7	13.2	17.4	10.4	9.8	13.9
42.8	30.1	37.3	45.8	54.3	33.4	29.6	35.4	39.0	36.4
2.7	2.5	2.6	2.8	2.9	2.7	2.5	2.8	2.9	2.8
0.6	0.6	0.6	0.6	0.7	0.5	0.5	0.5	0.5	0.6
51.8	25.6	43.5	59.0	68.5	28.5	16.3	35.5	42.1	39.6
6.9	3.5	5.3	8.0	9.6	4.0	2.3	4.4	8.0	12.2
39.5	67.2	49.3	31.4	20.7	65.8	79.5	58.4	48.4	45.6
1.8	3.6	2.0	1.6	1.3	1.8	2.0	1.6	1.5	2.7

children, which is consistent with the notion of socioeconomic bifurcation among recent immigrant cohorts. Again, sizable differences are seen across parental year of immigration and nativity groups, which mirror the poverty results by showing greater deprivation among more recent arrivals and foreign-born children.

The labor force behavior of immigrants and their effects on the U.S. labor market have historically generated great concern (Papademetriou and others, 1989). For immigrant children, the employment status of elders is critical for shaping both immediate economic fortunes and long-term norms and values regarding work. Table 5.3 reveals that both the average number of workers in the household and the number of workers per household member vary remarkably little across the groups of interest. Children of more recent immigrants have slightly fewer workers, but the differences are not great.

A final indicator of socioeconomic status is housing tenure—whether the family's residence is owned or rented. Second-generation children are less likely than native children to be in a household that owns its home (with or without a mortgage) and are much more likely to be living in rented households. Only about 23 percent of children of recent arrivals live in a family-owned home, while almost three out of four (74 percent) are in rented quarters. Foreign-born children are especially disadvantaged in this regard.

Household Heads

To further document the social and economic background of children, several tables describe the social and demographic characteristics, income sources, and labor force status of household heads.

Social and Demographic Characteristics. Table 5.4 shows means and percentage distributions for various social and demographic characteristics of household heads. On the whole, household heads of the second generation are older than those of native children (38.7 years and 35.1 years, respectively). Not surprisingly, more recently arrived household heads are younger than those who have been in the United States longer. The heads of households with second-generation children also are more likely to be male (83 versus 76 percent), a finding that is consistent with the differentials in marital status. Second-generation household heads are more likely to be married (87 percent) than are native ones (78 percent) and are correspondingly less likely to be divorced, separated, or never married. That children of immigrants are more likely to be found in married-couple families is an encouraging sign that may counteract, somewhat, their comparatively low socioeconomic status.

The data for race and ethnicity in table 5.4 clearly reflect the origins of the new immigration. Fully 84 percent of the household heads of native children are white, which compares with about half (53 percent) of those of second-generation children. The nonwhite household heads of native children are overwhelmingly black (15 percent overall). By contrast, among second-generation household heads, Asians are the modal nonwhite category (34 percent overall), followed by blacks (12 percent overall). The race distribution of household heads by year of immigration reflects the well-known shift toward Asian countries of origin. Almost half (46 percent) of children with a parent who arrived from 1985 to 1990 had an Asian household head. The corresponding percentage for children whose parents arrived before 1965 is only 7 percent. Results for Hispanicity are shown in a separate panel. About 45 percent of second-generation children have a Hispanic household head, and about two-thirds of these claim to be of Mexican ethnicity (31 percent overall). The data also reflect the decline in the proportion of Hispanics among recent immigrant cohorts as Asians have come to represent a larger portion of the immigrant stream.

Table 5.4 indicates that a disadvantage faced by children of more recent arrivals is that their parents are less likely to be citizens. About 76 percent of children who immigrated after 1984 had household heads who were not citizens. Among foreign-born children in this category, 89 percent of household heads were not citizens.

The distributions of two important human capital attributes, English-speaking ability and formal education, are also shown in table 5.4. For some groups, English ability is positively related to socioeconomic attainment. (See, for example, Bean and Tienda, 1987.) In 1990, only about 24 percent of second-generation household heads spoke English "not well" or "not at all." This compares with less than 1 percent among native household heads. The inability to speak English well is, not surprisingly, a liability more common among more recently arrived household heads and among those of foreign-born children. For example, of foreign-born children whose parents arrived between 1985 and 1990, nearly half (47 percent) of their household heads spoke English "not well" or "not at all."

Table 5.4 indicates that when compared to the household heads of native children, those of second-generation children are overrepresented among both the poorly educated and the very well educated. Over one-quarter of second-generation children have household heads who completed eight or fewer years of schooling. This compares with merely 3 percent of native children. Interestingly, these rates of low educational attainment are not worst among the most recent arrivals; those who arrived between 1985 and 1990 are not as poorly educated as those who arrived between 1975 and 1984. Foreign-born children are much more likely to have poorly educated parents than their native-born counterparts. At the other extreme, second-generation children are slightly more likely to have parents with graduate or professional degrees than their native counterparts. This reflects an immigration policy that continues to give priority to prospective immigrants with exceptional scientific, professional, or artistic credentials. While those with parents who arrived before 1965 have the highest percent with household heads who have bachelor's degrees or better, those from the most recent immigrant cohort (1985–90) are better off in this regard than those from the previous (1975–84) cohort.

Table 5.4 **Social and Demographic Characteristics of Children's Household Heads**

Household Variable	Native	Total	Parent's Year of Immigration			
			85–90	75–84	65–74	<1965
Age (mean)	35.1	38.7	36.1	37.2	40.4	42.0
Male household head	76.1	83.0	84.5	82.1	82.3	85.5
Marital status						
Married	78.1	86.9	89.8	85.7	85.9	89.0
Widowed	1.3	1.4	1.2	1.3	1.6	1.6
Divorced	10.2	4.4	2.1	3.8	5.8	5.8
Separated	4.2	3.5	2.7	4.0	3.8	2.2
Never married	6.1	3.9	4.3	5.2	3.0	1.4
Race						
White	83.8	53.2	42.0	38.0	58.0	88.4
Black	14.5	11.7	10.8	14.2	14.1	4.1
Native American	1.1	0.4	0.4	0.4	0.3	0.4
Asian	0.5	34.2	46.1	46.8	27.2	6.9
Other	0.1	0.5	0.7	0.6	0.4	0.2
Hispanicity						
Mexican	3.3	30.5	27.3	32.9	33.7	21.1
Puerto Rican	1.5	0.7	0.6	0.6	0.9	0.7
Cuban	0.0	2.4	0.9	1.5	3.4	4.5
Central American	0.0	4.6	6.3	6.2	2.8	1.4
South American	0.0	3.2	4.0	3.1	3.8	1.9
Other Hispanic	0.6	3.5	3.5	3.7	4.1	1.9
Not Hispanic	94.5	55.1	57.4	52.0	51.3	68.5
Citizenship						
Native	100.0	16.7	11.1	12.4	19.1	30.4
Naturalized citizen	0.0	33.3	12.7	30.2	40.9	49.5
Not a citizen	0.0	50.0	76.2	57.4	40.0	20.1
English ability						
Speaks only English	93.4	23.7	14.6	16.2	24.9	51.9
Speaks very well	4.8	30.2	24.7	29.0	34.8	30.9
Speaks well	1.2	22.1	22.0	25.6	23.0	11.1
Speaks not well	0.5	18.2	27.4	22.4	13.9	5.0
Speaks not at all	0.1	5.7	11.4	6.8	3.4	1.1
Completed education						
Eight years or less	3.4	25.7	26.3	30.7	25.7	11.4
High school or more	83.1	60.1	59.5	54.2	59.4	78.3
College or more	23.0	22.7	25.4	20.1	21.5	29.5
Graduate or professional	8.7	11.0	12.5	9.5	11.0	13.8

SOURCE: Public Use Microdata (PUMS) Sample A of the 1990 U.S. Census of Population and Housing. Sample includes children with at least one immigrant parent.

Table 5.4 *(continued)*

	Native-Born Children					Foreign-Born Children			
	Parent's Year of Immigration					Parent's Year of Immigration			
Total	85–90	75–84	65–74	<1965	Total	85–90	75–84	65–74	<1965
38.3	35.1	35.9	40.3	41.9	40.0	38.3	40.7	42.6	44.9
83.8	84.7	83.6	82.8	85.9	80.3	84.4	78.2	75.5	72.5
87.9	90.7	87.5	86.6	89.6	83.4	89.1	80.7	75.6	71.2
1.1	0.5	0.8	1.5	1.5	2.4	1.7	2.6	3.4	6.2
4.3	1.5	3.2	5.6	5.7	4.7	2.5	5.6	8.6	9.4
3.0	2.1	3.3	3.6	2.1	4.9	3.1	5.9	6.8	6.8
3.7	5.2	5.2	2.8	1.2	4.6	3.6	5.2	5.7	6.4
59.6	51.8	43.1	59.1	88.9	30.1	35.3	24.1	33.6	62.2
11.4	13.1	13.9	13.6	3.8	13.1	9.2	15.1	25.8	17.5
0.4	0.6	0.4	0.3	0.4	0.2	0.3	0.2	0.2	0.5
28.2	33.9	42.0	26.6	6.7	55.9	54.5	59.8	39.1	19.7
0.4	0.6	0.6	0.4	0.2	0.7	0.7	0.8	1.3	0.1
30.7	29.9	34.0	32.7	20.5	29.7	25.3	29.9	47.1	42.3
0.8	1.1	0.7	0.9	0.7	0.2	0.2	0.3	0.5	0.5
2.6	0.8	1.3	3.4	4.5	1.7	1.0	2.0	2.4	3.0
3.7	5.4	5.2	2.7	1.3	7.6	7.0	8.7	4.5	4.2
3.0	3.6	2.8	3.8	1.8	4.0	4.2	3.7	4.2	3.0
3.4	3.8	3.6	4.1	1.9	4.2	2.4	4.5	6.4	6.0
55.8	55.4	52.4	52.4	69.3	52.6	58.9	50.9	34.9	41.0
21.2	24.2	16.5	20.4	31.3	1.6	1.6	1.6	1.2	2.2
36.6	17.7	30.8	41.0	49.5	22.2	9.1	28.7	39.9	48.0
42.2	58.1	52.7	38.7	19.2	76.3	89.3	69.7	58.9	49.8
27.7	21.3	18.5	25.8	52.9	10.2	9.7	10.1	11.7	17.1
32.5	29.8	31.5	35.3	30.8	22.5	20.9	22.4	28.1	36.6
21.4	21.1	25.4	22.9	10.7	24.6	22.6	26.2	24.3	23.3
14.6	20.2	19.4	13.0	4.7	30.7	32.6	30.4	26.6	16.7
3.9	7.6	5.2	3.0	1.0	12.0	14.1	10.9	9.4	6.3
22.9	21.7	27.7	24.4	10.9	35.1	29.7	38.2	42.9	32.9
63.1	63.3	57.1	60.7	79.0	50.2	56.8	46.5	41.0	49.3
23.3	23.1	21.2	22.0	29.8	20.9	27.2	17.2	14.3	14.4
11.3	11.4	10.1	11.2	13.9	4.5	5.9	3.6	3.7	4.5

Together, these results on the household head's education suggest some caution when making assumptions about the poor and deteriorating "quality" (human capital characteristics) of recent immigrant cohorts (Keely, 1975; Borjas, 1990). The children of immigrants are much more likely to have poorly educated parents than are native children, but they also are somewhat more likely to have very well-educated parents. If not bimodal, this pattern is at least indicative of an immigrant population that is overrepresented among the worst and best endowed. Moreover, that children of the most recent arrivals are somewhat better off with respect to parental education than those of the immediately preceding cohort is suggestive more of improvement than of deterioration in the "quality" of recent immigrants.

Labor Force Characteristics.   In the aggregate, native children and second-generation children are remarkably similar with respect to the labor force status of their household heads. At the time of the 1990 census, second-generation household heads were slightly less likely to be at work, and they were more likely to be unemployed or out of the labor force altogether (table 5.5). Labor market dislocation is more apparent among second-generation children with more recently arrived parents and among those who are foreign born as compared to native born. Even at the extreme, the percent with household heads who are at work never falls below 74 percent (foreign-born children of recent arrivals). With respect to class of worker, again more similarity than difference is seen. Second-generation children are slightly more likely to have parents working in the private sector or self-employed and less likely to be working in the public sector than those of native children. The propensity to be self-employed is especially apparent among children of earlier immigrant cohorts. For example, about 16 percent of children of immigrants who arrived before 1965 have self-employed household heads, as compared with about 11 percent for native children.

Table 5.5 also shows that native and second-generation children are rather similar in the occupational distributions of their household heads, although the second generation have parents who are underrepresented in the comparatively well-paying professional occupations and overrepresented in service occupations and in operator and laborer occupations, where wages tend to be lower. Looking across immigrant cohorts, there is a general deterioration in the occupational distributions of children's household heads (a relative decline in professional and relative increase in service employment), though the 1985 to 1990 cohort has a higher percent professional than the immediately preceding cohort.

Income Characteristics.   Income characteristics of children's household heads are presented in table 5.6. The first panel shows the percent of children whose parents report income from any of eight separate sources: wages and salaries; self-employment; farming; assets (interest, dividends, and rents); Social Security; public assistance (Aid to Families with Dependent Children, Supplemental Security Income, and general assistance); retirement funds; and other. By far the most important income source is wages and salaries, which native children's parents are slightly more likely to report than second-generation ones (84 and 82 percent respectively). The only sizable difference is that for asset income, which household heads of second-generation children are less likely to receive (28 versus 21 percent). Second-generation household heads also are less than half as likely to report income from farming (2.1 versus 0.7 percent). Comparing second-generation children by parental year of immigration, children of recent arrivals are less likely to have household heads with earnings and are more likely to receive public assistance income.

Since much public concern over the new immigration is fueled by worries over the fiscal implications of rising poverty among immigrants, we felt it was important to compare poor native and second-generation children with respect to parental earnings and public assistance receipts. These data, also in the first panel of table 5.6, indicate that, compared with poor native children, poor second-generation children are more likely to have household heads with earnings (51 percent versus 59 percent) and are less likely to have household heads reporting public assistance or "welfare" (37 versus 22 percent). These findings are consistent with those from 1980 (Jensen, 1989) and suggest a preference for work over welfare that may be stronger among poor immigrant than poor native families.

The second panel in table 5.6 shows mean receipts (in thousands of dollars) for those who received income from a given source. The results show signs of both disadvantage and advantage for the second generation. The pattern for wage and salary income of household heads—the most important source of income for these households—is similar to that for total household income in table 5.3. Second-generation household heads have slightly lower earnings than do native ones, and earnings are much lower on average among the more recently arrived and those of foreign-born children. On the other hand, it is noteworthy that second-generation household heads have greater self-employment income (by over $3,000) than do those of native children. This suggests that entrepreneurship continues to be a survival strategy that carries somewhat greater reward in immigrant families

Table 5.5 Labor Force Characteristics of Children's Household Heads

		Total				
			Parent's Year of Immigration			
Household Variable	Native	Total	85–90	75–84	65–74	<1965
Labor force status						
At work	82.0	80.1	74.5	79.0	81.9	85.4
Unemployed	4.5	5.1	5.9	5.3	5.3	3.5
Not in labor force	10.7	11.4	15.7	12.1	9.6	8.5
Not at work/Armed forces	2.8	3.4	3.9	3.6	3.2	2.6
Class of worker[a]						
Employee in private sector	71.2	74.5	78.5	76.9	72.2	68.1
Local government employee	6.8	4.3	3.1	3.6	4.9	6.6
State government employee	4.3	2.8	3.2	2.4	2.7	3.5
Federal government employee	5.7	5.0	5.9	4.5	5.1	5.3
Self-employed/Not incorporated	7.8	8.2	5.8	8.0	8.8	9.8
Self-employed/ Incorporated	3.6	4.6	2.7	3.9	5.6	6.4
Unpaid family worker	0.2	0.4	0.6	0.4	0.3	0.3
Unemployed	0.3	0.3	0.3	0.3	0.3	0.2
Occupation						
Professional	26.0	22.9	21.6	19.4	23.8	32.2
Technical/Sales	23.2	18.7	17.8	17.6	18.9	22.4
Service	10.0	12.9	15.2	14.7	11.7	8.3
Farm	3.0	5.3	6.2	6.0	4.9	3.1
Crafts	18.4	17.7	16.2	17.6	18.3	18.5
Operatives/Laborers	18.7	21.6	21.9	24.0	21.6	14.8
Military	0.5	0.6	0.9	0.5	0.5	0.4

SOURCE: Public Use Microdata (PUMS) Sample A of the 1990 U.S. Census of Population and Housing. Sample includes children with at least one immigrant parent.
[a] Among those who worked in 1989.

than in native families. Interestingly also, while the second generation was less likely to have parents with interest, dividend, and rental income, those who did have such income received more from this source than did similarly situated native children. Finally, while second-generation household heads are less likely to receive public assistance, those who do receive about $2,000 more, on average, than do house-

Table 5.5 (*continued*)

	Native-Born Children					Foreign-Born Children			
	Parent's Year of Immigration					Parent's Year of Immigration			
Total	85–90	75–84	65–74	<1965	Total	85–90	75–84	65–74	<1965
81.2	74.9	79.5	82.1	85.7	76.3	74.2	77.7	78.7	74.0
4.9	5.6	5.2	5.2	3.5	5.8	6.1	5.6	6.1	5.4
10.2	13.0	11.3	9.4	8.2	15.6	17.7	14.3	12.7	18.3
3.7	6.5	4.0	3.3	2.6	2.3	2.1	2.4	2.6	2.3
73.1	75.3	76.3	71.9	67.9	79.3	80.9	78.6	77.6	72.8
4.6	3.0	3.6	4.9	6.7	3.5	3.2	3.5	4.7	4.4
2.8	3.2	2.4	2.8	3.5	2.6	3.2	2.1	2.4	3.0
5.6	8.9	5.4	5.3	5.3	2.8	3.7	2.1	2.8	4.4
8.4	6.2	7.7	8.9	9.8	7.4	5.5	8.8	7.5	8.9
4.9	2.8	3.9	5.7	6.4	3.6	2.7	4	4.5	4.6
0.3	0.4	0.3	0.3	0.2	0.6	0.7	0.5	0.3	0.9
0.3	0.2	0.3	0.3	0.2	0.4	0.3	0.4	0.3	1.2
24.2	20.9	20.7	24.4	32.6	18.4	22.2	15.9	15.8	17.0
19.4	18.9	18.1	19.2	22.6	16.4	17.0	16.2	14.9	18.7
11.8	14.5	13.3	11.4	8.2	17.0	15.7	18.3	16.3	13.1
5.0	6.3	5.9	4.7	3.0	6.4	6.1	6.1	9.1	8.1
18.0	16.5	17.7	18.5	18.5	16.6	15.9	17.1	16.4	19.0
20.8	21.2	23.3	21.2	14.6	24.6	22.4	26.0	27.0	22.6
0.6	1.5	0.7	0.5	0.4	0.2	0.4	0.1	0.2	0.4

hold heads of native children. This may simply reflect their greater prevalence in nonsouthern states, where welfare benefit levels tend to be higher.

Second-Generation Children

Our analysis is motivated by the assumption that the social and economic impact of immigration is determined not only by the character-

Table 5.6 Income Characteristics of Children's Household Heads

Household Variable	Native	Total	85–90	75–84	65–74	<1965
		Total				
			Parent's Year of Immigration			
Percent receiving income by source						
Wage/Salary	84.2	81.9	78.8	81.3	83.2	84.2
(among poor heads)	50.9	59.0	59.4	60.4	57.6	52.3
Self-employment	9.6	9.7	6.4	9.2	10.8	12.4
Farming	2.1	0.7	0.4	0.6	0.8	1.0
Interest/Dividend/Rent	28.2	21.2	14.6	17.5	23.7	33.6
Social Security	2.4	2.3	1.7	1.9	2.7	3.2
Public assistance	8.2	7.0	9.0	8.2	5.8	4.1
(among poor heads)	37.4	21.9	18.4	23.1	22.5	23.6
Retirement	2.5	2.3	1.3	1.8	3.1	3.2
Other	9.1	4.7	3.5	4.1	5.7	6.0
Mean receipt ($1,000s) by source						
Wage/Salary	30.2	28.3	22.9	25.0	30.9	37.9
Self-employment	23.5	26.7	19.1	24.7	28.8	31.4
Farming	14.6	12.9	9.6	10.1	14.7	15.5
Interest/Dividend/Rent	2.7	4.1	3.0	3.5	4.8	4.6
Social Security	5.9	5.3	4.0	4.6	5.6	6.4
Public assistance	4.2	6.3	6.7	6.7	5.5	5.5
Retirement	7.9	8.3	7.6	7.2	8.6	9.7
Other	3.9	4.8	5.2	4.7	4.7	4.7

SOURCE: Public Use Microdata (PUMS) Sample A of the 1990 U.S. Census of Population and Housing. Sample includes children with at least one immigrant parent.

istics of immigrants themselves but also by those of their offspring. A lagging cost (benefit) of immigration lies in the extent to which children of the new immigration compare unfavorably (favorably) with their native counterparts. This section compares the second generation with native children with respect to a limited number of sociodemographic and employment variables.

There is virtually no difference between native and second-generation children in mean age—both groups average 8.4 years (table 5.7). Because their parents are younger, the second-generation children of more recent arrivals are younger than those whose parents immigrated earlier. There also is very little difference in the sex ratio, which hovers close to 51 percent male and 49 percent female for all groups.

Table 5.6 (*continued*)

	Native-Born Children					Foreign-Born Children			
	Parent's Year of Immigration					Parent's Year of Immigration			
Total	85–90	75–84	65–74	<1965	Total	85–90	75–84	65–74	<1965
83.2	82.3	82.5	83.4	84.5	77.6	76.3	78.3	80.6	74.0
59.4	63.2	61.1	57.0	52.6	58.3	57.4	58.8	63.0	49.5
10.2	7.1	9.2	11.0	12.5	7.8	5.8	9.3	8.6	8.0
0.8	0.5	0.6	0.8	1.0	0.5	0.3	0.6	0.8	0.5
23.4	16.7	18.8	24.4	34.1	13.8	13.1	14.2	14.0	16.9
2.3	1.6	1.7	2.6	3.1	2.3	1.8	2.3	4.0	6.5
6.2	7.2	7.4	5.7	3.9	10.1	10.4	10.3	7.1	10.1
22.2	17.3	22.6	23.0	23.8	21.3	19.1	24.0	18.0	20.8
2.6	1.8	2.0	3.1	3.1	1.4	1.0	1.4	2.9	4.2
5.1	4.3	4.3	5.7	6.1	3.4	2.9	3.4	5.7	5.1
29.8	22.1	25.8	31.4	38.2	23.0	23.5	22.5	23.1	22.7
27.8	20.9	25.4	28.9	31.5	21.7	17.5	22.9	26.9	26.1
13.4	9.0	10.4	14.9	15.5	10.2	10.3	9.5	11.8	18.0
4.2	2.9	3.3	4.8	4.6	3.8	3.1	4.1	4.5	3.9
5.5	4.3	4.6	5.6	6.5	4.4	3.8	4.5	5.2	5.3
6.0	5.7	6.4	5.5	5.6	7.1	7.3	7.3	5.5	5.0
8.6	8.1	7.5	8.7	9.8	6.5	7.0	6.3	6.6	6.2
4.7	4.8	4.6	4.7	4.7	5.2	5.8	4.8	4.9	6.5

If the second generation is to compete successfully with native youth for employment, they will need to develop marketable skills through education and training. Table 5.7 shows little difference between native and second-generation children in the percent not in school—both around 13 percent. That the proportion not in school is substantially higher among children of more recent arrivals (17 percent among children of 1985 to 1990 arrivals) may simply reflect the fact that they are more likely to be of preschool age (ages four to five) but does bear further scrutiny. Unfortunately, because education was not coded in completed years (as it was in the 1980 PUMS), it is not possible with these data to discern whether second-generation children are more likely than native children to be behind in school.

Two variables in table 5.7 depict children's English-speaking ability. At about 66 percent, second-generation children are far more likely to

Table 5.7 Characteristics of Children

Household Variable	Native	Total	85–90	75–84	65–74	<1965
		Total				
		Parent's Year of Immigration				
Age (mean)	8.4	8.4	6.8	7.6	9.6	9.9
Male child	51.5	51.3	51.2	51.3	51.0	51.6
Schooling status						
Not in school	13.0	13.3	16.6	15.4	10.3	9.7
Attending public school	61.2	59.5	49.3	57.9	65.4	63.5
Attending private school	9.4	10.2	5.9	7.9	12.8	16.6
Not applicable (younger than 3)	16.3	17.0	28.2	18.8	11.5	10.3
Speaks another language at home	5.4	65.8	83.9	76.4	62.5	33.8
English ability[a]						
Very well	65.3	62.1	37.6	60.6	74.3	74.5
Well	22.2	24.1	31.5	26.4	18.5	17.5
Not well	11.9	11.4	24.1	10.9	6.4	7.4
Not at all	0.7	2.3	6.8	2.1	0.8	0.6
Labor force status[b]						
Employed	31.8	24.7	17.0	21.4	25.3	31.3
Not in the labor force	59.9	67.7	76.0	70.6	66.6	62.0
Other (including unemployed)	8.3	7.6	7.0	8.0	8.1	6.7
Weeks worked 1989 (mean)[c]	22.1	21.8	22.0	21.2	21.6	22.4
Hours worked per week 1989 (mean)[c]	21.7	22.5	24.2	23.9	22.3	21.2

SOURCE: Public Use Microdata (PUMS) Sample A of the 1990 U.S. Census of Population and Housing
[a] Among those who speak another language at home.
[b] Among those age 16 or older.
[c] Among those who worked in 1989.

Table 5.7 (*continued*)

	Native-Born Children					Foreign-Born Children			
	Parent's Year of Immigration					Parent's Year of Immigration			
Total	85–90	75–84	65–74	<1965	Total	85–90	75–84	65–74	<1965
7.7	3.7	6.0	9.5	9.9	10.8	9.1	11.9	11.8	10.9
51.2	51.3	51.1	51.0	51.6	51.6	51.2	51.9	51.0	51.1
13.8	17.6	18.2	10.2	9.6	11.5	15.8	8.0	11.8	13.6
54.8	22.7	49.1	65.0	63.3	75.5	68.7	81.5	72.5	68.4
11.2	4.1	8.4	13.0	16.7	7.1	7.1	6.5	9.0	10.9
20.2	55.6	24.4	11.9	10.4	6.0	8.3	3.9	6.8	7.2
57.7	63.6	70.6	60.9	32.4	86.7	88.8	86.1	83.5	79.4
68.5	56.7	60.1	75.7	75.6	51.2	34.3	61.3	61.2	59.8
21.7	26.4	26.4	18.0	16.9	28.5	32.3	26.5	24.0	24.9
8.9	14.1	11.7	5.9	7.1	15.9	25.9	9.7	10.9	11.7
1.1	2.9	1.8	0.5	0.4	4.5	7.5	2.5	3.9	4.1
27.6	22.4	24.0	25.5	31.7	20.2	16.2	20.7	24.4	22.0
64.8	70.1	67.1	66.5	61.6	72.2	76.9	71.6	67.4	71.7
7.6	7.5	8.9	8.0	6.7	7.6	6.9	7.7	8.2	6.3
21.8	20.8	20.2	21.7	22.4	21.6	22.3	21.5	21.4	21.7
21.7	24.0	23.2	21.9	21.1	24.3	24.3	24.2	24.8	25.6

speak a language other than English at home. This compares with 5 percent among native children. Among the second generation, the percentage is substantially higher among children of more recent immigrants and among the foreign born. When considering those who do speak a non-English language at home, only about 14 percent of second-generation children speak English "not well" or "not at all." The percent speaking English poorly obviously is much higher among children of recent arrivals and those born abroad.

Labor force status was obtained only for those children aged sixteen and seventeen. Among them, native children are more likely to be employed (32 percent) than are second-generation children (25 percent). The latter are correspondingly more likely to be out of the labor force altogether. Finally, among the sixteen- and seventeen-year-olds who were working, when measured as average weeks and hours worked, labor supply is remarkably similar between native and second-generation children.

Conclusions

The new immigration will have enormous effects on the U.S. economy and society well into the next century. The nature of these effects will depend greatly on how the children of these newest Americans fare over the life course. To understand the circumstances under which they are beginning this journey, we have provided a rough descriptive portrait of today's second generation by analyzing data on children drawn from the 1990 census.

We reiterate that the lack of information about parental nativity in the 1990 PUMS greatly inhibits our ability to provide a complete assessment of the second generation, since we are forced to examine only those children still residing with their parents. With this data constraint in mind, the picture that emerges is of a fragmented second generation that shows signs of both stress and hope. On the negative side, compared with native children, offspring of the new immigration are decidedly disadvantaged in a variety of ways. They are far more likely to be living near or below official poverty thresholds and in rented housing. Moreover, their household heads are overrepresented in the lowest education categories, have poorer or nonexistent English-speaking ability, are more likely to be unemployed or out of the labor force, have lower earnings, and have lower status occupations. The spouses of their household heads (data not shown) also are comparatively disadvantaged with respect to educational attainment and occupational status.

These pessimistic circumstances are counterbalanced to a degree by signs of advantage and hope for the new second generation. Compared with native children, their household heads are more likely to be married, are overrepresented among the best educated, and have higher self-employment and asset income (among those reporting income from these sources). Moreover, when poor children are examined separately, household heads of second-generation children are less likely to receive welfare income and more likely to receive earnings than their native counterparts. Finally, the second generation themselves are just as likely to be attending school.

An important dimension of this analysis is the comparison across year-of-immigration categories. Here the problem of selectivity (owing to differential rates of exit from families of orientation) becomes most acute and suggests caution. With this caveat, the evidence again provides mixed signals as to the fortunes of the second generation. On the one hand, by nearly every measure, circumstances appear far worse among children of more recent immigrants and children who were born abroad. In fact, in many instances children of earlier arrivals (those arriving between 1965 and 1974 or before 1965) are better off than native children. While some improvement in the circumstances of recent arrivals can be expected as their parents adjust to the U.S. labor market and climb the age-earnings profile, they cannot be expected readily to overcome their parents' comparatively low levels of education and lower-status occupations. On the other hand, there also is evidence that children of the most recent cohort, those arriving between 1985 and 1990, are better off in certain respects than are earlier arrivals. Specifically, they are more likely to have household heads who are very well educated and who are in professional occupations.

Notes

1. In cases where a child had two immigrant parents who fell into different year-of-immigration categories, the year of immigration of the child's mother was used. The results did not differ meaningfully when, as an alternative, we used the year of immigration of the more recently arrived parent.

2. The term linguistically isolated is a misnomer in those circumstances where a non-English-speaking household is embedded within a linguistically homogeneous non-English-speaking community.

6

The Households of Children of Immigrants in South Florida: An Exploratory Study of Extended Family Arrangements

Lisandro Pérez

THE STRUCTURE of households has long been recognized as critical to family welfare, especially to the well-being of children. In studies of African American families, for example, family structure has been linked to educational opportunities, employment prospects, and delinquency and crime (Taylor, 1994: 33). The manner, however, in which family structure, and especially female headship, is associated with adverse consequences for children has been difficult to articulate and the source of some controversy. Research indicates that poverty is the critical variable, not family structure per se, since the purported negative effects of female headship disappear at the upper socioeconomic levels (Aschenbrenner, 1978).

Perhaps because a great deal of research on household structure has focused precisely on the relationship between female headship and socioeconomic variables among minority families, a more ample spectrum of possible analyses on the relationship between family structure and the lives of children, broadly conceptualized, has not been fully developed in the literature. This is especially true of the body of knowledge on immigrant households in the United States. Among immigrants, both the antecedents and consequences of household structure can be expected to be enmeshed in a complex interplay of ethnicity and socioeconomic factors. One of the salient issues regarding immigrant households is their evident extension beyond the nuclear unit. Since the bulk of contemporary immigrants to the United States originates in the developing countries of Latin America and Asia, the assumption is that extended family arrangements are culturally determined, the continuation of patterns from traditional societies. Even when socioeconomic factors are considered in explaining the formation of immigrant households, they are clearly regarded as secondary to cultural explanations. For example, Pérez (1986b) explains the importance of grandparents in Cuban immigrant households in the context of cultural norms regarding the care of dependent elderly. The conclusion that grandparents form an integral part of a household that is well adapted to facilitate upward mobility is presented almost as an unintended consequence or latent function of a culturally determined pattern.

Without necessarily questioning the validity of ethnicity in explaining the structure of immigrant households, it is notable that it contrasts with the predominant explanations applied to the study of extended family arrangements among U.S. minority households. In those analyses, socioeconomic factors prevail. Research on African American families, for example, tends to view the presence of grandparents, uncles, and aunts in the household as a successful adaptation to adverse economic conditions and the relatively high incidence of female headship (Billingsley, 1968; Hill, 1971; Hays and Mindel, 1973).

The analysis presented here represents an initial approach to this topic using data that promise to yield answers on the antecedents of extended family arrangements among immigrant households with children. The intention here is not to exhaust a phenomenon that has complex interrelationships. Instead it explores the manner in which extended family arrangements, especially the presence of grandparents, are related to national origin, cultural assimilation, and socioeconomic variables. This chapter is regarded as a first approach simply because it cannot present the full breadth of the analyses possible with the data. As is suggested later, it is possible in subsequent analyses to draw conclusions not only about the antecedents of extended family arrangements but also about their consequences.

Data

The data used here were derived from the South Florida sample of the Children of Immigrants Survey, conducted from 1992 to 1993. The universe for the sample consisted of all eighth and ninth graders in the public school systems of Dade and Broward counties, the counties that contain Miami and Fort Lauderdale, respectively. Interviews also were conducted in selected private schools in Miami. The sample was limited to those children with at least one foreign-born parent and who had been born in the United States or lived here for at least five years. A total of 2,844 students were interviewed in 25 schools. (See Portes, 1994, for more details on the survey.)

The questionnaire used in the survey had 113 questions, including a set regarding the child's household situation: number of persons in the household, adult guardianship arrangement, number of siblings, and the presence of other relatives and nonrelatives. The respondents could specify the number of grandparents, aunts, and uncles residing with them. It should be emphasized that the data offer the advantage of limiting the analysis to those immigrant households with children, that is, those households of special relevance for policy-oriented analysis. On the other hand, the disadvantage is that they are household data derived exclusively from the children's reporting. Subsequent interviews with a limited number of parents, however, tended to confirm the accuracy of the children's reports.

The mean number of persons residing in the respondents' households was 4.77. This is considerably higher than the 2.63 figure provided by the U.S. Bureau of the Census for all households in the United States in 1990 (U.S. Bureau of the Census, 1992: 49). Quite apart from the possibility that more immigrant than nonimmigrant households are extended, the contrast with the national figure can be attributed primarily to the fact that, by definition, the sample is limited to households with at least one child. The number of children in the respondents' households, however, is not large. Respondents reported they had 1.48 siblings on average.

Table 6.1 shows the number of relatives reported by the children in the sample, according to the "type" of relative (grandparents, aunts and uncles, or others). Relatives are understood to be persons other

Table 6.1 Number and Percent of Respondents According to Number of Relatives Residing with Them[a]

Number of Relatives	Grandparents		Aunts/Uncles		Other Relatives	
	Number	Percent	Number	Percent	Number	Percent
None	2,330	83.5	2,558	91.7	2,603	93.2
One	321	11.5	161	5.8	111	4.0
Two	134	4.8	59	2.1	44	1.6
Three or more	5	0.2	11	0.4	33	1.2
Total	2,790	100.0	2,789	100.0	2,791	100.0

[a]Relatives are all those persons related to the respondent, other than parents and siblings.

than parents or siblings. Clearly, the households of children in the sample were more likely to be extended vertically, across generations, than horizontally. Extended households were more likely to include a grandparent than an uncle, aunt, or other relative. More than 16 percent of the respondents lived with at least one grandparent.

As might be expected, the percentages of "aunts or uncles" and "other relatives" are not very dissimilar from each other. Although there is no further information on who are the "other relatives," it can be expected that a large number of them might be connected with the aunt or uncle—that is, cousins of the respondents.

Bivariate Analysis

This section presents the analysis of the relationship between selected variables and the extension of households beyond the nuclear family. The selected variables are as follows: guardianship arrangement, national origins, and assimilation-related measures. For the sake of clarity, the results are presented using graphs. The significance of the relationship is further explored, however, with statistical tests that focus exclusively on the presence of grandparents in the household, given their importance in the sample. The presence of grandparents is treated as a two-category (or dummy) variable, with zero indicating the absence of grandparents and one indicating households with any grandparents present.

Guardianship Arrangement

Guardianship arrangement refers to the adult guardian or guardians with whom the children reside. Figure 6.1 presents the five most important response categories, divided further by type of relative: grandparent or aunt/uncle. It is obvious that households with single parents are more likely to include another relative. This is consistent with the literature on the relationship between single parenthood and extended families.

In proportional terms, grandparents have a greater likelihood to be present in single-parent households than in households with two guardians. Furthermore, "father alone" households had the highest proportion of relatives, especially grandparents. Obviously, when the responsibility for child rearing falls exclusively on a male, he is more likely to have a relative present, typically one or both of his parents. There is a parallel situation among households with two adult guardians: father/stepmother households had the highest proportion of relatives.

**Figure 6.1 Percent of Respondents Residing with at Least One Grand-
parent or One Aunt/Uncle by Guardianship Arrangement**

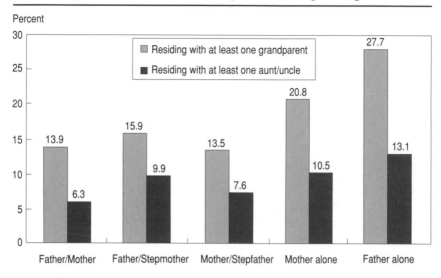

Focusing specifically on the relationship between the presence of grandparents and single parenthood, a bivariate means comparison found an F-ratio significant at the .05 level, confirming the general tendency found in the graph.

National Origins

There were several measures for country of origin, including the birthplaces of the father and mother. For the purposes of this analysis, however, respondent's ethnic self-identification was used. Figure 6.2 presents data on the three largest nationality groups in the sample: Cubans, Nicaraguans, and Haitians, in addition to an "other Hispanic" category that combines all other Latin American nationalities and those who answered "Hispanic" as their ethnic identification. Each of the nationality groups was arrived at by combining the unhyphenated identification (for example, Cuban) with the hyphenated one (for example, Cuban-American).

It is evident that the type of relative who extends the family varies considerably by national origin. Among Nicaraguans and Haitians, aunts and uncles are more likely than grandparents to be members of the households. In the Haitian case, "other relatives" have a proportionally greater likelihood than all others to be present in households. "Other Hispanics" have a slightly higher incidence of grandparents in

Figure 6.2 Percent of Respondents Residing with One or More Relatives, by Type of Relative and Respondent's Ethnic Identification, Selected Nationalities[a]

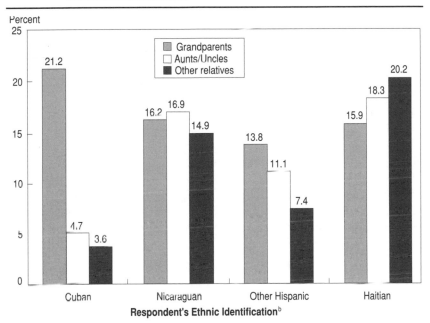

Percent

Legend:
- Grandparents
- Aunts/Uncles
- Other relatives

Cuban: 21.2, 4.7, 3.6
Nicaraguan: 16.2, 16.9, 14.9
Other Hispanic: 13.8, 11.1, 7.4
Haitian: 15.9, 18.3, 20.2

Respondent's Ethnic Identification[b]

[a] Relatives are persons related to respondent other than parents or siblings.
[b] Hyphenated or unhyphenated identification.

the household than any other group. But the most obvious feature of the figure is the large proportion of Cuban households with grandparents and the contrast between that figure and the proportion of aunts and uncles and of other relatives. More than one-fifth of the Cuban respondents' households had at least one grandparent.

This is consistent with the results of the U.S. decennial censuses, which clearly show the importance of the three-generation household among Cuban Americans (Pérez, 1986b: 13–17). It is a phenomenon that has its origins in the nature of migration from socialist Cuba. Dissatisfaction with revolutionary change was probably highest among the elderly. In issuing exit permits, especially during the airlift (1965 to 1973) period of this exodus, the Cuban government gave preference to the dependent elderly while restricting the migration of males of military age (Pérez, 1986a: 132). Consequently, the median age of the Cuban-origin population of the United States and the percent over 65 are higher than the comparable figures for the U.S. population as a whole. Without any retirement or pension benefits in the United States, they have traditionally lived with their children. In comparing the different nationality groups according to the mean number of households with grandparents present, the resulting F-ratio was significant at the .05 level.

Does the presence of so many grandparents in Cuban households also reflect an adaptation to single-parent households? In fact, could single parenthood be determining the patterns found in figure 6.2? Table 6.2 shows the degree of single-parent guardianship found in each of the nationality groups. Despite the extraordinary presence of grandparents in Cuban households, Cubans do not exhibit the highest percentage of single-parent households. Furthermore, the Nicaraguan case also does not follow the expected pattern, for it has high proportions of all types of relatives but the lowest incidence of single-parent guardians. The opposite pattern, also contrary to expectation, holds for other Hispanics. Only the figures for Haitians are consistent with a relationship between single parenthood and extended family arrangements.

Cultural or "Assimilation-Related" Factors

Two indicators of assimilation are used in this section: year of mother's arrival in the United States and ability to speak a language other than English. Figure 6.3 shows the percentage of respondents residing with one grandparent, divided in quinquennial years by date of arrival of the mother. The relationship is far from linear. If the expectation is that the presence of grandparents will increase with a decrease in parents' years of residence in the United States, the pattern in figure 6.3 does not support it.

Figure 6.4 presents an intriguing pattern. There is a definite linear increase in the presence of grandparents across the categories of language proficiency. Respondents who do not speak a foreign language have the lowest percentage of grandparents, while those who indicated they speak another language "well" or "very well" have the highest incidence of grandparents in the home. It could be argued that the presence of grandparents is higher because the household may

Table 6.2 **Percent of Respondents with a Single Guardian, by Respondent's Ethnic Identification, Selected Nationalities**

Cuban	19.6
Nicaraguan	17.4
Other Hispanic	20.5
Haitian	27.9

**Figure 6.3 Percent of Respondents Residing with at Least One Grand-
parent, by Year of Mother's Arrival in the United States**

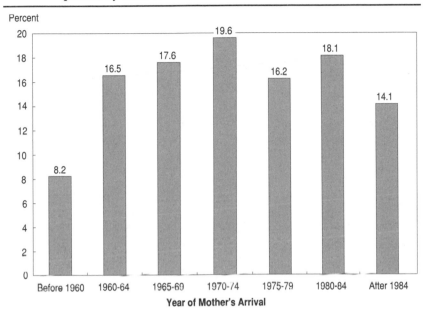

**Figure 6.4 Percent of Respondents Residing with at Least One Grand-
parent or One Aunt/Uncle, by Ability to Speak a Language
Other Than English**

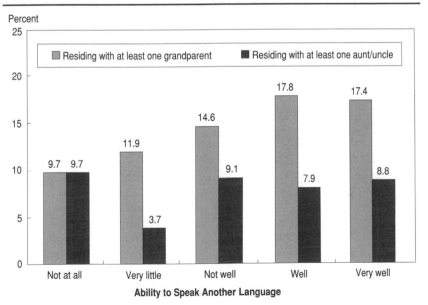

have a lower degree of assimilation (as measured, at least, by respondent's proficiency in a foreign language) and therefore a greater tendency to follow extended family norms from the country of origin. If that is the case, however, it should be a pattern echoed by the figures on presence of aunts and uncles; yet those results show no relationship at all to language ability. The pattern is literally random. The tendency for immigrant households with grandparents present to retain foreign-language proficiency is not statistically significant at the .05 level.

In conclusion, simple relationships were found among extended family relationships, parenting arrangements, and national origins. There was little evidence, however, of a similar association with cultural or assimilation variables.

Multivariate Analysis

The analysis in the previous section clearly shows the need to go beyond the variables thus far examined as correlates of extended family arrangements. The multivariate design in this section uses the presence of grandparents as the sole dependent variable. The independent variables were selected to reflect a range of household, ethnic, assimilation, and socioeconomic measures. They are as follows:

1. *Parenting arrangement.* This has been recorded as a two-category variable: one for single-parent households (father or mother); zero for all other parenting arrangements.

2. *National origin.* Cuban, Nicaraguan, other Latin, or Haitian.

3. *Year of father's arrival in the United States.* Years grouped into seven intervals of five years each.

4. *Year of mother's arrival in the United States.* Same as above.

5. *Knowledge of a language other than English.* Four categories, ranging from "poor" to "very well."

6. *Knowledge of English.* Same as above.

7. *Respondent's age.* Values ranging from 12 to 17.

8. *Respondent's length of stay in the United States.* Three categories: "All my life," "ten years or more," "five to nine years."

9. *Mother's highest level of education.* Six categories, ranging from "elementary school or less" to "college graduate or more."

10. *Home ownership.* "Yes" or "no."

11. *Father's SEI score.* Composite index of socioeconomic status.

To measure the combined effect of these eleven variables on the presence of grandparents in the household, the statistical model used is logistic regression. Because of the evident differences shown earlier in the incidence of the dependent variable among the different nationality groups, the second independent variable, national origins, is designated in the logistic regression model as categorical. Each nationality effect represents a deviation from the average for all categories.

Table 6.3 presents the results of a forward stepwise application of this model with presence of grandparents as the dependent variable. The table lists only those independent variables whose effects are significant at the .05 level. These variables are single parenthood, mother's educational level, father's SEI score, and Cuban national origin.

The most important overall finding is the failure of any of the "assimilation-related" variables to emerge as significant in the analysis. Mother's year of immigration, length of residence of the respondent in the United States, and language abilities in either English or the parental language did not emerge as significant variables, confirming the results of the bivariate analyses. At the same time, this multivariate analysis brings forward the importance of at least two socioeconomic variables that had not been considered earlier: mother's education and father's SEI.

Discussion and Conclusion

The importance of single parenthood as a predictor variable is not surprising, given what the literature has shown about its relationship with extended family arrangements in other populations. Nor is it surprising to find a strong association with Cuban national origin, given what we know about the antecedents and the extent of the presence of

Table 6.3 Logistic Regression of Presence of Grandparents on Selected Predictors (Significant Effects Only)

	Coefficient	Odds	Significance
Parenting arrangement (single parenthood)	.0835	1.9147	.0001
Mother's educational level	.0602	1.1518	.0028
Father's SEI score	−.0392	.9927	.0263
National origin	−.0902		.0001
Cuban	.0665	1.5044	.0012
Nicaraguan	.0000	.9642	.8723
Haitian	.0000	1.0312	.9243
Other Latin	.0107	.7989	.1362

grandparents in Cuban households. What poses a greater interpretive challenge is the insignificance of the "cultural" or "assimilation-related" variables and the relative prominence of certain socioeconomic variables. Obviously, the results underscore the complexity of the correlates of household arrangements. Although the culture and assimilation variables selected for analysis did not demonstrate an association with household structure, it is also evident that a Cuban background had a strong positive effect on three-generation families. More important than culture and the extent of assimilation may be the conditions of migration and the socioeconomic status of the immigrant group. The nature and selectivity of the exodus from Cuba have largely determined the relatively high incidence of three-generation families in this population. That exodus included a disproportionately large number of elderly persons, not a typical situation for international migrants. The assumption has always been, however, that the importance of three-generation families among Cubans reflects, more than anything else, the retention of cultural patterns and norms regarding care for the dependent elderly. This analysis may force a reexamination of that assumption, at least in the direction of considering certain socioeconomic variables—mother's education and father's SEI score—important determinants.

It would appear that the importance of parenting arrangements and socioeconomic variables in determining household structure among nonimmigrant groups also may hold true for immigrant households, despite the tendency to attribute immigrant patterns primarily to cultural variability. Obviously, this analysis is not definitive. One avenue of research would be to undertake qualitative research on the functions of grandparents in immigrant households. A focus on the Cuban case would be especially illustrative, given the prevalence of the phenomenon in that group and the complex interplay among culture, conditions of migration, and socioeconomic variables. Another avenue for research, left totally unexplored by this analysis, is to treat the presence of grandparents as an independent variable. The implications of the presence of grandparents for the adaptation patterns of the second generation would represent a unique look at the noneconomic consequences of household structure.

7

The Crucible Within:
Ethnic Identity, Self-Esteem,
and Segmented Assimilation
Among Children of
Immigrants

RUBÉN G. RUMBAUT

I wish I knew some other way to render the mental life of the immigrant child of reasoning age. . . . What the child thinks and feels is a reflection of the hopes, desires, and purposes of the parents who brought him overseas, no matter how precocious and independent the child may be. . . . My parents knew only that they desired us to be like American children. . . . In their bewilderment and uncertainty they needs must trust us children to learn from such models as the tenements afforded. More than this, they must step down from the throne of parental authority, and take the law from their children's mouths; for they had no other means of finding out what was good American form. The result . . . makes for friction, and sometimes ends in breaking up a family. . . . This sad process of disintegration of home life may be observed in almost any immigrant family of our class and with our traditions and aspirations. It is part of the process of Americanization. . . . It is the cross that the first and second generations must bear—Mary Antin (1912: 198, 271–272)

IRONICALLY, Mary Antin's popular autobiography, written before she was thirty, was serialized in *The Atlantic Monthly* in the same year the Immigration (Dillingham) Commission presented its forty-two-volume report to the U.S. Congress, including five volumes on children of immigrants, fueling fears about the danger to the nation posed

---

The author gratefully acknowledges support provided by research grants from the Andrew W. Mellon Foundation, the Spencer Foundation, the National Science Foundation, and the Russell Sage Foundation.

by a putatively inferior stock of inassimilable "new" immigrants from eastern and southern Europe. A Russian Jew who immigrated at a young age to Boston with her family in 1894 and went to public schools in Chelsea, Antin was the precocious and independent daughter of a petty trader confined to the "Pale of Settlement" in the empire of the tsars, and her book is at once perceptive about "the mental life of the immigrant child" and pregnant with the unabashed patriotism and newfound freedom of a former stateless person who finds in America, despite many hardships, "a nest to homeless birds" (1912: 231).

Nearly a century later, a huge new generation of immigrant children, now from Asia, Latin America, and the Caribbean, is growing up in American cities in contexts that seem both familiar and sharply different from those reported long ago by Antin. Once again questions are raised about the assimilability of the newcomers—because of their race, language, culture, or supposed unwillingness to speak English. Procrustean, one-size-fits-all panethnic labels—such as Asian, Hispanic, black—are imposed willy-nilly by the society at large to lump ethnic groups together that may hail variously from Vietnam or Korea, India or China, Guatemala or Cuba, Haiti or Jamaica, and that differ widely in national and class origins, phenotypes, languages, cultures, generations, migration histories, and modes of incorporation in the United States. Their children, especially adolescents in the process of constructing and crystallizing a social identity, are challenged to incorporate what is "out there" into what is "in here," often in dissonant social contexts. In California, on the opposite coast from Mary Antin's home, a ninth-grade Filipino immigrant girl, eager to fit in her new milieu, reports that "our parents don't come [to school functions] because they don't know any English. I don't even tell them when they are supposed to come. They dress so different and I don't want our parents to come because the others will laugh at them and tease us. We are ashamed" (Olsen, 1988: 82). When Lao teens in a San Diego junior high school are teased by white classmates and told to "go back to China," the Lao kids fire back: "Go back to Europe!" And a sixteen-year-old Cambodian girl, a survivor of Cambodia's "killing fields" of the late 1970s living in an inner-city neighborhood in San Diego with her widowed mother and unlikely to finish high school, is puzzled by a question about American identity: "How could I be American? I have black skin, black eyes, black hair . . . My English not good enough and my skin color black" (quoted from case histories in Rumbaut and Ima, 1988; compare Hatcher and Troyna, 1993).

Background

In some respects, especially in the racial-ethnic diversification and stratification of the American population, the current transformation may be unprecedented in the American experience. Class, not color, shaped the fates of the "white ethnics"—Italians, Poles, Greeks, Russian Jews, and many others—whose arrival by the millions during the previous peak period of immigration preceding World War I culminated in the restrictionist national-origins quota laws of the 1920s. The groups that had occasioned such vitriolic alarms were European whites whose assimilation, amalgamation, and absorption into the mainstream of American life over the succeeding decades, notably in the aftermath of World War II, was aptly captured in the subtitle of Richard Alba's 1985 study, *Italian Americans: Into the Twilight of Ethnicity*. For those white Americans, at least, one outcome of widespread social mobility and intermarriage in a span of three or more generations is that ethnic identity has become an optional, familial, leisure-time form of symbolic ethnicity (Gans, 1979; Alba, 1990; Waters, 1990). Our conventional models of immigrant acculturation and self-identification processes largely derive from the historical experience of those (and earlier) European immigrants and their descendants.

Today's new and rapidly accelerating immigration to the United States is extraordinary in its diversity of color, class, and national origins. The 1990 census counted 19.8 million immigrants, an all-time high. In terms of color, most new immigrants reported themselves to be nonwhite in the census. The proportion of white immigrants declined from 88 percent of those arriving before 1960, to 64 percent in the 1960s, to 41 percent in the 1970s, and to 38 percent in the 1980s.[1] This changing racial-ethnic makeup will change in still more complex ways due to rapidly increasing rates of ethnic intermarriage.[2] In terms of class, today's immigrants include by far the most educated groups (Asian Indians, Taiwanese) and the least educated groups (Mexicans, Salvadorans) in American society, as well as the groups with the lowest poverty rates in the United States (Filipinos) and the highest (Laos and Cambodians)—a reflection of polar-opposite types of migration embedded in very different historical and structural contexts. They also differ greatly in their English-language skills, age and sex structures, patterns of fertility, and forms of family organization. In terms of national origins, and for the first time in U.S. history, Latin American and Caribbean peoples by 1990 had definitively replaced Europeans as the largest immigrant population in the country, and the total born in Asia also surpassed the total born in Europe. Over half of these non-European immigrants arrived during the 1980s alone. Mexicans accounted for 22 percent (4.3 million) of the total foreign-born population and for 26 percent of all immigrants arriving since 1970. Filipinos ranked second, with close to one million immigrants and 5 percent of the total. Mexicans and Filipinos constitute, as a result, the largest Hispanic and Asian immigrant groups in the United States today. In fact, just over a dozen countries have accounted for over two-thirds of all immigrants since 1970: Mexico, Cuba, El Salvador, Guatemala, Nicaragua, the Dominican Republic, Jamaica, and Haiti in the Caribbean Basin; and the Philippines, Vietnam, South Korea, China, Taiwan, and India in Asia. Given current trends, the immigrant population will grow at a still faster rate and its composition will diversify further during the 1990s (Rumbaut, 1994).

Research about these new immigrants and refugees has focused largely on first-generation adults. However, much less is known about their children, even though they are a very visible presence in the schools and streets of many American communities and will form an increasingly important part of American society. Few in-depth studies have been conducted on the adaptation process of immigrant children and their prospects for the future, and what is known about their actual adaptation patterns is fragmentary. Even less is known about the subjective aspects of the children's experience, as processed within their phenomenal field—what I refer to here as the "crucible within"—including their modes of ethnic or national self-identification, perceptions of discrimination, aspirations for their adult futures, cultural preferences, forms of intergenerational cohesion or conflict within their families, self-esteem and psychological well-being, and how all these may be related to more objective indices of their experience, such as their school and work performance and language shifts from the mother tongue to English, in given social contexts.

This chapter is an effort to contribute to the empirical knowledge about immigrant psychosocial adaptation, focusing on identity formation during adolescence. The findings reported are from a 1992 survey—the first wave of an ongoing longitudinal study—of over 5,000 teenage children of immigrants in the San Diego and Miami metropolitan areas. Most of the major groups of new immigrants—from Asia, Latin America, and the Caribbean—are amply represented in San Diego and Miami; in fact, for many of those groups, San Diego and Miami are either the primary area of settlement in the United States (for example, the Lao in San Diego; the Cubans and Nicaraguans in Miami) or among the top urban areas in degree of concentration (Mexicans, Filipinos, Vietnamese, and Cambodians in San Diego; Haitians,

Colombians, and Jamaicans in the greater Miami area). This permits a broad comparison—both east and west coasts, inner-city and suburban communities, and ethnically homogeneous and heterogeneous communities—of children of immigrants.

For this diverse sample, the chapter addresses these principal research questions: What are their ethnic (or panethnic) self-identity choices? What characteristics distinguish the different national-origins groups from each other, and the different types of ethnic (or panethnic) identities from each other? And among those characteristics, which are the main predictors of different types of ethnic identities, and of self-esteem, depressive symptoms, and parent-child conflict?

Theoretical Perspectives

It is of more than passing interest to note that the concept of identity—which, like ethnicity, was not in common use as recently as 1950—was developed by an immigrant, Erik H. Erikson, in his well-known *Childhood and Society* (1950) and many subsequent works. Indeed, Erikson observed that his coinage of "identity" and "identity crisis" was inspired by "the experience of emigration, immigration, and Americanization," in a country "which attempts to make a super-identity of all the identities imported by its constituent immigrants" (quoted in Gleason, 1980: 31). But he applied the concepts to adolescent development rather than immigrant adaptation. According to Erikson (1968), adolescence spans a period of identity crisis, a passage to adulthood marked by major physical, emotional, and social changes. An essential task of development during this time of heightened self-consciousness, when the self-concept is most malleable, is the formation of a healthy sense of identity (Rosenberg, 1979; see Phinney, 1990, for a review of various developmental models of identity formation). For children of immigrants, that developmental process can be complicated by experiences of intense acculturative and intergenerational conflicts as they strive to adapt in social-identity contexts that may be racially and culturally dissonant.

Recent scholarship has suggested that the incorporation of today's new second generation is likely to be segmented and that different groups will take different pathways to adulthood, depending on a variety of conditions and contexts, vulnerabilities and resources (Gans, 1992; Portes and Zhou, 1993; compare Abramson, 1980). As Portes and Zhou argue, "the question is to what sector of American society a particular immigrant group assimilates" (1993: 82). Thus, one path may follow the relatively straight-line theory (or "bumpy-line theory," as

Gans [1992] suggests, may be a more apt term) of assimilation into the white middle-class majority; an opposite type of adaptation may lead to downward mobility and assimilation into the inner-city underclass; yet another may combine upward mobility and heightened ethnic awareness within solidary immigrant communities. We would expect that such divergent modes of incorporation will be accompanied by changes in the character and salience of ethnicity—from linear to reactive processes of ethnic solidarity and identity formation (Portes and Rumbaut, 1990)—and hence by divergent modes of ethnic self-identification. Thus, ethnicity may for some groups become optional and recede into the social twilight, as it did for the descendants of the white Europeans, or it may become a resilient resource or an engulfing master status. Still other variants may range from the formation of bilingual-bicultural-binational identities to panethnogenesis and the eventual acceptance of such officially constructed supranational categories as Hispanic and Asian (compare Espiritu, 1992).

Theories of social identity and self-esteem have suggested various social psychological mechanisms underlying the formation of ethnic self-images (compare Rosenberg, 1979; Tajfel, 1981; Phinney, 1991; Bernal and Knight, 1993; Porter and Washington, 1993). Youths see and compare themselves in relation to those around them, based on their social similarity or dissimilarity with the reference groups that most directly affect their experiences—for example, with regard to such visible and socially categorized markers as gender, race, accent, language, class, religion, and nationality. Ethnic self-awareness is either heightened or blurred, depending on the *dissonance or consonance of the social contexts* that are basic to identity formation. For youths in a consonant context, ethnicity is not salient; while for those facing contextual dissonance the salience of ethnicity and ethnic group boundaries increases, all the more so when it is accompanied by disparagement and discrimination. In theory, self-esteem should be lower in dissonant social contexts—that is, where social dissimilarity is greater along with exposure to negative stereotypes and reflected appraisals about one's group of origin—but mechanisms of perceptual defense are deployed to protect self-esteem (which is seen as a basic human drive; compare Rosenberg, 1979). The youth may cope with the psychological pressure by seeking to reduce conflict and to assimilate (literally, to become similar) within the relevant social context. An alternative and opposite reaction may lead to the rise and reaffirmation of ethnic solidarity and self-consciousness—as has occurred among Korean American youths in Los Angeles in the aftermath of the 1992 riots (Min, 1995; compare Portes, 1984).

Historical and contemporary field studies have portrayed the complexity of multiple paths to identity resolution in the second generation. Such segmented or divergent adaptations have been observed within the same ethnic group, the same ethnic neighborhood, the same school, and even the same family. For example, in a classic psychological study of second-generation Italian immigrants in New Haven in the late 1930s, Child (1943) described three main reactions to the dilemma of maintaining relations with the immigrant family of origin—the "rebel" (who assimilates into the American milieu), the "in-group" type (who retains an Italian ethnicity), and the "apathetic" or marginal reaction—each shaped by a set of centripetal and centrifugal social forces. Another classic ethnography, done at about the same time in Boston's Italian "slum district" (Whyte, 1955 [1943]), detailed the divergent trajectories of the "college boys," who assimilated out of the ethnic colony and into the larger society, and the "corner boys," who were loyal to their peers above all and who stayed behind. (See MacLeod, 1995, for a parallel recent ethnography of divergent ethnic fates in an inner-city neighborhood.) Fieldwork in the 1980s with Mexican-origin students in a California high school distinguished five different ethnic identity types—from recently arrived to longer term Mexican immigrants, who did especially well in school, to assimilated U.S.-born Mexican Americans, to the more troubled Chicanos and Cholos—all of whom differed profoundly in their achievement and aspirations (Matute-Bianchi, 1986). Other field studies of Mexican-origin youth have observed that, even in the same family, each child may resolve identity issues and conflicts differently and occupy a spectrum from Cholo to anglicized, from bilingual to Spanglish-speaking or English-only-speaking, from assimilated youth to gang member (Vigil, 1988; Suárez-Orozco and Suárez-Orozco, 1995).

For the purposes of this study, some specific hypotheses can be derived from the available theoretical literature on ethnic identification and assimilation. In perhaps the most influential statement on assimilation in American life, Gordon (1964) considered "identification assimilation"—that is, a self-image as an unhyphenated American—as the end point of a process that begins with acculturation, proceeds through structural assimilation and intermarriage, and is accompanied by an absence of prejudice and discrimination in the core society. For Gordon, once structural assimilation has occurred, either in tandem with or subsequent to acculturation, "the remaining types of assimilation have all taken place like a row of tenpins bowled over in rapid succession by a well placed strike" (1964: 81). For the children of white European immigrants, the acculturation process was so "overwhelmingly triumphant" that "the greater risk consisted in alienation from family ties and in role reversals of the generations that could subvert normal parent-child relationships" (1964: 107). If predictions from so-called straight-line assimilation theory (see also Warner and Srole, 1945; but compare Abramson, 1980; Gleason, 1980; Glazer, 1993) apply to the current waves of immigrants from Asia and the Caribbean Basin, then we would expect that the greater level of acculturation—as indicated by fluency in, preference for, and use of English in social life, as well as by U.S. nativity and citizenship—the greater the probability of identification assimilation.

A variant of assimilation theory predicts that identity shifts would tend to be from lower- to higher-status groups; where social mobility is blocked by prejudice and discrimination, lower-status group members may instead reaffirm their ethnic identity or adopt a panethnic label, even despite a high degree of acculturation (Yinger, 1981 and 1994). As a corollary, all other things being equal, I hypothesize that the children of higher-status immigrant parents (who form a sizable proportion of contemporary immigrants) will be less likely to assimilate into the dominant group ethnicity and more likely to identify with the ethnicity of their parents.

Segmented identificational assimilation, however, takes issue with the assumption of a relatively unilinear if not unidirectional process of identification into the dominant group ethnicity. Instead, as described earlier, multiple ethnic identities may emerge, corresponding to distinct modes of immigrant adaptation and social contexts of reception. One of those paths leads to assimilation into white middle-class society, and we would expect the predictions of straight-line theory to apply. However, as Portes and Zhou (1993) have argued, some of the contextual factors that are most likely to shape the prospects of the new second generation have to do with the presence or absence of racial discrimination, location in or away from inner-city areas (and hence differential association with the reactive adversarial subcultures of underclass youths), and the presence or absence of a strong receiving coethnic community. Contexts that combine the positive features of those factors (as in Cuban Miami, a well-established economic enclave that provides a wide range of resources and role models to their children, including private bilingual schools, and insulates them from both native minorities and general prejudice) may lead to a resilient sense of ethnic identity. By contrast, contexts that combine the negative features of those factors (as in Miami's Little Haiti, a large but disadvantaged ethnic community, facing official hostility and widespread racial discrimination, whose children are concentrated in inner-city schools where native peer groups undercut the immigrant ethos of their parents) may lead to assimilation into the oppositional identities of native racial minorities (Portes and Zhou, 1993; compare Fordham and Ogbu, 1987).

In this study, we are concerned with the influence of relevant social contexts on self-concept, self-regard, and psychological well-being. So far the discussion has focused attention on contexts and processes outside the family that may influence modes of ethnic self-definition. How these youths think and feel about themselves, however, is critically affected by the parents' modes of ethnic socialization and by the strength of the attachment that the child feels to the parents and the parents' national origins. Ethnic self-identity is, among other things, a measure of how strongly a child identifies with his or her parents. Indeed, we expect that family structure, parental characteristics, and the quality of parent-child relationships should have significant effects on all aspects of the psychosocial adaptation process (compare Rumbaut, forthcoming). Psychologically, we hypothesize that factors that may reduce contextual dissonance—acculturation (especially in English competency), U.S. nativity, and citizenship—would have positive effects on self-esteem and psychological well-being. Those that increase contextual dissonance and expose youth to negative reflected appraisals from parents and peers especially—such as discrimination and conflictual relations—would have negative effects. We expect that the most recently arrived immigrant families will be most exposed to dissonant social contexts and dissonant messages about themselves; hence we would expect the psychosocial adaptation of teens from these families to be more difficult and to affect their sense of self-worth. These general hypotheses will be tested through multivariate analyses of ethnic self-identifications, self-esteem, and depressive symptoms, controlling for gender, age, national origin, and a variety of individual and family characteristics. We turn first, however, to a brief discussion of the sample and measures used in this research.

Data and Methods

The data to be presented are derived from the first phase of a study of children of immigrants enrolled in schools in southern California and South Florida. The students sampled in the initial survey were eighth and ninth graders, grade levels at which dropout rates are still relatively low, to avoid the potential bias of differential dropout rates among ethnic groups at the senior high school level. The survey was conducted during the spring of 1992 in collaboration with the unified school districts of San Diego, California, and Dade (Miami) and Broward (Fort Lauderdale) Counties in South Florida. As mentioned, the groups sampled include most of the major immigrant and refugee populations in the United States today and reflect their diverse origins and patterns of concentration in those sites. In San Diego, the sample includes children of the two largest immigrant groups in the United States—Mexicans and Filipinos—as well as children of the largest refugee populations to be resettled in the United States since 1975—the Vietnamese, Laotians, and Cambodians (compare Rumbaut, 1990, 1991, 1995). In Miami, where immigrants form a majority of the metropolitan area and have fundamentally transformed it over the past three decades, the sample represents a huge and highly diversified Cuban exile community, as well as the second largest concentration of immigrants from the Afro-Caribbean, who have entered under very different circumstances—especially those from Haiti, Jamaica, and the English-speaking West Indies—and sizable, recently arrived groups from Nicaragua, Colombia, and elsewhere in Latin America (see Portes and Stepick, 1993; Portes and Zhou, 1993). Florida's Broward County provides a different, less ethnically concentrated, setting from Miami and Hialeah but is also the home of more than half of the Jamaican students in the sample.

Sample Selection

To be eligible for inclusion in the study, a student had to be either foreign born or U.S. born with at least one foreign-born parent. Since the school districts do not collect information on the nativity or immigration status of parents, a brief initial survey of *all* eighth and ninth graders was carried out to determine eligibility. All eligible students then took parental consent forms home; these were signed and returned by three-fourths of the parents in San Diego and two-thirds of the parents in South Florida. Those students, in turn, were administered the survey questionnaire at school during the spring semester of 1992. The final sample of students who completed the survey totaled 5,264: over 2,400 Mexican, Filipino, Vietnamese, Cambodian, Lao, and other Asian and Latin American students in San Diego city schools, and over 2,800 Cuban, Haitian, Jamaican, Nicaraguan, Colombian, and other Latin American and West Indian students in Dade and Broward Counties. About 200 of the students in the Miami sample (primarily upper-middle-class Cubans) were enrolled in two bilingual private schools. All others attended public schools, which ranged from predominantly nonwhite central-city schools to predominantly white suburban schools, including middle, junior high, and magnet schools. The sample represents dozens of different nationalities, roughly corresponding to the varying concentrations of particular immigrant groups in the San Diego and Miami metropolitan areas. However, for the purposes of this chapter, we exclude from the analysis a small mixed group of 137 respondents in the Miami area with a parent born in any one of several dozen countries in the Middle East, Africa, Europe, Australia, and Canada. Thus, we report data for the 5,127 children of immigrants from Asia, Latin America, and the Caribbean, focusing analytically on the ten largest national-origin groups from these regions.[3]

At the time of the survey, most of the respondents were fourteen or fifteen years old (the mean age was 14.2, with an age range from twelve to seventeen) and were born in 1977 or 1978. The total sample is evenly split by gender, grade, and generation: half are U.S.-born children of immigrant parents (the second generation) and half are foreign-born youths who immigrated to the United States before age twelve (what Thomas and Znaniecki refer to in their classic work as the half-second generation [1958: 1776], and I have called the one-and-a-half, or 1.5, generation [see Rumbaut and Ima, 1988; Rumbaut, 1991]). Among the foreign-born youth, the sample is also evenly split by age at arrival: About half had lived in the United States for ten years or more (that is, they were preschool age at arrival), while the other half had lived in the United States nine years or less (that is, they had reached elementary school age in their native country but arrived in the United States before reaching adolescence). Thus, time in the United States for these immigrant children is not solely a measure of exposure to American life but also an indicator of different developmental stages at the time of immigration. (On the importance of these different ages and stages at arrival among immigrant children, see Cropley, 1983.)

Measures

The items and response formats composing the major scales used in the analysis, along with their scoring and reliability coefficients (Cronbach's alphas), are detailed in table 7.1. Some are standardized instruments widely used in the research literature. Self-esteem was measured using the ten-item Rosenberg scale (Rosenberg, 1965, 1979). Depressive symptoms were measured with a four-item subscale from the Center for Epidemiological Studies-Depression (CES-D) scale; these items have been found to be predictive of major depression among adolescents (Vega, Hough, and Romero, 1983; compare Vega and Rumbaut, 1991). The correlation between self-esteem and depression was $-.39$ ($p < .0001$) for the sample as a whole. An English proficiency index was developed using four items measuring the respondent's self-reported ability to speak, understand, read, and write English well, scoring each item from 1 to 4 (1 = not at all, 2 = not well, 3 = well, 4 = very well), with an overall index score calculated as the mean of the four items. This English proficiency index was strongly

Table 7.1 Composition and Reliability of Scales

Scale and Scoring	Cronbach's Alpha[a]	Items and Measures
English Proficiency Index (four items: scored 1 to 4)	.92	How well do you (speak, understand, read, write) English? 1 = Not at all; 2 = Not well; 3 = Well; 4 = Very well
Foreign Language Index (four items: scored 1 to 4)	.93	How well do you (speak, understand, read, write) [parental non-English language]? 1 = Not at all; 2 = Not well; 3 = Well; 4 = Very well
Educational Aspirations Scale (two items: scored 1 to 5)	.80	What is the highest level of education you would like to achieve? And realistically speaking, what is the highest level of education that you think you will get? 1 = Less than high school; 2 = High school; 3 = Some college; 4 = Finish college; 5 = Finish a graduate degree
Rosenberg Self-Esteem Scale (ten items: scored 1 to 4)	.81	I feel I am a person of worth, at least on an equal basis with others. I feel I have a number of good qualities. I am able to do things as well as most other people. I take a positive attitude toward myself. On the whole, I am satisfied with myself. All in all, I am inclined to think I am a failure [*reverse score*]. I feel I do not have much to be proud of [*reverse score*]. I wish I could have more respect for myself [*reverse score*]. I certainly feel useless at times [*reverse score*]. At times I think I am no good at all [*reverse score*]. 1 = Disagree a lot; 2 = Disagree; 3 = Agree; 4 = Agree a lot

Scale	α	Items
Depression Subscale (CES-D) (four items: scored 1 to 4)	.74	[*How often during the past week:*] I did not feel like eating; my appetite was poor. I could not "get going." I felt depressed. I felt sad. 1 = Rarely; 2 = Some of the time (1 or 2 days); 3 = Occasionally (3 or 4 days); 4 = Most of the time (5 to 7 days)
Familism Scale (three items: scored 1 to 4)	.57	One should find a job near his or her parents even if it means losing a better job somewhere else. When someone has a serious problem, only relatives can help. In helping a person get a job, it is always better to choose a relative rather than a friend. 1 = Disagree a lot; 2 = Disagree; 3 = Agree; 4 = Agree a lot
American Preference Scale (three items: scored 1 to 4)	.57	How often you believe there is no better country to live in than the United States. How often you prefer American way of doing things. How often your parents prefer American way of doing things. 1 = Never; 2 = Sometimes; 3 = Most of the time; 4 = All of the time
Parent-Child Conflict Scale (three items: scored 1 to 4)	.56	In trouble with parents because of different way of doing things. My parents are usually not very interested in what I have to say. My parents do not like me very much. 1 = Not true at all; 2 = Not very true; 3 = Partly true; 4 = Very true

[a]Cronbach's alpha is an indicator of the internal consistency of a composite measure. It ranges from 0 to 1. Values of .7 and above are generally interpreted as indicating high internal consistency and reliability.

correlated (.42, p < .0001) with the objective Stanford reading achievement test score, providing evidence of its validity. A foreign-language proficiency index was similarly constructed, assessing the respondent's ability to speak, understand, read, and write the parental native language, also scoring each of the four items from 1 (not at all) to 4 (very well), with the overall index score as the mean of the four items. Educational aspirations are measured as the mean of two items asking for the highest level of education the respondent would like to achieve and the highest level realistically expected; the score ranges from 1 (less than high school) to 5 (a graduate degree), with 4 equal to finishing college. Finally, as a data reduction technique, sets of attitudinal variables were also factor-analyzed using varimax rotation, and main factors with eigenvalues greater than one and factor loadings greater than .50 were identified. We report findings from three scales thus created, each containing three items and measuring familism, American preferences, and parent-child conflict. (See table 7.1 for specific items composing these scales, response formats, and scoring.)

Perceptions and experiences of discrimination were measured by several items. Here we report results from responses to a direct question about actually having been discriminated against (and if yes, why and by whom) and to a key item about expected discrimination: "No matter how much education I get, people will still discriminate against me" (scored from 1 = not true at all, to 4 = very true). Respondents' perceptions of their family's economic situation compared with five years ago were measured on a scale from 1 = much better, to 5 = much worse. Hours per weekday spent doing homework and hours per weekday spent watching television are here scored: 0 = less than 1 hour; 1 = 1 to 2 hours, and so on through 5 = 5 or more hours. Finally, an item measuring feelings of being embarrassed by one's parents, a not uncommon experience among immigrant children (as illustrated at the outset of the chapter), reads as follows:

> [Question:] Linda and Luis are both students whose parents are foreign-born. Linda says, "I am sometimes embarrassed because my parents don't know American ways." Luis says, "I am never embarrassed by my parents; I like the way they do things." Which comes closest to how you feel? [Linda, Luis, or neither].

In this analysis, answers checking Linda were scored 1 and the others were scored 0.

Findings

Results are summarized in six tables of data. Table 7.2 presents the various types of ethnic self-identification chosen by the respondents, broken down by the nativity of the children (U.S. born versus foreign born) and the national origins of their parents. Table 7.3 then provides a detailed portrait of the major national-origin groups, including all of the measures discussed earlier plus other characteristics and the type and location of schools. Table 7.4 breaks down those same variables by the different types of self-reported ethnic identities. Table 7.5 presents logistic regressions predicting the odds of selecting four main types of ethnic self-identity. Finally, table 7.6 presents the results of multiple linear regressions predicting self-esteem scores and depressive symptoms, while table 7.7 provides a similar analysis of parent-child conflict outcomes.

Perhaps the first result to be highlighted concerns the determination of ethnic groups by national origins, and the assignment of the respondents to their respective ethnic groups. Who is Cuban, Filipino, Haitian, Lao, or Mexican turns out to be a complicated methodological problem rather than a simple matter of fact. In principle, the determination of ethnicity should be straightforward and unambiguous, based in the first instance on the birthplace of foreign-born respondents, or, if U.S. born, on the birthplace of their parents. However, reflecting the fluidity of ethnicity and the increasing patterns of intermarriage noted, only three-fourths (76.9 percent) of the children in the sample had parents who were conationals. (These rates of homogamy vary widely by nationality, as is shown in table 7.3). In 12.6 percent of the cases, one parent was U.S. born; sometimes these involved coethnic marriages (for example, a Mexican immigrant married to a U.S.-born woman of Mexican descent), but often they did not (for example, a black American serviceman married to a Filipina woman, a Cuban-born man married to an Anglo wife, a Haitian married to a Dominican). Other cases reflected a variety of mixed nationalities; in some, ethnicity cut clearly across nationality (for example, a Chinese man from Hong Kong married to an ethnic Chinese woman from Burma) but not in most. In still others, birthplace was not a proxy for ethnicity (for example, those involving ethnic minorities from the countries of origin, such as the Hmong from Laos and ethnic Chinese from Vietnam, or those involving unique historical circumstances, such as the fact that many Cambodian and Lao children in the sample were born in refugee camps in Thailand or elsewhere in Southeast Asia). In these cases, languages spoken, surnames, and other indicators had to be checked to determine ethnicity. Where none of these steps resolved the ambiguity involved in ethnic assignment—especially in cases of mixed marriages and in stepfamilies—the nationality of the mother took precedence (unless she was U.S. born), reflecting both the mother's more influential role in the children's socialization (a pattern that is documented in the text that follows) and the fact that fathers were absent in fully 30 percent of the homes in the sample. In the much smaller number of mixed cases where the mother was absent but the father was not, the nationality of the father was given precedence (unless he was U.S. born) in assigning respondents by national origin. As should become clear, what is a methodological problem to the researcher is a central psychosocial problem to an adolescent in arriving at a meaningful ethnic self-definition.

Ethnic Identities

An open-ended question was asked to ascertain the respondent's ethnic self-identity, and the answers were subsequently coded and quantified. The results (and the wording of the question) are presented in table 7.2, broken down by the respondents' nativity and their parents' nationality. Four main types of ethnic self-identities became apparent: (1) an ancestral, immigrant, or national-origin identity (for example, Jamaican, Nicaraguan, or Hmong); (2) an additive, syncretic, or hyphenated identity (for example, Cuban-American, Filipino-American, or Vietnamese-American); (3) an assimilative or American national identity, without the hyphen; and (4) a dissimilative racial or panethnic identity (for example, Hispanic, Latino, Chicano, black, or Asian). The first two explicitly identify with the immigrant experience and original homeland, if at different degrees of closeness, whereas the last two are identities exclusively "made in the U.S.A." The first three also focus chiefly on national identifications (whether of origin or of destiny, or a bridging of both); the fourth reflects a denationalized identification with racial-ethnic minority groups and self-conscious differences from the white Anglo majority population. For the sample as a whole (N = 5,127), without regard to the nativity of the respondents, just over a quarter (27 percent) identified by national or ethnic origin; a plurality (40 percent) chose a hyphenated American identification; just over a tenth (11 percent) identified as "American"; and over two-tenths (21 percent) selected racial or panethnic self-identifications (less than 4 percent of these respondents indicated a "mixed or other identity" not classifiable by the three other types given). Seen another way, two-thirds of the respondents ethnically self-identified with their or their parents' immigrant origins; the remaining one-third reported either assimilative or dissimilative identities that are not connected to those origins but to their American present.

Whether the respondent was born in the United States or not—that is, whether the respondent is a member of the second generation or of the half-second, or 1.5, generation—makes a great difference in the type of ethnic identity selected. Among the foreign born, as table 7.2

shows, 43 percent identify by their own national origin, but that proportion drops sharply to 11 percent among the U.S. born. By contrast, hyphenated American identities increase from 32 percent among the foreign born to a prevailing 49 percent among the U.S.-born second generation. Assimilative "American" self-identifications jump sharply from a minuscule 3 percent among the foreign born to over 20 percent among the U.S. born—double the proportion of the U.S. born who identify in terms of their parents' nationalities. These findings are suggestive of a significant assimilative trend in ethnic self-identification from one generation to the next. The most assimilative groups in this regard appear to be the Latin Americans, with the very notable exception of Mexicans. Among the U.S. born, less than 4 percent of Mexican-descent youth identified as American (the lowest proportion of any group), in sharp contrast to 29 percent of the Cubans, 32 percent of the Colombians, and even higher proportions of the Nicaraguans and other Latin Americans. Asian-origin groups, especially the Vietnamese and Filipinos, are the most likely to opt for additive or hyphenated ethnic identities, as are the Cubans; Jamaicans are most likely to sustain a national-origin identity into the second generation, even though among them the percentage so identifying drops from 63 percent among those born in Jamaica to 23 percent among those born in the United States.

At the same time, a substantial proportion of the sample—about one-fifth of the foreign born and an equal proportion of the U.S. born—opt for racial or panethnic modes of self-definition, but again there are significant variations within as well as between national-origin and regional-origin groups. Among the 1,655 Asian-origin youth surveyed, only 11 chose the panethnic labels Asian or Asian American; among the Asian-origin adolescents, at least so far, Asian panethnicity is a moot issue (but see Espiritu, 1992). By contrast, of the 3,033 youth of Spanish-speaking Latin American origins, 631 (21 percent) identified as Hispanic, and another 28 (0.9 percent) as Latino. The Hispanic identity appears to be tied to Spanish-language use among the less sizable and more recently arrived Latin American immigrant groups and declines very rapidly (as does Spanish-language use) from the foreign-born 1.5 generation to the U.S.-born second generation. It remains, however, a significant label for all Latin American nationalities except the Cubans. Among the Cubans, who form a numerical majority in the Miami area, racial or panethnic forms of self-definition are the least common of all the groups in the study. Among the 757 Mexican-origin youth, a very substantial number (123) identified as Chicano, virtually all of them U.S. born and all of them in California; in fact, a quarter of all Mexican-descent second-generation students self-

Table 7.2 Self-Reported Ethnic Identity of Children of Immigrants in Southern California and South Florida, 1992, by Nativity of the Children and National Origin of Their Parents

Ethnic Identity by Nativity[a]	Foreign or U.S. Born	Latin America and Caribbean								Asia						
		Mexico	Cuba	Nica-ragua	Colom-bia	Latin America	Haiti	Jamaica	West Indies	Philip-pines	Viet-nam	Laos		Cam-bodia	Other	Total
												Lao	Hmong			
Total foreign born (N)	FB	301	354	318	105	236	101	93	35	368	313	153	50	93	76	2,596
Total U.S. born (N)	US	456	873	26	122	242	77	62	71	450	58	2	3	3	86	2,531
Percent identifying as "American"	FB	0.0	3.7	5.0	1.9	9.3	3.0	7.5	8.6	0.5	2.2	1.3	4.0	2.2	1.3	3.2
	US	3.9	28.5	50.0	32.0	35.5	26.0	22.6	28.2	5.8	10.3	0.0	0.0	33.3	20.9	20.2
Hyphenated American[b]	FB	16.3	46.3	13.2	24.8	17.8	31.7	22.6	31.4	51.6	41.9	27.5	26.0	45.2	35.5	32.0
	US	38.8	55.8	23.1	34.4	21.1	44.2	40.3	29.6	65.6	67.2	50.0	33.3	33.3	58.1	48.6
National origin[c]	FB	36.2	39.8	35.8	39.0	33.9	42.6	63.4	48.6	39.4	48.6	61.4	62.0	40.9	56.6	42.6
	US	8.1	6.2	0.0	9.8	10.3	13.0	22.6	14.1	21.8	19.0	50.0	66.7	33.3	10.5	11.2
Racial/Panethnic/Mixed identity[d]	FB	47.5	10.2	45.9	34.3	39.0	22.8	6.5	11.4	8.4	7.3	9.8	8.0	11.8	6.6	22.1
	US	49.1	9.5	26.9	23.0	33.1	16.9	14.0	28.2	6.9	3.4	0.0	0.0	0.0	10.5	20.0

136

Identity	Nativity	757	1,227	344	227	478	178	155	106	818	371	155	53	96	162	5,127
"Hispanic"[e]	FB	41.2	7.6	42.5	29.5	36.0	0.0	0.0	0.0	0.0	0.0	0.0	0.0	0.0	0.0	15.5
	US	20.6	7.9	19.2	19.7	26.4	0.0	0.0	0.0	0.0	0.0	0.0	0.0	0.0	0.0	10.1
"Chicano"[f]	FB	3.7	0.0	0.0	0.0	0.0	0.0	0.0	0.0	0.0	0.0	0.3	0.0	0.0	0.0	0.4
	US	24.6	0.0	0.0	0.0	0.0	0.0	0.0	0.0	0.0	0.0	0.0	0.0	0.0	0.0	4.4
"Black"	FB	0.0	0.0	0.0	0.0	0.0	8.9	3.2	5.7	0.5	0.0	0.0	0.0	0.0	0.0	0.6
	US	0.4	0.1	0.0	0.8	0.8	14.3	9.7	15.5	0.7	0.0	0.0	0.0	0.0	0.0	1.5
Mixed identity, other	FB	2.7	2.5	3.5	4.8	3.0	13.9	3.2	5.7	7.9	7.3	9.8	8.0	11.8	6.6	5.6
	US	3.5	1.5	7.7	2.5	5.8	2.6	4.8	12.7	6.2	3.4	0.0	0.0	0.0	10.5	4.0
Total sample (N)		757	1,227	344	227	478	178	155	106	818	371	155	53	96	162	5,127

[a] Responses to the open-ended survey question: "How do you identify, that is, what do you call yourself?" See text for analysis.

[b] For example, "Mexican-American," "Cuban-American," "Filipino-American," "Hmong-American," and so on.

[c] For example, "Mexican," "Cuban," "Filipino." The Hmong are an ethnic minority group from Laos who identified as Hmong, not as Lao; they are here distinguished from the Lao (the ethnic majority group from Laos). Similar distinctions, though not reflected in the table, apply to ethnic Chinese from Vietnam and elsewhere in Southeast Asia.

[d] For example, "Hispanic," "Chicano," "Latino," "Black." Only eleven respondents (0.2 percent) identified as "Asian" or "Asian-American"; they are included here under "Mixed, other."

[e] A total of 631 respondents indicated a "Hispanic" ethnic identity, while only 28 (18 of Mexican origin) chose "Latino." The latter are here included under "Hispanic."

[f] The 123 respondents choosing "Chicano" were all Mexico-origin youth in San Diego. They differ significantly from those choosing "Latin," "Hispanic," or other identities.

identified as Chicano, a historical and problematic identity unique to that group, which adds to the complexity of Mexican ethnic identities in the U.S. context. (See Matute-Bianchi, 1986, 1991; Sánchez, 1993; Hurtado, Gurin, and Peng, 1994; Suárez-Orozco and Suárez-Orozco, 1995). Finally, a black or black American racial identity is observable only among the youth from the Afro-Caribbean: Haiti, Jamaica, and the other English-speaking West Indies. Here, however, the pattern is the reverse of that seen for Hispanic self-identification: that is, the choice of a black identity significantly increases for all of these groups among the U.S. born, although it is chosen by a relatively small minority and is particularly rare among the Jamaicans. Of the 439 youths born in the Afro-Caribbean in our sample, only 10 percent identified as black. Still, among the U.S. born, more Haitian-origin and West Indian youths identified as black than they did as Haitian or West Indian. This pattern appears likely to expand over time and may reflect processes of identificational assimilation with native minority peer groups in inner-city areas (compare Woldemikael, 1989).

Differences by National Origin

Table 7.3 sketches a broad psychosocial portrait of all of the major national-origin groups. These data make clear, first of all, the distinct patterns of geographic concentration of these groups and their basic demographic characteristics. All of the groups from the Afro-Caribbean differ from the others in the disproportionately high number of females in the sample (compare Foner, 1987). The Nicaraguans and the Indochinese are the most recent arrivals, the majority coming during the 1980s, and few of the teenagers are U.S. born. (The relatively small number of U.S.-born Vietnamese are children of the elite first wave of 1975 refugees.) The Cubans, on the other hand, have been here the longest, and over 70 percent of them were born in the United States— a higher proportion by far than any other. The large size of the Cuban sample (1,227) accurately reflects their preponderance in Dade County schools; indeed, the Cubans were the only ethnic group in the sample who constituted a majority in their communities.

There are wide differences in socioeconomic status among them. Levels of parental education are lowest for the Mexicans, Haitians, and Indochinese, especially the Laotians and Cambodians; the Indochinese have the highest proportion of parents not in the labor force, a reflection of the fact that they exhibit the highest rates of poverty and welfare dependency in the United States (Rumbaut, 1994). The Filipinos and the other Asians (mainly Chinese, Japanese, Koreans, and Indians) show the highest proportions of college graduates among mothers and fathers, and their families are much more likely to own rather than rent their homes. Reflecting their families' lower-class status, Mexican and Indochinese respondents (especially the Cambodian, Hmong, and Lao youths, then the Vietnamese) were the most likely to attend inner-city schools in San Diego, followed by Haitian students in the Miami area. The Filipinos, Jamaicans, and Colombians were the least likely to be schooled in inner-city contexts, while a much higher proportion of the Cubans were enrolled in private schools.

Table 7.3 also presents information on patterns of English and foreign-language use and proficiency. With the obvious exception of immigrants from the English-speaking Caribbean, and a nontrivial number of Filipinos and other Asians, very few of the respondents spoke English only (7.3 percent of the total sample). However, nearly three-fourths of the total sample preferred English, including substantial majorities in every group and nearly nine out of ten Filipinos; the single exception is the Mexicans, who are the most loyal to their mother tongue, although even among them 45 percent preferred English. More than one-third speak only English with their parents, although, interestingly, a smaller proportion speak only English with their close friends (in most cases also children of immigrants). The Hmong are perhaps the most dramatic opposite example: Virtually no Hmong parent speaks English with his or her children, and these families are the most linguistically isolated of any in the United States, according to 1990 census data; but over one-third of the Hmong children report speaking only English with their friends. The Laotians and Cambodians also have the lowest scores in both the four-item English-language proficiency index and the Stanford reading achievement test scores. (The Stanford standardized test data in table 7.3 reflect national percentiles.) The Latin American groups have higher scores in the four-item foreign-language proficiency index (Spanish) than any other group, with the Mexicans scoring highest in their self-reported Spanish ability.

Various indicators of educational attainment and aspirations are provided in table 7.3. The other Asians show a level of ability in the Stanford math achievement test that is well above national norms, followed by the Vietnamese, Filipinos, Cubans, and Colombians; the Hmong, Mexicans, and Cambodians are well below national math norms, followed by the Lao and the Haitians. The student rankings in math scores generally reflect the socioeconomic status of their parents. The association between social class and educational attainment does not similarly extend, however, to academic grade point averages (GPAs). For example, despite their poor performance on achievement tests, the Hmong earned the highest academic GPAs of all the groups

Table 7.3 Social Characteristics of Children of Immigrants in Southern California and South Florida, 1992, by National Origin of Parents[a]

| | Latin America and Caribbean | | | | | | | | Asia | | | | | | |
Social Characteristic	Mexico	Cuba	Nica-ragua	Colombia	Latin America	Haiti	Jamaica	West Indies	Philip-pines	Vietnam	Lao	Hmong	Cambodia	Other Asia	Total
Number in sample	757	1,227	344	227	478	178	155	106	818	371	155	53	96	162	5,127
Location (in percent)															
San Diego County	96.3	0.2	1.2	1.8	11.9	0.6	5.8	8.5	98.7	97.8	99.4	100.0	99.0	72.2	46.9
Dade County	3.2	97.5	97.7	88.1	75.7	80.9	41.9	61.3	1.0	1.3	0.6	0.0	1.0	19.1	47.6
Broward County	0.5	2.4	1.2	10.1	12.3	18.5	52.3	30.2	0.4	0.8	0.0	0.0	0.0	8.6	5.6
Gender and age															
Percent male	51.6	52.6	48.6	48.0	44.8	37.6	36.1	33.0	49.8	52.3	48.4	50.9	43.7	50.0	49.0
Age (years)	14.2	14.1	14.4	14.2	14.4	14.4	14.2	14.2	14.1	14.3	14.6	14.1	14.5	14.1	14.2
Nativity and citizenship (in percent)															
U.S. born	60.2	71.1	7.6	53.7	50.6	43.3	40.0	67.0	55.0	15.6	1.3	5.7	3.1	53.1	49.4
U.S. citizen	69.2	77.8	27.0	63.0	66.9	53.9	54.8	81.1	78.0	34.5	17.4	9.4	11.5	66.0	62.8
Less than 10 years in U.S.	28.4	9.0	57.9	26.9	30.2	28.8	36.1	20.7	28.7	42.4	44.5	33.9	48.0	27.7	27.8
Both parents conationals	73.1	76.3	85.8	63.4	75.3	82.0	76.8	49.1	76.3	89.5	94.8	90.6	80.2	66.7	76.9
One parent is U.S. born	17.3	10.1	1.5	11.9	19.0	5.6	11.6	23.6	19.6	3.2	0.6	0.0	0.0	27.2	12.6
Socioeconomic status (in percent)															
Father is college graduate	7.3	25.4	38.4	24.2	28.0	10.1	23.9	17.9	29.0	15.1	10.3	1.9	5.2	42.0	22.3

Mother is college graduate	4.2	20.9	28.5	19.4	22.0	11.2	30.3	23.6	38.1	8.6	3.9	0.0	4.2	25.9	20.0
Father not in labor force	21.1	17.0	22.7	19.4	20.5	30.3	27.1	30.2	17.4	45.6	67.1	75.5	78.1	13.0	24.7
Mother not in labor force	44.8	29.7	29.4	26.9	27.2	27.5	18.1	19.8	13.9	59.6	74.2	88.7	87.5	37.0	33.8
Own home	32.5	67.2	33.4	53.3	57.3	64.6	63.9	58.5	73.7	34.5	24.5	1.9	11.5	71.0	53.7
Language (in percent)															
speak English only	2.4	0.7	0.6	1.3	4.2	4.5	47.1	56.6	18.0	1.6	0.0	0.0	0.0	19.1	7.3
prefer English	45.2	82.3	74.4	70.5	73.6	80.9	71.0	85.9	88.3	51.5	52.3	64.2	65.6	75.3	71.7
speak English with parents	19.9	56.8	11.1	19.8	33.1	44.4	74.8	88.7	84.4	9.7	7.7	1.9	12.5	53.1	38.3
speak English with friends	12.3	17.4	15.4	25.6	26.8	29.2	59.4	76.4	62.8	29.4	15.5	34.0	13.5	69.1	30.5
English proficiency index (1–4)	3.47	3.85	3.69	3.82	3.79	3.80	3.91	3.93	3.84	3.35	3.27	3.13	3.37	3.70	3.70
Foreign Language Index (1–4)	3.24	3.06	3.15	3.10	3.00	2.34	2.07	1.65	2.12	2.61	2.38	2.67	2.42	2.18	2.76
Education															
Stanford reading test (percentile)	26.6	47.5	38.0	44.7	42.9	30.4	47.8	43.0	51.1	37.6	22.3	15.2	14.0	62.0	41.2
Stanford math test (percentile)	31.9	58.5	55.4	58.4	55.3	45.0	55.5	49.8	59.1	60.4	42.1	29.7	35.7	74.3	52.9
Grade point average	2.24	2.28	2.32	2.33	2.31	2.28	2.58	2.45	2.93	3.04	2.86	2.95	2.72	3.24	2.52
Hours daily on homework (0–5)	1.16	1.21	1.28	1.24	1.21	1.82	1.90	1.46	1.87	2.00	1.84	2.32	1.73	1.96	1.48
Hours-of-homework-to-TV ratio	0.88	0.81	0.82	0.89	0.87	0.88	1.06	0.87	1.02	1.31	1.24	1.53	1.29	1.29	0.96
Educational aspirations (1–5)	3.90	4.42	4.41	4.42	4.36	4.44	4.51	4.41	4.40	4.18	3.70	3.52	3.93	4.51	4.29

(continued)

Table 7.3 (continued)

Social Characteristic	Latin America and Caribbean								Asia						
	Mexico	Cuba	Nica-ragua	Colombia	Latin America	Haiti	Jamaica	West Indies	Philip-pines	Vietnam	Lao	Hmong	Cambodia	Other Asia	Total
Family and parents															
Both natural parents at home (in percent)	59.3	58.7	62.8	58.6	57.3	44.9	39.4	46.2	79.5	73.1	71.6	77.4	68.8	77.8	63.3
Father absent from home (in percent)	35.3	34.7	29.4	33.5	37.7	44.9	51.0	51.9	14.9	19.1	16.8	18.9	25.0	16.1	30.1
Household size	4.8	3.4	4.5	3.7	3.7	5.0	3.8	3.9	4.5	5.3	5.7	6.9	5.4	3.5	4.3
Familism values scale (1–4)	2.07	1.79	1.83	1.81	1.83	1.79	1.77	1.77	1.87	2.09	2.15	2.12	2.11	1.77	1.89
Parents are main school help (in percent)	24.0	36.4	29.1	29.1	33.3	23.0	38.1	37.7	27.4	13.2	7.1	1.9	6.3	30.9	28.0
Embarrassed by parents (in percent)	8.1	16.5	16.9	16.3	12.1	25.3	6.5	13.2	17.2	25.9	20.7	35.9	31.3	33.3	16.7
Parent-child conflict scale (1–4)	1.69	1.63	1.63	1.67	1.67	1.91	1.71	1.76	1.76	1.85	1.80	1.96	1.94	1.72	1.71
Ethnic identity of mother (in percent)															
"American"	20.2	24.1	15.7	18.1	33.5	16.3	26.5	45.3	20.8	15.6	5.8	17.0	10.4	24.7	21.8
Hyphenated American	12.0	29.6	9.3	22.5	13.8	25.3	9.0	12.3	27.9	16.2	21.9	9.4	20.8	15.4	20.4

National origin	58.3	65.1	43.4	55.1	41.6	55.1	57.4	35.8	47.8	59.8	67.1	69.8	64.6	55.6	51.7
Racial/Panethnic/ Mixed	9.5	11.9	2.9	4.4	11.0	3.4	7.1	6.6	3.6	8.3	5.2	3.8	4.2	4.4	4.1
Schools (in percent)															
Inner-city schools	61.0	23.8	20.0	8.4	23.0	36.0	8.4	24.5	5.5	48.5	66.5	83.0	91.7	18.5	29.5
Bilingual private schools	0.1	1.2	14.9	3.1	2.3	0.0	0.0	0.0	0.0	0.0	0.0	0.0	0.0	0.0	4.0
Discrimination and views of U.S.															
Percent discriminated against	64.9	51.2	38.1	45.3	48.7	62.7	74.2	61.9	63.5	67.2	72.1	55.8	59.6	59.4	55.1
Expects discrimination (1–4)	2.12	1.81	1.67	1.74	1.83	2.37	2.59	2.31	2.21	2.15	2.31	2.28	2.09	2.13	2.00
U.S. is best country (1–4)	2.65	2.57	3.03	2.50	2.70	2.11	2.04	2.31	2.81	2.90	2.91	2.89	2.77	2.86	2.75
American preference scale (1–4)	2.33	2.33	2.56	2.27	2.45	2.21	2.20	2.47	2.60	2.49	2.41	2.55	2.39	2.61	2.46
Psychological status															
Self-esteem scale (1–4)	3.17	3.37	3.40	3.41	3.33	3.36	3.49	3.44	3.25	3.10	3.07	2.99	3.07	3.32	3.29
CES-D depression subscale (1–4)	1.68	1.68	1.60	1.66	1.66	1.75	1.70	1.68	1.68	1.69	1.59	1.65	1.66	1.56	1.66

[a] All the differences between national-origin groups are significant at the .0001 level for all variables, except for the CES-D depression score, which is significant at the .05 level. See text and table 7.1 for description of items composing specific scales and their scoring.

except for the high-achieving Vietnamese and other Asians. Table 7.3 provides one main reason: The Hmong devote more hours per day to homework than any other group. In general, Asian-origin students put in the most homework time and Latin American students the least, with those from the Afro-Caribbean in between. The highest GPAs are found for students with the highest ratios of homework-to-television-watching hours (all the Asian-origin groups plus the Jamaicans). Significantly, over time and generations in the United States, reading achievement test scores go up but the number of hours spent on homework goes down, as do GPAs—a finding that confirms similar findings among immigrant students in California and elsewhere (Sung, 1987; Olsen, 1988; Rumbaut and Ima, 1988; Gibson, 1989; Suárez-Orozco, 1989; Rumbaut, 1990, 1995, forthcoming; Caplan, Choy, and Whitmore, 1991). Most of the national-origin groups report very high educational aspirations, led by the Jamaicans and other Asians; the Laotians, Cambodians, and Mexicans, on the other hand, exhibit notably lower aspirations than other groups.

Table 7.3 also presents data on family size and structure and on the quality of parent-child relationships. Notably, all Asian-origin groups have a higher proportion of families with both natural parents at home; the somewhat higher incidence of father absence among the Hmong, and especially the Cambodians, is due not to divorce but to the death of the father prior to the family's arrival in the United States, a reflection of their extraordinarily harsh contexts of exit (Rumbaut, 1991). About one-half of all families from the Afro-Caribbean have no father at home. The research literature has pointed to the high levels of familism—a deeply ingrained sense of obligation and orientation toward the family—among Mexican immigrants in particular (for example, see Vega, Hough, and Romero, 1983; Suárez-Orozco and Suárez-Orozco, 1995). These collectivistic obligations to the family contrast with the individualistic values in the American milieu. Our data confirm that Mexican respondents exhibit significantly higher scores on the familism scale than any other group, with one major exception: All of the Indochinese groups, who also have the largest family households, score even higher on that scale. Yet the lack of parental resources among the Indochinese is underscored by the fact that their parents are least likely to be the main source of help to their children with their schoolwork. At the same time, Indochinese children are the most likely to report feeling embarrassed by their parents (including 36 percent of the Hmong) and to exhibit the highest parent-child conflict scores, along with Haitian children. Cuban parents, along with English-speaking Jamaican and other West Indian parents, are the most likely to be the principal source of school-related help to their children. Cubans and Nicaraguans report the lowest levels of parent-child conflict as measured by our scale. Jamaican and Mexican youths are the least likely to feel embarrassed by their parents.

A crucial dimension of our exploratory study involves racial-ethnic discrimination perceived or experienced by our respondents. Substantial majorities of practically every group—including about three-fourths of the Jamaicans and two-thirds of the Mexicans, Haitians, Filipinos, and Indochinese—reported having felt discriminated against, and many also expected to be discriminated against no matter how much education they earn. Cuban, Colombian, Nicaraguan, and other Latin Americans in Miami reported lower levels of prejudice and generally disagreed with the statement that people would discriminate against them regardless of educational merit. The Cubans and then the Indochinese—state-sponsored refugee groups who have been the recipients of substantial public assistance—reported the highest level of agreement with the statement that "There is no better country to live in than the United States." Those groups, along with the Filipinos and other Asians, also scored highest on the American preference scale (indicating preferences for "American ways"). Haitians and Jamaicans, at the other extreme, scored the lowest on those measures.

Finally, table 7.3 presents the scores on the Rosenberg self-esteem scale and the CES-D depression subscale for all nationality groups. The Mexicans and especially the Indochinese showed the lowest global self-esteem scores, with the lowest score in the sample found for the Hmong. The highest self-esteem scores were found among the respondents from Jamaica and the other English-speaking West Indies, followed by Haiti, Cuba, and the other Latin American groups. However, the Haitians and the Jamaicans—the principal groups from the Afro-Caribbean, who reported the most experiences with and expectations of racial discrimination in the sample—also exhibited the highest depression scores. Self-esteem and depression are inversely related, but they are *not* simply two sides of the same psychological coin; this issue will be examined later through multiple regression analyses of these two variables.

Differences by Ethnic Identity

Table 7.4 presents data on the same set of variables as in table 7.3, broken down by the major types of ethnic identities reported by the respondents. Table 7.4 makes it quite clear that each identity type has a statistically significant and distinct social profile. Briefly, a few main points should be highlighted and then examined more closely in logistic regressions.

Table 7.4 Social Characteristics of Children of Immigrants in Southern California and South Florida, 1992, by Self-Reported Ethnic Identity[a]

Social Characteristic	"American"	Hyphenated American	National Origin	Racial/ Panethnic/ Mixed Identity
		Ethnic Identity Types		
Number in sample	592	2,062	1,391	1,082
Location (in percent)				
San Diego County	12.8	49.4	54.9	50.5
Dade County	82.3	45.4	37.6	45.5
Broward County	4.9	5.6	7.5	4.1
Gender and age				
Percent male	63.0	47.1	47.1	47.2
Age (years)	14.1	14.2	14.3	14.3
Nativity and citizenship (in percent)				
U.S. born	86.2	59.6	20.4	46.9
U.S. citizen	91.1	74.0	36.3	60.0
Less than 10 years in U.S.	8.9	19.8	43.3	33.7
Both parents conationals	53.7	76.8	90.2	72.6
One parent is U.S. born	25.8	14.6	3.5	13.3
Socioeconomic status (in percent)				
Father is college graduate	30.6	23.3	22.9	15.3
Mother is college graduate	25.7	22.5	19.4	12.7
Father not in labor force	17.9	23.4	28.0	26.8
Mother not in labor force	28.7	30.0	39.6	36.6
Own home	67.9	61.7	46.2	40.2

[a] All differences between ethnic identity groups are significant beyond the .0001 level for all variables, except for the CES-D depression subscale score and the parent-child conflict scale, which are significant at the .01 level. See text and table 7.1 for description of items composing specific scales and their scoring.

Table 7.4 (*continued*)

Racial/Panethnic or Mixed Identity Types

"Hispanic"	"Chicano"	"Black"	Mixed/Other	Total Sample
659	123	53	247	5,127
37.6	100.0	26.4	65.2	46.9
58.1	0.0	67.9	29.6	47.6
4.2	0.0	5.7	5.3	5.6
43.1	60.2	37.7	53.9	49.0
14.4	14.1	14.3	14.4	14.2
38.9	91.1	69.8	40.9	49.4
52.5	95.9	81.1	57.5	62.8
40.6	13.8	13.2	29.6	27.8
77.7	76.4	56.6	60.3	76.9
8.5	16.3	28.3	21.5	12.6
17.0	4.1	18.9	15.8	22.3
12.6	3.3	17.0	16.6	20.0
23.2	22.8	30.2	37.7	24.7
33.2	51.2	28.3	40.1	33.8
38.4	29.3	47.2	49.0	53.7

(*continued*)

Table 7.4 (*continued*)

Social Characteristic	"American"	Ethnic Identity Types		
		Hyphenated American	National Origin	Racial/ Panethnic/ Mixed Identity
Language				
Percent speak English only	10.6	8.8	5.8	4.8
Percent prefer English	89.9	78.4	60.6	63.4
Percent speak English with parents	55.2	47.1	28.2	25.2
Percent speak English with friends	42.1	34.1	26.4	22.6
English Proficiency Index (1–4)	3.87	3.79	3.58	3.60
Foreign Language Index (1–4)	2.61	2.62	2.85	2.99
Education				
Stanford reading test (percentile)	49.2	44.3	38.9	34.1
Stanford math test (percentile)	60.8	55.4	52.8	44.0
Grade point average	2.39	2.61	2.63	2.29
Hours daily on homework (0–5)	1.37	1.59	1.56	1.23
Hours-of-homework-to-TV ratio	0.89	0.96	1.05	0.85
Educational aspirations (1–5)	4.42	4.37	4.25	4.12
Family and parents				
Both natural parents at home (in percent)	61.5	66.4	66.2	54.8
Father absent from home (in percent)	31.9	28.0	26.0	38.4
Household size	3.6	4.1	4.6	4.4
Familism values scale (1–4)	1.81	1.84	1.95	1.95

Table 7.4 (*continued*)

Racial/Panethnic or Mixed Identity Types

"Hispanic"	"Chicano"	"Black"	Mixed/Other	Total Sample
0.3	2.4	28.3	13.0	7.3
61.6	43.9	88.7	72.5	71.7
16.7	14.6	75.5	42.5	38.3
13.1	8.9	67.9	44.9	30.5
3.58	3.56	3.90	3.62	3.70
3.23	3.14	1.98	2.47	2.76
34.8	22.0	35.9	38.3	41.2
45.9	27.8	47.0	47.1	52.9
2.30	1.93	2.23	2.49	2.52
1.19	0.89	1.64	1.39	1.48
0.84	0.66	0.73	0.99	0.96
4.20	3.63	4.36	4.09	4.29
55.7	59.4	41.5	53.0	63.3
38.2	34.2	50.9	38.1	30.1
4.3	4.7	4.5	4.4	4.3
1.93	2.10	1.82	1.98	1.89

(*continued*)

Table 7.4 (*continued*)

Social Characteristic	"American"	Ethnic Identity Types		
		Hyphenated American	National Origin	Racial/ Panethnic/ Mixed Identity
Parents are main school help (in percent)	35.1	31.7	22.7	23.8
Embarrassed by parents (in percent)	20.6	17.2	17.9	12.3
Parent-child conflict scale (1–4)	1.68	1.70	1.75	1.72
Ethnic identity of mother (in percent)				
"American"	50.2	21.7	9.2	22.6
Hyphenated American	23.3	33.1	5.9	13.3
National origin	22.6	41.2	80.9	50.3
Racial/Panethnic/ Mixed	3.9	4.0	4.0	13.7
Schools (in percent)				
Inner-city schools	19.9	24.3	31.1	42.5
Bilingual private schools	11.5	5.6	0.9	0.8
Discrimination and views of U.S.				
Percent discriminated against	37.9	54.0	62.2	57.5
Expects discrimination (1–4)	1.75	1.98	2.13	2.00
U.S. is best country (1–4)	3.08	2.86	2.55	2.62
American preference scale (1–4)	2.78	2.53	2.27	2.38
Psychological status				
Self-esteem scale (1–4)	3.41	3.31	3.23	3.27
CES-D depression subscale (1–4)	1.59	1.64	1.69	1.68

Table 7.4 (*continued*)

Racial/Panethnic or Mixed Identity Types

"Hispanic"	"Chicano"	"Black"	Mixed/Other	Total Sample
24.9	15.4	28.3	24.3	28.0
9.7	9.8	11.3	20.7	16.7
1.67	1.85	1.71	1.78	1.71
22.0	10.6	41.5	26.3	21.8
12.4	12.2	17.0	15.4	20.4
52.0	64.2	30.2	42.9	51.7
13.5	13.0	11.3	15.4	4.1
42.8	66.7	43.4	29.6	29.5
1.2	0.0	0.0	0.4	4.0
54.3	71.5	63.5	57.9	55.1
1.89	2.27	2.49	2.06	2.00
2.60	2.72	2.51	2.67	2.75
2.32	2.34	2.58	2.49	2.46
3.28	3.15	3.45	3.25	3.29
1.69	1.63	1.75	1.67	1.66

While less than one-half the sample is in the Dade County (Miami) area, 82 percent of all respondents identifying as American were in Dade County (as were most phenotypically white respondents). Respondents self-identifying as American are much more likely to be U.S.-born males, with at least one U.S.-born parent who also (especially if it is the mother) self-identifies as American, living in smaller households and higher-social-status families. These respondents are more linguistically assimilated, have high educational aspirations despite comparatively mediocre grades and lesser effort invested in homework (but more in leisure-time activities, such as television), are least likely to be attending schools in the inner city or to have experienced discrimination, and are most likely (1) to view the United States as the best country in which to live, (2) to endorse individualistic values (lowest familism scores), and (3) to have a robust psychosocial profile (higher self-esteem, lower depression). This general picture describes rather well the hypothesized expectation of assimilation into the white middle-class mainstream (compare Alba, 1990; Gans, 1992; Portes and Zhou, 1993).

Predictors of Ethnic Identities: An Odds Ratio Analysis

Table 7.5 presents the results of maximum-likelihood logistic regressions predicting the odds of selecting each of the four main types of ethnic self-identification. Several sets of predictor variables—measuring gender, nativity and citizenship, aspects of relationships with parents and ethnic socialization, language and acculturation, and experiences and expectations of discrimination—are entered to test their hypothesized effects on ethnic identity choices. A measure of socioeconomic status is provided by a dummy variable for parents who work in high-status professions. (Parents' education and home ownership are not included in table 7.5 but had no significant effects in earlier runs.) Dummy variables for all of the major national-origin groups are also included in the equations (Cubans serve as the comparison group), as well as for San Diego and Broward County locations (Dade County serves as the comparison group) and for inner-city and private school contexts. Especially with measures of subjective perceptions and preferences, ethnic self-identification may influence as well as be influenced by those perceptions; with cross-sectional data it is not possible to disentangle such reciprocal effects unambiguously. For our purposes, the multivariate results presented in table 7.5 should be construed not as direct causal influences but as relationships between ethnic identity and selected factors.

A first intriguing finding is that gender makes a significant difference in most forms of ethnic self-identification. Males are more likely to identify in unhyphenated terms, as American or their national origin, whereas females are more likely to express an additive binational (hyphenated) identity. Moreover, in separate analyses of different types of racial or panethnic identities among the Latin American–origin youths, females were significantly more likely to choose a Hispanic identity; among Mexican-origin youths, males were much more likely to identify as Chicano. In a review of seventy empirical studies in the relevant research literature, Phinney (1990) found only fragmentary results about gender differences in ethnic identity, allowing no firm conclusions. However, in a recent study of the intersection of gender, race, and ethnicity among adolescent children of black Caribbean immigrants in New York, Waters (forthcoming) reports that gender shapes the meanings attached to different types of ethnic self-identity, including an American identity. She suggests that the boundaries between different types of identity are more fluid and permeable for girls than for boys and that the task of developing a racial and ethnic identity is bound up with issues of gender identity as well.

Nativity (the word shares a common root, meaning birth, with "nation" and "nature") is very closely linked to identity. Indeed, the evidence of generational discontinuities in the self-identity profiles of U.S.-born versus foreign-born children of immigrants—and of their varying attachment to the homeland of their parents—is a finding that merits underscoring in our analysis. Table 7.5 shows that being born in the United States (that is, second-generation rather than 1.5-generation status) is by far the strongest predictor of identifying as American (odds or probability ratio of 7.48 to 1). It is a significant positive predictor of selecting a hyphenated-American label (odds ratio of 1.84 to 1). In addition, U.S. birth is the strongest negative predictor of identifying by national origin (odds of 1 in 5), controlling for all other variables in the equations.

Becoming a naturalized U.S. citizen (which for legal immigrants requires a minimum waiting period of five years after arrival or admission to permanent residency) adds moderately to this pattern. Citizenship matters, over and above nativity. It may be interpreted here as signaling a stake in the society as a full-fledged member, legally as well as subjectively, with an accompanying shift in one's frame of reference. Indeed, these variables—nativity and citizenship—have far stronger effects on ethnic self-identification than our measure of years in the United States, suggesting that it is not so much the length of time in the country but the nature of one's sociopolitical membership that shapes the psychology of identity.

Table 7.5 Predictors and Odds of Selecting Four Types of Ethnic Identity Among Children of Immigrants Results of Maximum-Likelihood Logistic Regressions[a]

	"American"		Hyphenated American		National Origin		Racial/Panethnic/Mixed	
	B	Odds	B	Odds	B	Odds	B	Odds
Gender, nativity, and citizenship								
Gender (1 = male, 0 = female)	0.54***	1.71	−0.26***	0.77	0.20*	1.22	−0.11	
U.S. born	2.01***	7.48	0.61***	1.84	−1.56***	0.21	0.07	
Naturalized U.S. citizen	0.57*	1.77	0.44***	1.56	−0.46***	0.63	0.08	
Parents and ethnic socialization								
Both parents conationals	−0.84***	0.43	0.33**	1.39	0.58***	1.79	−0.42**	0.66
One parent U.S. born	−0.49**	0.61	0.25*	1.29	0.18		−0.28	
Mother identifies as								
"American"	0.68***	1.97	0.05		−0.26*	0.77	0.23**	1.26
Hyphenated American	0.26		0.66***	1.95	−0.71***	0.49	...	
National origin	−0.11		−0.11		0.56***	1.74	0.10	
Racial/panethnic minority	0.39		−0.17		−0.71**	0.49	0.87***	2.39
Mixed or other ethnic	...		...		...		0.64***	1.90
Parents are professionals	0.04		−0.19**	0.83	0.19**	1.21	−0.06	
Parents are main homework help	−0.24*	0.79	0.26**	1.29	−0.00		−0.32**	0.73
Embarrassed by parents	0.38**	1.46	0.01		0.00		−0.18	
Language and acculturation								
Speaks English with friends	0.41**	1.50	−0.19	0.83	−0.06		0.00	
Prefers English	0.52**	1.68	0.13		−0.28**	0.76	0.08	
English Proficiency Index (1–4)	−0.16		0.37***	1.45	−0.13		−0.16	
Foreign Language Index (1–4)	−0.06		−0.11**	0.89	0.09*	1.10	0.02	
American preference scale (1–4)	0.66***	1.94	0.03		−0.45***	0.64	−0.04	

154

Discrimination								
Been discriminated against	-0.37**	0.69	-0.04		0.12	1.09	0.12	1.43
Expects discrimination (1–4)	-0.03		-0.04		0.08*		-0.00	0.39
Location								
Inner-city school	0.05		-0.06		-0.31**	0.74	0.36***	
Private school	0.17		0.04		-0.70*	0.50	-0.94**	
San Diego County	-1.60***		-0.52**	0.59	0.20	1.54	1.24***	3.46
Broward County	-0.94**		0.33*	1.39	0.43*		-0.23	
Dade County	⋯		⋯		⋯		⋯	
National origin of parents								
Cuban	⋯		⋯		⋯		⋯	
Mexican	-0.82*	0.44	0.01		-0.68*	0.51	0.50*	1.65
Nicaraguan	0.42		-1.36***	0.26	-0.34*	0.71	1.83***	6.21
Other Latin American	0.56**	1.75	-1.16***	0.31	-0.04		1.28***	3.61
Haitian	0.16		-0.54**	0.59	0.25	2.15	0.66**	1.93
Jamaican	0.58		-0.85***	0.43	0.77**		-0.02	
Other West Indies	-0.39		-0.93***	0.39	0.78*	2.18	0.89**	2.45
Filipino	-0.77*	0.46	0.89***	2.44	0.59*	1.81	-1.45***	0.24
Vietnamese	0.46		0.93***	2.54	0.39		-2.22***	0.11
Laotian and Cambodian	0.98		0.45		0.69*	2.00	-1.80***	0.16
Other Asian	-0.11		0.60*	1.82	0.42		-1.14**	0.32
Model X² (degrees of freedom)	1,158(35)	***	561(35)	***	1,580(35)	***	1,002(35)	***
Number of cases in analysis	4,936		4,936		4,936		4,936	
Mean of dependent variable	.115		.402		.271		.211	

[a] All differences between ethnic identity groups are significant beyond the .0001 level for all variables, except for the CES-D depression subscale score and the parent-child conflict scale, which are significant at the .01 level. See text and table 7.1 for description of items composing specific scales and their scoring.
Statistical significance: *** = p < .001 level; ** = p < .01; * = p < .05. Ellipses indicate that a variable was omitted from the regression and served as a reference for the others in the set.

The parents' own nativity itself exerts a strong influence in the ethnic socialization of the child. Having both parents born in the same nation significantly boosts the odds of the child identifying with the parents' nationality and, more moderately, the odds of identifying binationally. It also significantly decreases the odds of self-defining assimilatively as an unhyphenated American. Having one parent born in the United States and the other foreign born significantly increases the probability that the children will choose a binational rather than an unhyphenated American identity. An even stronger and very clear-cut pattern evident in table 7.5 is the influence of the mother's own ethnic identity. Respondents who perceive their mother identifying as American increase their odds of identifying as American. By roughly similar two-to-one odds, they increase their chances of identifying as a hyphenated American, by national origin, or of adopting a racial or panethnic minority label if they believe their mother self-identifies in that way as well. (See Alba [1990: 187–194] for related results on the effects of parents' ethnic identity status.) The effect of the mother's perceived identity was stronger than the father's, pointing to the possibly stronger effect of mothers in ethnic (and other) socialization processes, along with the actual absence of fathers in a substantial number of these families.

Having immigrant parents who are higher-status professionals is significantly more likely to increase the odds of choosing a national-origin identity. In such upper-middle-class immigrant families, the child may have more reason to associate social honor with and to feel pride in the national identity of the parents. As Rosenberg has observed (1979: 13), the child's sense of self-worth is in part contingent on the prestige of the elements of social identity. In this instance, the net result suggests a linear extension and reaffirmation of the cultural past rather than an emergent reaction to the American present. This finding is in accord with theoretical expectations that identity shifts tend to be from lower- to higher-status groups, all other things being equal (Yinger, 1981; see chapter 8 for a related analysis of the relationship of status and identity). In addition, parents who are the main source of help with their children's schoolwork—and hence perhaps more involved, interested, and influential in other aspects of their children's lives, including their ethnic socialization—significantly reduce the odds that their children will pick up either an American self-identity or a racial or panethnic label. On the other hand, respondents who report feeling embarrassed by—and hence not proud of—their parents are much more likely to identify assimilatively as American.[4] In short, the preceding set of variables involving parental resources and the quality of parent-child relationships underscores the fundamental influence of the family as a crucible of ethnic socialization processes (compare Rumbaut and Rumbaut, 1976; Alba, 1990).

Language also is closely, and affectively, connected to the formation and maintenance of ethnic identity—both within and without the family (see Cropley, 1983; Phinney, 1990, 1991; Suárez-Orozco and Suárez-Orozco, 1995). Respondents who prefer English and who speak only English with their close friends are significantly more likely to identify as American and less likely to self-define by national origin. Conversely, youths who do not prefer English and who report greater fluency in their parents' native languages are most apt to identify by national origin. Indeed, acquiring English may entail abandoning not only a mother tongue but also a personal identity. In the middle are the bilingual children who choose additive or hyphenated-American identities. The likelihood of selecting that type of identity is associated with a greater level of English proficiency and with having close friends (also children of immigrants) with whom they do not speak only in English. Thus, these identity choices reflect not only linguistic acculturation patterns but also how and which languages are used with close friends in interpersonally relevant social contexts. After controlling for language preferences, another measure of acculturation in our data set was also significantly associated with ethnic self-identity—those youths with higher scores in the American preferences scale (those who prefer American ways) are more apt to identify themselves as unhyphenated Americans; youths with lower scores are apt to self-identify by ancestral origin.

What are the effects of discrimination on ethnic self-identity among these youths? As table 7.5 shows, respondents who have experienced discrimination are significantly less likely to identify as American. Respondents who expect that people will discriminate against them no matter the level of education they achieve are also more likely to maintain a national-origin identity. Such perceptions of exclusion and rejection on racial-ethnic grounds—on ascribed rather than achieved statuses—clearly undercut the prospect of identificational assimilation into the mainstream. On the other hand, among the various racial and panethnic identity types, perceptions of discrimination were significantly associated only with the selection of a Chicano self-identity.

Location—that is, the social contexts of school and community in which these youths grow up—also counts a great deal, as table 7.5 shows. Attending inner-city schools where most students are racial-ethnic minorities significantly increases the odds of developing a racial or panethnic identity (particularly for youths reporting a black self-identity) while decreasing the odds of identifying ancestrally by national origin. Precisely the opposite effect is seen for those attending the two upper-middle-class private schools. These results provide empirical support for a segmented-assimilation perspective (Portes and Zhou, 1993), here applied to the process of ethnic self-definition. In addition, compared with the Miami area, respondents in San Diego are much less likely to identify as American, with or without a hyphen, but much more likely to identify in racial or panethnic minority terms. Ironically, the Miami area, despite its extraordinarily high proportion of immigrants, turns out to be more conducive to the development of assimilative mainstream identities among the teenage respondents in our sample than expected.

Finally, with all other predictor variables controlled in these equations, table 7.5 examines the influence of national origins on the mode of ethnic self-identification. This is an important issue, since if ethnic identification was determined by acculturation, discrimination, and related social processes, we would expect to find few if any nationality effects. To a large extent this is the case for the two unhyphenated national identities (American and national origin). Becoming American, in particular, is largely accounted for by predictor variables already discussed; almost all nationalities wash out of that analysis, with the notable exceptions of Mexicans and Filipinos (who are less likely to call themselves mainstream Americans). The Jamaicans emerge here as the group most likely to identify in national-origin terms.

However, the effects of particular nationalities are very pronounced in the selection of additive or hyphenated and racial or panethnic identities. Two broad patterns emerge here. First, compared with Cubans in Miami (the reference group in these analyses), the Asian-origin groups, especially the Vietnamese and Filipinos, are far more likely to develop additive binational identities; all of the Latin American and Afro-Caribbean groups, except for the Mexicans, are significantly less likely to do so. On the other hand, coming from any of the Asian-origin nations greatly decreases the odds of self-defining in racial or panethnic minority terms; coming from certain Latin American countries, as well as Haiti and the other West Indies groups, significantly increases those odds.[5] Why this is so poses intriguing theoretical and policy questions. National-origin indicators are proxies for the complex and diverse histories, social structures, and cultures of these immigrant communities, which, while not reducible to the variables employed in this study, nonetheless significantly shape the self-definitions of their youth. To delve into these issues will require extensive comparative-historical and ethnographic research (see chapter 3).

Predictors of Self-Esteem and Depressive Symptoms

Table 7.6 shifts our focus to a multiple regression analysis of two key psychological dependent variables: self-esteem (the ten-item Rosenberg scale) and depressive symptoms (CES-D subscale). Both equations examine the effects of several sets of variables hypothesized to influence those cognitive and affective dimensions of psychosocial adaptation: gender, age, and nativity; family socioeconomic status and parent-child relations; English and foreign-language proficiency; school attainment; experiences and expectations of discrimination; and ethnic identity and national origins. In both equations, the variable most strongly associated with lower self-esteem (beta = −.267) and higher depression (beta = .281) was our measure of parent-child conflict. For that reason, given the importance of such intergenerational conflict in psychosocial adaptation processes among children of immigrants, the results of a multiple regression analysis to identify the principal correlates of parent-child conflict are presented separately in table 7.7.

Gender emerges here as the next strongest predictor of psychological well-being. Significantly lower self-esteem, and much higher levels of depressive symptomatology, are found among females in this sample, a finding consistent with other studies of adolescents (see Rosenberg, 1979: 287; Phinney, 1991), as well as of adults among both immigrants and nonimmigrants and among both majority and minority populations (see Vega and Rumbaut, 1991). Interestingly, lower self-esteem also is associated with being U.S. born (second-generation status), a finding that parallels research in Britain showing that the self-esteem of West Indian girls born in Britain was lower than that of those born in the West Indies (Cropley, 1983: 107–108). That may be related to differing comparative frames of reference between the foreign born and the native born, and to the generational shift from immigrant into ethnic minority status (compare Suárez-Orozco and Suárez-Orozco, 1995). By contrast, a significant though relatively weak effect is seen in the net association between recent arrival in the United States and depressive symptoms, a finding consistent with the expectations of theories of acculturative stress among immigrants (Laosa, 1990; Vega and Rumbaut, 1991).

More than the other objective measures of socioeconomic status, the respondents' perception that their family's economic situation had worsened in the past five years was significantly associated with decreased self-esteem as well as increased depression and parent-child conflict—a result that points to the psychological costs of downward

Table 7.6 Predictors of Self-Esteem and Depressive Symptoms Among Children of Immigrants: Results of Least-Squares Multiple Regressions

	Self-Esteem			Depressive Symptoms		
	B	Std. Error	Beta[a]	B	Std. Error	Beta[a]
Gender, age, and nativity						
Gender (1 = male; 0 = female)	.118	.014	.113***	−.281	.017	−.222***
Age (years)	.022	.008	.035**			n.s.
U.S. born	−.028	.014	−.027*			n.s.
Foreign born (<10 years in U.S.)			n.s.	.051	.021	.035*
Family socioeconomic status						
Father's educational level (1–6)	.008	.004	.026*			n.s.
Father not employed			n.s.	.052	.022	.035*
Father absent from home	−.046	.015	−.040**	.106	.020	.076***
Worse family economic situation	−.026	.008	−.039**	.044	.011	.054***
Parents						
Parent-child conflict scale (1–4)	−.225	.012	−.267***	.288	.015	.281***
Embarrassed by parents	−.068	.009	−.097***	.042	.011	.050**
Parents are main homework help			n.s.			n.s.
No one helps with homework	−.031	.016	−.026*	.060	.020	.040**

Language and schooling						
English Proficiency Index (1–4)	.210	.017	.193***	−.053	.020	−.040**
Foreign Language Index (1–4)			n.s.			n.s.
Limited-English-Proficient (LEP)	−.150	.023	−.102***			n.s.
Grade point average (GPA)	.057	.008	.098***	−.063	.010	−.089***
Discrimination						
Been discriminated against	−.028	.007	n.s.	.090	.018	.071***
Expects discrimination (1–4)			−.055***	.022	.009	.036**
Ethnic identity/National origin[b]						
Black	.169	.065	.033**			n.s.
Filipino	−.138	.019	−.099***			n.s.
Vietnamese	−.083	.026	−.042**			n.s.
Explained variance			Adjusted R^2 = .281			Adjusted R^2 = .200

[a] Standardized regression coefficients. Statistical significance: *** = $p < .0001$; ** = $p < .01$; * = $p < .05$. The n.s. stands for not significant.
[b] No other self-reported ethnic identities (American, Hyphenated American, Hispanic, Chicano) or national-origin group has statistically significant effects in these equations.

mobility and economic stress for the adolescents in our sample. The unemployment of the father and, even more, the absence of the father from the home are related to a higher incidence of depression and lower self-esteem. The father's level of education (but not the mother's) is significantly and positively related to self-esteem. Both psychological dependent variables—self-esteem and depression—worsen when the respondent has no one at home or elsewhere to help with school work, when the respondent feels embarrassed by his or her parents, and, especially, when parent-child conflict and derogation exists. Family contexts clearly shape psychological outcomes among these youths; the findings in this regard are unexceptional and in line with conventional theories.

English-language competence and educational achievement are significantly and positively related to self-esteem and psychological well-being. Specifically, the higher the English-language proficiency index and the higher the academic GPA, the higher the self-esteem score and the lower the depression score. Knowledge of English in particular showed a very strong positive association with self-esteem, underscoring the psychological importance of linguistic acculturation for children of immigrants in American social contexts, especially in schools. Indeed, after controlling for the level of English-language proficiency, being labeled and assigned to classes as a Limited English Proficient (LEP) student is significantly associated with diminished self-esteem (although not with depressive symptoms). A LEP status is a common designation for non-English-speaking immigrants in public schools, as well as a stigmatized status that typically places them outside the mainstream English-language curriculum and exposes them to teasing and ridicule by other students. By contrast, the foreign-language proficiency index score was not significantly associated with either dependent variable. Also, although not shown in table 7.6, higher self-esteem is strongly associated with higher educational aspirations.

With cross-sectional data, we cannot untangle unambiguously the causal dynamics in all these associations—particularly with subjective variables such as educational aspirations, but also with objective variables such as GPA. It may be that reciprocal effects are involved (Rosenberg, Schooler, and Schoenbach, 1989; Owens, 1994; also of interest is Faunce, 1984), and the sample is being reinterviewed in 1995–96 to add a longitudinal dimension to our study in order to sort out more clearly the temporal ordering of variables and effects.

The noxious psychological effects of racial-ethnic discrimination are apparent in the results shown in table 7.6. Having been discriminated against elevates depressive symptoms significantly—although, interestingly, it does not have a significant effect on self-esteem. However, expected discrimination—that is, agreeing with the statement that "people will discriminate against me regardless of how far I go with my education"—is significantly associated with both increased depression and decreased self-esteem. With perceived discrimination and the other variables controlled for, only one type of ethnic self-identity was significantly associated with self-esteem, and none with depression scores. Specifically, a black self-identity was positively associated with higher self-esteem, a result suggesting that such a mode of self-identification serves a psychologically protective function (compare Porter and Washington, 1993). No other reported ethnic self-identity showed any significant positive or negative relationship with self-esteem. That finding is in accord with the available research (Rosenberg, 1979; Phinney, 1991) and debunks the enduring but erroneous folk wisdom that minority or lower-status children must have lower self-esteem. Indeed, the broad implication is that ethnic self-identifications may be chosen to the extent that they protect the youth's self-regard in relevant social contexts. Conversely, among national-origin groups, the Vietnamese and especially the Filipinos were the only nationalities still reflecting statistically significantly lower self-esteem scores, suggesting that in comparison with other groups certain psychosocial vulnerabilities or dynamics among Vietnamese and Filipino children of immigrants not captured by our data may be linked to a diminished sense of self-worth. All other nationalities, however, washed out of the regression equation analyzing self-esteem outcomes.

Predictors of Parent-Child Conflict

Finally, table 7.7 presents the results of a multiple regression analysis predicting parent-child conflict scale scores. We examined a broad array of potential objective and subjective predictors and briefly highlight some of the most noteworthy findings. Here again, gender is a significant determinant. The daughters of immigrant parents are more likely than the sons to be involved in such conflicts and instances of parental derogation—a possible reflection of the clash between restrictive parental standards for behavior and dating and the girls' increasing sense of and desire for individuality and independence from parental control in the transition to adulthood (compare Rumbaut and Ima, 1988; Woldemikael, 1989; Matute-Bianchi, 1991; Gibson, 1995; Waters, forthcoming). Controlling for other factors, age and U.S. nativity are not significantly related to parent-child conflict. Instead, such conflicts appear more likely to occur among the most recently arrived immigrant families in our sample.

Several objective and subjective features of the family are particularly associated with frictions in the parent-child relationship. Table 7.7 suggests that such frictions are more likely to occur in families where the mother is less educated and where the economic situation of the family has perceptively worsened. Parent-child conflict is significantly reduced in families with both natural parents at home and where both parents and siblings are available and serve as main sources of help with schoolwork—all of which may be interpreted not only as indicators of available family resources and social support but also of family cohesion. Conversely, conflict with parents is exacerbated when the youth feels embarrassed by his or her parents and when the youth has no one to seek out for help with schoolwork.

Language and education are central issues in the relationship of immigrant parents and their children, which may spark conflict and derogation between them. As table 7.7 shows, conflict is increased significantly in cases where the child prefers English and also has a poor command of the parental native language—a recipe for communication problems, as well as problems of parental control and authority. In Vietnamese families, to take one example, parents are sometimes infuriated when a teenage son deliberately switches to English, with its egalitarian pronoun "you," in order to avoid speaking Vietnamese, which would require the son to use the numerous pronouns through which due deference is paid to the authority of the parents (Rumbaut and Ima, 1988). Conflict with parents also is exacerbated by the greater the number of hours the children spent watching television, the fewer the hours they spent on homework, the lower their academic GPA, and the lower their educational aspirations—variables that paint a fairly vivid picture of the nature of the clashing discourses and competing concerns over which tensions develop in the parent-child relationship.

Last, as table 7.7 shows, the issue of discrimination is itself associated strongly with parent-child conflict: The more the youth has experienced discrimination and the more the youth perceives that "people will discriminate against me regardless of how far I go with my education," the more conflict there appears to be in the parent-child relationship—perhaps because the implicit outlook that sees discrimination as trumping education contradicts immigrant parents' own theories of success (Ogbu, 1991; Gibson, 1995). That is, immigrant parents tend to define the situation in instrumental terms (extolling the virtues of hard work and good grades), whereas their children, who seek to fit in socially, tend to experience in expressive terms the impact of disparagement within an ethnic minority status.

None of the different ethnic self-identity types, however, had statistically significant associations with parent-child conflict, and only a

Table 7.7 Predictors of Parent-Child Conflict Among Children of Immigrants

Predictor Variable	Parent-Child Conflict		
	B	Std. Error	Beta[a]
Gender, age, and nativity			
Gender (1 = male; 0 = female)	−.101	.017	−.081***
Age (years)			n.s.
U.S. born			n.s.
Foreign born (<10 years in U.S.)	.059	.021	.041**
Family socioeconomic status			
Mother's educational level (1–6)	−.018	.006	−.049**
Worse family economic situation	.041	.011	.051***
Parents			
Both natural parents at home	−.053	.018	−.041**
Embarrassed by parents	.168	.011	.206***
Parents are main homework help	−.107	.023	−.078***
Siblings are main homework help	−.078	.024	−.050**
No one helps with homework	.088	.023	.060**
Language and schooling			
English Proficiency Index (1–4)			n.s.
Foreign Language Index (1–4)	−.018	.009	−.031*
Limited-English-Proficient (LEP)	.076	.029	.044**
Prefers English (1 = yes, 0 = no)	.083	.021	.060***
Grade point average (GPA)	−.101	.011	.148***
Educational aspirations (1–5)	−.034	.011	−.045**
Hours per day doing homework	−.016	.007	.034**
Hours per day watching TV	.010	.005	.028*
Discrimination			
Been discriminated against	.121	.018	.097***
Expects discrimination (1–4)	.101	.009	.167***
National origin[b]			
Haitian	.112	.048	.032*
Filipino	.074	.026	.045**
Vietnamese	.162	.035	.069***
Laotian and Cambodian	.124	.040	.048**
Explained variance		Adjusted R^2 = .190	

[a]Standardized regression coefficients. Statistical significance: *** = p < .0001; ** = p < 01; * = p < .05. The n.s. stands for not significant.
[b]No other self-reported ethnic identities (American, Hyphenated-American, Hispanic, Chicano, black) or national-origin group had statistically significant effects in these equations.

handful of nationalities did: the Haitians, the Filipinos, and the Indochinese (Vietnamese, Cambodians, and Laotians). The degree of parent-child conflict was shown earlier (in the bivariate results by nationality) to be more intense among those particular national-origin groups; that remains the case in the multivariate analysis even after controlling for a variety of explanatory factors. It is worth repeating that multivariate results also show that the Vietnamese and Filipinos were the only nationalities significantly associated with lower self-esteem, even with parent-child conflict controlled, suggesting that psychosocial adaptation processes may be particularly problematic for both parents and children in those ethnic groups.

In any event, these data suggest a range of issues around which tension, derogation, and conflict—the "friction" that Mary Antin refers to at the outset of this chapter—are produced in the adolescents' relationship with their immigrant parents, conflicts that in turn affect the children's self-esteem, psychological well-being, and social identities.

Conclusion

This chapter has touched on multiple aspects of the psychosocial adaptation of children of the new immigration to the United States, focusing on the formation of ethnic identities during adolescence. Among the many empirical results presented in the preceding analysis, certain findings are especially noteworthy. The data show major differences in patterns of ethnic self-identification among teenage children of immigrants from Asia, Latin America, and the Caribbean—both between and within groups from diverse national origins—growing up in two distinct corners of the United States. Instead of a uniform assimilative path, this study found multiple or segmented paths to identity formation and resolution. Several major patterns emerged from multivariate analyses of factors theoretically expected to shape the process of ethnic self-identification and other aspects of psychosocial adaptation such as self-esteem and depression.

First, ethnic self-identification is a gendered process. Among the adolescents in the sample, gender was a significant predictor of virtually every type of ethnic self-identity chosen, suggesting that issues of gender and ethnic identity may be connected. Girls were much more likely to choose additive or hyphenated identities as well as a Hispanic panethnic self-label; boys were more likely to choose an unhyphenated national identity (whether American or national origin), except those of Mexican descent who were more likely to identify as Chicano. In addition, gender was a main determinant of psychological well-being, with girls being much more likely than boys to report lower self-esteem, higher depression, and a greater level of parent-child conflict.

Second, partly in line with expectations drawn from classic assimilation theory, acculturation strongly affects the process of identificational assimilation. Being born in the United States (second-generation status) greatly increases the propensity for an assimilative self-definition, as does naturalized U.S. citizenship and a preference for fluent use of English with close friends. Conversely, being foreign born (1.5 generation) and not a U.S. citizen and having a preference for and fluency in the parental native language are associated with an ancestral or national-origin identity. The strength and significance of the effects of acculturative processes on the odds of self-identifying as a hyphenated American lie between those two poles. In general, the hyphenated identity emerges less as a qualitatively different mode of ethnic self-definition than as a bridge or middle position along the identificational spectrum between an American national identity and that of national origin.[6] Still, whereas parental nationality tends to wash out in our models as a predictor of the children's propensity to identify either as American or by national origin, parental nationality has very strong effects on the choice of a hyphenated identity. Children of all Asian-origin nationalities are much more likely to do so, whereas most of those coming from Latin America and the Caribbean are less likely to add the hyphen.

Third, perceptions of discrimination affect the way children define their ethnic identities. Those who report having been discriminated against are less likely to identify as American; those who perceive that people will discriminate against them no matter the level of education they achieve are more likely to remain loyal to a national-origin identity. Such experiences and perceptions of social injustice undercut the prospect of identificational assimilation into the mainstream. They also are associated with higher levels of depressive symptoms and greater parent-child conflict.

Fourth, the determination of dissimilative racial or panethnic self-identities follows a different logic, having relatively little to do with acculturative processes. Location and nationality matter more here. Youths in inner-city schools where most students are racial-ethnic minorities are more likely to define themselves in terms of those identities, particularly black and Chicano, and less likely to identify ancestrally by national origin. Precisely the opposite effect is seen for those attending upper-middle-class private schools. The results support a segmented-assimilation theoretical perspective. Virtually no Asian-origin youth chose the panethnic labels Asian or Asian American. A black or black American racial identity was chosen by only 10 percent of the youth from Afro-Caribbean backgrounds, but its use increased among the U.S. born. A Hispanic identity was picked by over 20 percent of those from Spanish-speaking countries, but it declines rapidly among the U.S. born. Children of immigrants in San Diego are much more likely to identify in racial or panethnic minority terms. The Miami area, despite its extraordinarily high proportion of immigrants, turns out to be more conducive to the development of assimilative mainstream identities, an ironic result that may be connected to race (the overwhelming proportion of phenotypically white youth in the sample reside in Miami) and to the effects of American racial categories and racism on perceived identity options.

Fifth, children's psychosocial adaptation is shaped by the family context. The likelihood of identificational assimilation is moderated by parental ethnic socialization, social status, and parent-child relationships. The children's ethnic self-identities strongly tend to mirror the perceptions of their parents' (and especially their mother's) own ethnic self-identities, as if they were reflections in an ethnic looking-glass. Children who feel embarrassed by their parents are significantly more likely to identify assimilatively as unhyphenated Americans, whereas higher-status professional parents are more likely to influence their children to identify by their national origin. Parent-child conflict emerged as the strongest determinant of poorer self-esteem and depressive affect.

"Becoming American" takes different forms, has different meanings, and is reached by different paths. But the process is one in which all children of immigrants are engaged: defining an identity for themselves—which is to say, finding a meaningful place in the society of which they are the newest members. To be sure, the process is complex, conflictual, and stressful, and profoundly affects the consciousness of immigrant parents and children alike. The process also is shaped within a much larger historical context, of which the participants may be no more conscious than fish are of water, and within an American crucible that has been shaping identities since the origins of the nation. In the final analysis, it is the crucible without that shapes the crucible within.

Notes

1. Black immigrants increased from 2 percent of pre-1960 arrivals to over 8 percent in the 1980s; Asians from 5 percent before 1960 to 31 percent in the 1980s; and other-race groups from 5 percent before 1960 to 23 percent in the 1980s. Immigrants from the Americas are the most racially mixed, with less than 45 percent reporting as white (mostly from Argentina and Cuba,

then Colombia and Nicaragua), 13 percent as black (most from Haiti, Jamaica, the English-speaking Caribbean, and the Dominican Republic), and 41 percent as other (predominantly mixed populations of mestizos from Mexico and certain countries in Central and South America; mulattoes from the Spanish-speaking Caribbean). Significantly, half of all black immigrants in the United States are concentrated in the New York metropolitan area and another 16 percent in Miami; half of the mestizo and Asian populations are concentrated in California, principally along the megalopolitan corridor from San Diego to Los Angeles (Rumbaut, 1994).

2. Hirschman (1994) has recently reported that, according to unpublished 1990 census data on married persons, the proportions of Hispanics married to non-Hispanic persons were 25 percent for those identifying as Cubans, 28 percent for Mexicans, 35 percent for Puerto Ricans, and 44 percent for other Hispanics; those figures do not include the significant number of Hispanics married to a member of a different Hispanic group (such as a Cuban-Mexican intermarriage). The proportion of Asians married to non-Asians was similar: 25 to 50 percent for different nationalities and generational groups. The number of black-white intermarriages has been edging upward as well, from 1.9 percent in 1970 to 3.4 percent in 1980 and 6.2 percent in 1990. Current intermarriage rates seem bound to rise even further in the future, creating a growing pool of persons with mixed ethnic ancestry and raising significant questions about the meaning and construction of ethnic identities among their children and of classifications based on ascriptive and increasingly tenuous categories such as Hispanic and Asian.

3. In the data presented in later tables, smaller national-origin groups from these regions are aggregated for ease of analysis and presentation. Other Latin Americans include most Central and South American countries, but primarily Dominicans, Hondurans, Argentinians, Peruvians, Ecuadoreans, Chileans, Salvadorans, and Guatemalans. Other West Indians come mainly from Trinidad and Tobago, the Bahamas, and Belize. Other Asians include mainly Chinese (from the mainland as well as Taiwan and Hong Kong), Japanese, Koreans, and Indians.

4. This familiar result reflects Child's (1943) depiction of the "rebel" reaction to intergenerational conflicts among second-generation Italian Americans.

5. Separate logistic regressions were run for selected subsamples to explore the association of variables with specific types of racial or panethnic self-identities, such as Hispanic and Chicano. For an analysis of the odds of selecting a Hispanic identity, I examined the subsample of 3,033 respondents of Latin American origins. The results show that a Hispanic self-identification is significantly more likely to be made by females; who are foreign born, living in the United States less than ten years, whose English is poor but whose Spanish is very good, and who speak in Spanish with their parents and close friends; who are not embarrassed by their parents; and whose parents are not conationals and themselves identify

in panethnic terms or as a mixed identity. The smaller-size Latin-origin groups—the Nicaraguans, Colombians, and other Latin Americans (but not Cubans or Mexicans)—are shown to be much more likely to select Hispanic as an ethnic identity.

In a separate analysis of the odds of selecting a Chicano identity, I focused on the subsample of 729 respondents of Mexican origin in San Diego. The results show that a Chicano self-identification is significantly more likely to be made by males who are U.S. born (the odds are 37 to 1) and whose close friends are also U.S.-born. They are significantly more likely to feel that they have been discriminated against. Moreover, among these 729 teenagers, the lower their academic grade point averages and the lower their educational and occupational aspirations, the greater the odds of their identifying as Chicano. This significant association of flattened aspirations and low educational attainment with a Chicano ethnic identity is not found for any other type of ethnic self-identification in our data set. It supports related findings in the literature that link a Chicano self-identification among U.S.-born high school youth with the development of adversarial modes of reaction. These include defensive nonlearning strategies in the classroom, anticipation of bleak adult futures, rejection of behaviors defined as acting white, and rejection of school and of teachers, in contrast to the more optimistic outlook and valuation of schooling reported among Mexican-born immigrant youth (Matute-Bianchi, 1986, 1991; Vigil, 1988; De Vos and Suárez-Orozco, 1990; Suárez-Orozco, 1991; Suárez-Orozco and Suárez-Orozco, 1995).

6. Harold J. Abramson puts it this way: "The hyphenate synthesizes a larger loyalty to America with a historic loyalty to the ethnic past" (1980: 156).

8

Ethnic and Racial Identities of Second-Generation Black Immigrants in New York City

MARY C. WATERS

THE GROWTH of nonwhite voluntary immigrants to the United
States since 1965 challenges the dichotomy that once explained
different patterns of American inclusion and assimilation—
the ethnic pattern of assimilation of European immigrants and
the racial pattern of exclusion of America's nonwhite peoples. The
new wave of immigrants includes people who are still defined
racially in the United States but who migrate voluntarily and often
under an immigrant preference system that selects for people with
jobs and education that puts them well above their co-ethnics in
the economy. Do the processes of immigration and assimilation
for nonwhite immigrants resemble the processes for earlier white
immigrants? Or do these immigrants and their children face very
different choices and constraints because they are defined racially by
other Americans?

This research was supported by a grant from the Russell Sage Foundation and by a John Simon Guggenheim Fellowship. I would like to thank
Maggie Apollon, Kayode Owens, Crystal Byndloss, Jimmy Phillippe,
and Lisa Walke for research assistance. I am grateful for comments on
an earlier version of this chapter from Christine Williams, Carolyn
Boyes-Watson, Nancy Foner, Niobe Way, Bonnie Leadbeater, and three
anonymous reviewers.

This chapter examines a small piece of this puzzle—the question of the development of an ethnic identity among the second generation of black immigrants from the Caribbean. While there has been a substantial amount of interest in the identities and affiliations of these immigrants, very little research has been conducted on the identities of their children. The children of black immigrants in the United States face a choice about whether to identify as black American or whether to maintain an ethnic identity reflecting their parents' national origins. First-generation black immigrants to the United States have tended to distance themselves from American blacks, stressing their national origins and ethnic identities as Jamaican or Haitian or Trinidadian, but they also face overwhelming pressures in the United States to identify only as blacks (Sutton and Makiesky, 1975; Foner, 1987; Stafford, 1987; Woldemikael, 1989; Kasinitz, 1992). In fact, they have been described as "invisible immigrants" (Bryce-Laporte, 1972), because rather than being contrasted with other immigrants (for example, contrasting how Jamaicans are doing relative to Chinese), they are compared with black Americans. The children of black immigrants, because they lack their parents' distinctive accents, can choose to be even more invisible as ethnics than their parents. Second-generation West Indians in the United States most often will be seen by others as merely "American"—and must actively work to assert their ethnic identities.

The types of racial and ethnic identities adopted by a sample of second-generation West Indians[1] and Haitian Americans in New York City are explored here, along with subjective understandings these youngsters have of being American, being black American, and being their ethnic identity. After a short discussion of current theoretical approaches to understanding assimilation among the second generation, three types of identities adopted by the second generation are described and the different experiences of race relations associated with these identities are traced. Finally this chapter suggests some implications for future patterns of identity development.

Immigration from the English-speaking islands of the Caribbean has been substantial throughout the twentieth century, but the number of immigrants coming from the West Indies and Haiti really grew following the 1965 change in the immigration law (Bryce-Laporte, 1987; Kasinitz, 1992). According to the 1990 census, there were 1,455,294 foreign-born blacks living in the United States, or 4.8 percent of blacks nationwide. The vast majority of them are from the Caribbean. Miami and New York City are the chief destinations for these immigrants, and the concentration of foreign-born blacks and their children is much higher in these cities. Currently, about 25 percent of the black population in New York is foreign born, with a substantial and growing second generation. (Because the census does not ask a birthplace-of-parents question, it is impossible to know exactly how many second-generation West Indians currently reside in the United States.) Between 1990 and 1992, I conducted in-depth interviews of immigrants and their children in New York City that were designed to explore assimilation patterns and issues of racial and ethnic identity.

The overall study was designed to explore the processes of immigrant adaptation and accommodation to the United States, to trace generational changes in adaptation and identification, and to explore the reactions of immigrants and their children to American race relations. Interviews with black and white Americans who interacted with the first and second generations were included in order to understand the dynamic and interactive processes of self- and other-identification and the development of ethnic attitudes and stereotypes. The first-generation respondents and their American coworkers were drawn from two work sites—unskilled workers at a food service company in downtown Manhattan and middle-class schoolteachers in the New York City school system. The entire study included in-depth interviews with seventy-two first-generation immigrants, eighty-three second-generation immigrants, twenty-seven whites, and thirty native-born black Americans.[2] In total, the study draws from 212 in-depth interviews that lasted between one and two hours. They were conducted by myself (a white female) and a team of three research assistants, two of whom are second-generation Caribbean Americans and one a black American.

Interviews with first-generation immigrants and their American coworkers reveal a great deal of tension between foreign-born and American-born blacks in both the working-class and the middle-class work sites. Long-standing tensions between newly arrived West Indians and American blacks have left a legacy of mutual stereotyping. (See Kasinitz, 1992.) The immigrants see themselves as hardworking, ambitious, militant about their racial identities but not oversensitive or obsessed with race, and committed to education and family. They see black Americans as lazy, disorganized, obsessed with racial slights and barriers, with a disorganized and laissez-faire attitude toward family life and child raising. American blacks describe the immigrants as arrogant, selfish, exploited in the workplace, oblivious to racial tensions and politics in the United States, and unfriendly and unwilling to have relations with black Americans. The first generation believes that their status as foreign-born blacks is higher than American blacks, and they tend to accentuate their identities as immigrants. Their accent is usually a clear and unambiguous signal to other Americans that they are foreign born.

The dilemma facing the second generation is that they grow up exposed to the negative opinions voiced by their parents about American blacks and to the belief that whites respond more favorably to foreign-born blacks. But they also realize that because they lack their parents' accents and other identifying characteristics, other people, including their peers, are likely to identify them as American blacks. How does the second generation handle this dilemma? Do they follow their parents' lead and identify with their ethnic identities such as Jamaican or Haitian or West Indian? Or do they try to become "American" and reject their parents' ethnic immigrant identities? The second-generation sample included eighty-three adolescents drawn from four sources designed to tap a range of class backgrounds and class trajectories:

1. Public school sample: teenagers attending two inner-city public high schools in New York City where I did extensive interviewing and participant observation (forty-five interviews).

2. Church school sample: teenagers attending Catholic parochial schools in the same inner-city neighborhoods; most of these students were not themselves Catholic (fourteen interviews).

3. Street-based sample: teenagers living in the same inner-city neighborhoods in Brooklyn who could not be reached through the school—either because they had dropped out or would not have responded to interviews conducted in a formal setting (fifteen interviews).

4. Middle-class sample: teenagers who had ties to these neighborhoods; they were either living there and attending magnet schools or colleges outside of the district or their families had since moved to other areas of the city or suburbs (nine interviews).

The young people we talked to included teens who are facing very limited socioeconomic mobility or downward social mobility (the inner-city public school students and the street group), students who are on an upward social trajectory and have a high chance of going to college (the parochial sample), and teens whose families are doing well and who themselves would seem to have bright futures. Overall, 16 percent of the eighty-three teens were from very poor families on public assistance, 49 percent were from families with at least one parent working at a low-wage job, and 35 percent were from middle-class families with at least one parent in a job requiring a college degree. The age of respondents ranged from fourteen to twenty-one. The average age was seventeen. The vast majority were aged sixteen to eighteen. We included teenagers who had spent at least three years in the United States and who had immigrated before age sixteen. They included thirty-four youths (41 percent) who compose the classic second generation—born in the United States of immigrant parents. Another fourteen (17 percent) immigrated to the United States before age seven. The rest of the sample, thirty-five young people, had immigrated after age seven and had spent at least three years in the United States. The actual age at immigration for these more recent immigrants varied from seven to fifteen.[3]

Theoretical Approaches to Assimilation

Theories derived from the experiences of European immigrants and their children in the early twentieth century predicted that the more time spent in the United States, the more likely second-generation youths were to adopt an "American identity" and to reduce ties to the ethnic identities and culture of their parents. This "straight-line" assimilation model assumes that with each succeeding generation, the groups become more similar to mainstream Americans and more economically successful. For instance, Warner and Srole's (1945) study of ethnic groups in Yankee City (Newburyport, Massachusetts) in the early 1930s describes the generational march from initial residential and occupational segregation and poverty to residential, occupational, and identificational integration and Americanization.

However, the situation faced by immigrant blacks in the 1990s differs in many of the background assumptions of the straight-line model. The immigrants do not enter a society that assumes an undifferentiated monolithic American culture but rather a consciously pluralistic society in which a variety of subcultures and racial and ethnic identities coexist. In fact, if these immigrants assimilate, they become not just Americans but black Americans. The immigrants generally believe that it is higher social status to be an immigrant black than to be an American black. Second, the economic opportunity structure is very different now from what it was at the beginning of the twentieth century. The unskilled jobs in manufacturing that enhanced job mobility for immigrants' children at the turn of the century have been lost as economic restructuring in the United States has shifted to a service economy (Gans, 1992). The immigrants also are quite varied in the skills they bring with them. Some arrive with advanced educations and professional qualifications to take relatively well-paying jobs, which put them ahead of native American blacks (for example, Jamaican nurses). Others are less skilled and face difficulties finding work in the United States. Finally, the degree of residential segregation faced by blacks in the United States, whether foreign born or American born, has always been, and continues to be, of a much higher order than the segregation faced by foreign-born white immigrants (Lieberson, 1980; Massey, 1990). Thus, even with occupational mobility, it is not clear that blacks would be able to move into higher-status neighborhoods in the orderly progression that Warner and Srole (1945) describe in their Yankee City study of European ethnic succession. A further complication for the black second generation is that part of being a black American involves dealing with American racism. Because immigrants and black Americans report a large difference in the perception and expectation of racism in American society, part of becoming American for the second generation involves developing a knowledge and perception of racism and its subtle nuances.

A few researchers have examined the self-identification of second-generation Caribbean blacks. In a study of Haitian Americans in Evanston, Illinois, in the 1970s, Woldemikael (1989) found that the second generation mostly identified as American black. He found that the first generation stressed their differences from American blacks, but the second generation faced pressure to become "not so much American, but Afro American"; "Afro American students pressured the Haitian students to adopt their dialect, speech and dress styles and ways of behavior" (Woldemikael, 1989: 94). In an in-depth study of several West Indian children in New York City schools, Michael (1990) also stresses the influence on these children of the Afro American children in school and on the streets.

New theories describing the experiences of becoming American for recent immigrants and their children (Gans, 1992; Portes and Zhou, 1993) stress the multiple and contradictory paths that second-generation children can follow. Some achieve socioeconomic success while retaining strong ethnic attachments and identities, while others assimilate to American subcultures with limited socioeconomic mobility. In a 1992 article entitled "Second Generation Decline," Herbert Gans outlines several scenarios of the socioeconomic and social integration of the post-1965 second generation. He speculates that the children of the new immigrants could face socioeconomic decline relative to their parents' positions because they might refuse to accept the low-level, low-paying jobs at which their parents work.

The other possibility is that the youngsters who do not "become American" and who reject the negative attitudes toward school, opportunity, hard work, and the "American dream" that their American peers have adopted, but rather stay tied to their parents' ethnic community and values, will end up doing better. Gans (1992) thus suggests that straight-line theory could be turned on its head, with "the people who have secured an economically viable ethnic or other niche acculturating less than did the European second and third genera-tions" and those without such a niche "experiencing the poverty and joblessness of second-generation decline and becoming American faster than other second-generation ethnics" (p. 188).

Using material from a number of different ethnographic case stud-ies, as well as a survey of second-generation school children in Miami and San Diego, Portes and Zhou (1993) make a similar argument. They describe the different outcomes of different groups of second-genera-tion youth as "segmented assimilation." They argue that how the first generation adapts to living in the United States creates differential op-portunities and social capital in the form of ethnic jobs, networks, and values that, in turn, create differential pulls on the allegiances of the second generation. For those immigrant groups that face extreme dis-crimination in the United States and that reside in close proximity to American minorities who have faced a great deal of discrimination, re-active ethnicity emerges in the first generation. The second-generation youth whose ties to American minorities are stronger and whose parental generation lacks sufficient social capital to advance the second generation are likely to develop the "adversarial stance" that American minorities, such as poor blacks and Hispanics, hold toward the domi-nant white society. This adversarial stance stresses that discrimination in the United States is very strong and devalues education as a vehicle of advancement. For those groups that maintain strong ethnic net-works, access to capital, and fewer ties to minorities in the United States, linear ethnicity characterizes the first generation. Linear ethnic-ity creates social capital—the networks of social ties from church and voluntary organizations that lead to job opportunities and the interlac-ing ties that reinforce parental authority and values vis-à-vis the second generation. These groups resist acculturation to the United States and end up providing better opportunities for the second generation.

Portes and Zhou (1993) use the experiences of Chinese and Koreans as examples of immigrants who develop linear ethnicity and strong ethnic communities in the United States. They are contrasted with the Haitians in Florida, who are pressured to adapt to the black American peer culture in their schools. Portes and Zhou stress that the adver-sarial stance of this latter peer culture directly contradicts the immi-grant parents' expectations of upward mobility and educational suc-cess for their offspring. The second generation that casts their lot with America's minority groups risks downward social mobility. Associa-tion with ethnic minorities could prove "a ticket to permanent subor-dination and disadvantage for the youngsters who adopt it" (p. 96).

Both Gans and Portes and Zhou stress the negative consequences in terms of aspirations and ultimate socioeconomic outcomes of adopting an "American" minority attitude toward school and work opportunities. Portes and Zhou call this an "adversarial outlook." John Ogbu (1990) describes a similar "minority" outlook as an oppositional frame of reference that he ties to historical roots in the involuntary incorporation of minority groups into society. These ideas are enormously helpful in explaining and understanding the experiences of the second-generation West Indian youth in this study. In fact, the youth described here, who seem to be on different socioeconomic trajectories, understand their racial and ethnic identities differently. Some of the adolescents we interviewed agree with their parents that the United States holds many opportunities for them. Others disagree with their parents because they believe that racial discrimination and hostility from whites will limit their abilities to meet their goals. By contrasting the ideas these youngsters have about their own identities and the role of race in American society, I suggest that social capital among the first generation and the type of segmented assimilation among the second generation vary within ethnic groups as well as between them. Some Jamaican Americans, for example, are experiencing downward social mobility while others are maintaining strong ethnic ties and achieving socioeconomic success.

The key factor for the youth I studied is race. The daily discrimination they experience, the racial socialization they receive in the home, and the understandings of race they develop in their peer groups affect strongly how they react to American society. The ways in which these youngsters experience and react to racial discrimination influences the type of racial and ethnic identity they develop.

Patterns in the Second Generation

The interviews suggest that while the individuals in this study vary a great deal in their identities, perceptions, and opinions, they can be sorted into three general types: identifying as Americans, identifying as ethnic Americans with some distancing from black Americans, or identifying as an immigrant in a way that does not reckon with American racial and ethnic categories.

A black American identity characterized the responses of approximately 42 percent of the eighty-three second-generation respondents interviewed. These youngsters identified with other black Americans. They did not see their "ethnic" identities as important to their self-image. When their parents or friends criticized American blacks or described what they perceived as fundamental differences between Caribbean-origin people and American blacks, these youngsters disagreed. They tended to downplay a national-origin identity and described themselves as American.

Another 30 percent of the respondents adopted a very strong ethnic identity that involved a considerable amount of distancing from American blacks. It was important for these respondents to stress their ethnic identities and for other people to recognize that they were not American blacks. These respondents tended to agree with parental judgments that there were strong differences between Americans and West Indians. This often involved a stance that West Indians were superior to American blacks in their behaviors and attitudes.

A final 28 percent of respondents had an immigrant attitude toward their identities, as opposed to American-identified youth or ethnic-identified youth. Most, but not all, of these respondents were more recent immigrants themselves. A crucial factor for these youngsters is that their accents and styles of clothing and behavior clearly signaled to others that they were foreign born. In a sense, their identity as an immigrant people precluded having to make a "choice" about what kind of American they were. These respondents had a strong identity, such as Jamaican or Trinidadian, but did not evidence much distancing from American blacks. Rather their identities were strongly linked to their experiences on the islands, and they did not worry much about how they were seen by other Americans, white or black.

A number of factors influence the type of identity the youngsters develop. They include the class background of the parents, the social networks in which the parents are involved, the type of school the child attends, and the family structure. All of these factors affect the ability of parents and other family members to shield children from neighborhood peer groups that espouse antischool values.

The type of identity and outlook on American race and ethnic relations that the youngsters developed was strongly related to their social class and its trajectory. The ethnic-identified youngsters were most likely to come from a middle-class background. Of the eighty-three second-generation teens and young adults interviewed, 57 percent of the middle-class teens identified ethnically, whereas only 17 percent of the working-class and poor teens identified ethnically.[4] The poorest students were the most likely to be immigrant or American identified. Only one out of the twelve teens whose parents were on public assistance identified ethnically. The American identified, perhaps not surprisingly, were also more likely to be born in the United States—67 percent of the American identified were born in the United States, as opposed to only 13 percent of the immigrant identified and 42 percent of the ethnically identified.

Parents with more education and income were able to provide better schools for their offspring. Among the respondents, some of the middle class had moved from the inner-city neighborhoods they had originally settled in to middle-class neighborhoods in the borough of

Queens or to suburban areas where the schools were of higher academic quality and more likely to be racially integrated. Other middle-class parents sent their children to Catholic parochial schools or to citywide magnet schools such as Brooklyn Tech or Stuyvesant. Thus, the children were far more likely to attend schools with other immigrant children and with other middle-class whites and blacks, although some of the Catholic high schools were all black in enrollment.

The children of middle-class parents who did attend the local high schools were likely to be recent immigrants who had an immigrant identity. Because of their superior education in the West Indies, these students were the best in the local high schools, attended honors classes, and were bound for college. The children of middle-class parents who identified as American and were pessimistic about their own future opportunities and adopted antischool ideologies were likely to have arrived early in their lives and to have attended New York City public schools in inner-city areas from an early age.

The social networks of parents also influenced the type of identity the children developed. Regardless of social class, parents who were involved in ethnic voluntary organizations or heavily involved in their churches seemed to instill a strong sense of ethnic identity in their children. Parents whose social networks transcended neighborhood boundaries seemed to have more ability to provide guidance and social contacts for their children.

The two neighborhood schools where we interviewed the teenagers were among the five most dangerous schools in New York City—they were inadequate facilities with crumbling physical buildings, high dropout rates, and serious problems with violence. Both schools were all minority, with over 90 percent of the student body composed of black students, both American and foreign born. The students who attended these schools and were not in the separate honors tract (which was overwhelmingly filled with newly arrived immigrants) faced very limited future options, even if they managed to graduate.

Finally, the family structure and the experience of migration itself have a profound effect on the degree of control parents have over teenage children. Many families are composed of single working mothers and children. These mothers have not been able to supervise their children as much as they would like, and many do not have any extended family or close friends available to help with discipline and control. Even families with two spouses present often have been apart for long periods because one spouse preceded the family in migration. Often children have been left in the islands or sent ahead with relatives to New York, with the parents often struggling to reassert authority after the family reunites. The generational conflict that ensues tends to create greater pressure for students to want to be "American" to differentiate themselves from parents.

Ethnic Response

All of the teenage respondents reported comments by their parents about American blacks that were very similar to those recorded in our interviews with the first generation. The differences were in how the teens interpreted what their parents were saying. In general, the ethnic-identified teens agreed with their parents and reported seeing a strong difference between themselves and black Americans, stressing that being black is not synonymous with being black American. They accept their parents' and the wider society's negative portrayals of poor blacks and wanted to avoid any chance that they will be identified with them. They described the culture and values of lower-class black Americans as lacking discipline, a work ethic, good child-rearing practices, and respect for education. They contrast these failures with the values of their parents' ethnic groups, which include an emphasis on education, strict discipline for children, a strong work ethic, and social mobility. They try to impress that they are Jamaican or Haitian and most definitely not black American. This allows them less dissonance with their parents' negative views of American blacks. They do not reject their parents' culture and identities but rather reject the American social system that would identify them as black American and strongly reject the African American peer group culture to which they would be assigned by whites and others if they did not consciously transmit their ethnic identities.

Although society may define the second generation on the basis of skin color, the second-generation ethnic teens believed that being black American involves more than merely having black skin. One young woman criticized American blacks in this way:

> Some of them [black Americans] think that their heritage includes not being able to speak correctly or walk correctly, or act loud and obnoxious to make a point. I don't think they have to do that. Just when I see black Americans, it depends on how I see you on the street. Walking down the street with that walk that moves a little bit too much. I would say, I'd think you dropped out of high school.

These teens also differentiated themselves from black Americans in terms of their sensitivity to racism, real or imagined. Some of the ethnic-identified second generation echo the feelings we heard from the first generation that American blacks are too quick to use race as an explanation or excuse for not doing well:

There was a time back in the '40s and '50s and '60s or whenever when people was actually trying to keep down black people and stuff like that. But, you know, some black people now, it's like they not actually trying to make it better, you know? Some are just like, people are like, oh, this place is trying to keep me down, and they sulk and they cry about it, and they're not really doing that much to help them-selves. . . . It's just like hyping the problem if they keep [saying] every-thing is racial, everything is racial.

The second-generation teens who are doing well try to understand how it is that they are so successful when black Americans are not—and often they chalk it up to family values. They say that their immi-grant families have close-knit family values that stress education. Aware of, and sometimes sharing, the negative images of black Amer-icans that the whites they encounter believe, the second generation also perceives that whites treat them better when they realize they are not "just" black Americans. When asked if they benefited ever from their ethnicity, they responded "yes": "It seems white Americans don't tend to put you in the same category as black Americans." Another re-spondent said:

The West Indians tend to go that extra step because they, whites, don't usually consider them really black Americans, which would be working class. They don't consider them, I guess, as black. They see them as a person.

The dilemma for the second generation is that while they have a strong sense of their own identities as very different from black Amer-icans, this was not clear to other people. Often both whites and blacks saw them as just black Americans and did not notice that they were ethnically different. When people did comment on their ethnic differ-ence it was often because of the way they talked and the way they walked. These two characteristics were cited as reasons that whites and other blacks gave for thinking those of the second generation were not "really black." Whites tend to let these children know that they think of them as exceptions to the rule, with the rule being that most blacks are not good people. However, these young people also know that unless they tell people of their ethnicity, most whites have no idea they are not black Americans.

Many of these teens coped with this dilemma by devising ways to telegraph their identities as second-generation West Indians or Haitians. One girl carried a Guyanese map as part of her key chain so that when people looked at her keys they would ask her about it and she could tell them that her parents were from Guyana. One young woman described having her mother teach her an accent so that she could use it when she applied for a job or a place to live. Others just try to work it into conversation when they meet someone. This means that their self-identification is almost always at odds with the identifications others make of them in impersonal encounters in American society and that, as a result, they must consciously try to accentuate their ethnic identity:

Q. When a form or survey asks for your race what do you put down?

A. Oh boy, that is a tough one. It's funny because, you know, when we fill applications I never know what to check off, you know. I'm serious. 'Cause they have Afro-American, but they never have like Caribbean. They do have white, Chinese. To tell the truth, I would like to be called Caribbean, West Indian. Black West Indian.

The teens who were around many black Americans felt pressure from their peers to be part of the group and identify as black American. These teens would consciously talk about passing for American at some points and passing for Haitian or Jamaican at others by changing the way they talked or acted:

When I'm at school and I sit with my black friends and, sometimes I'm ashamed to say this, but my accent changes. I learn all the words. I switch. Well, when I'm with my friends, my black friends, I say I'm black, black American. When I'm with my Haitian-American friends, I say I'm Haitian. Well, my being black, I guess that puts me when I'm with black Americans, it makes people think that I'm lower class. . . . Then, if I'm talking like this [regular voice] with my friends at school, they call me white.

American-Identified Second Generation

The American-identified second-generation teenagers differed in how little they stressed their immigrant or ethnic identities to the interviewers. They follow a path that is more similar to the model posed in the straight-line theory. They stress that they are American because they were born here, and they are disdainful of their parents' lack of understanding of the American social system. Instead of rejecting black American culture, it becomes their peer culture, and they embrace many aspects of it. This brings them in conflict with their parents' generation, most especially with their parents' understandings of American blacks. They most definitely assimilate to black America; they speak black English with their peers, they listen to rap music, and they accept the peer culture of their black American friends. They are aware of the fact that they are considered black American by others and that they can be accused of "acting white" if they don't speak black English and behave in particular ways. Most included their ethnic identities as background, but none of them adopted the stance that they were not, in a major sense, black American. When asked about ethnic background and how other people think of it, one respondent replied:

Q. What is your ethnic background?

A. I put down American because I was born up here. I feel that is what I should put down. . . .

Q. What do other people think you are?

A. Black American because if I don't say. . . . Like if they hear my parents talk or something they always think they are from Jamaica. . . . But they just think I am black American because I was born up here.

Many of these teens discuss how they do not control how others see them:

Some people just think I am American because I have no accent. So I talk like American people. I don't talk Brooklynese. They think I am from down south or something. . . . A lot of people say you don't look Haitian. I think I look Haitian enough. I don't know, maybe they are expecting us to look fresh off the boat. I was born here and I grew up here, so I guess I look American and I have an American accent.

Q. If people think you are black American do you ever do anything about it?

A. No, I don't. If they ask me if I am American, I say yes. If they ask me where my parents are from, I tell them Haiti.

In fact, they imply that being a black American is more stylish and "with it" than being from the islands:

I consider myself a black American. When I think of a black American I don't think of them as coming from the West Indies.

Q. Any characteristics that come to mind?

A. I would not think of someone in a suit. I would think of a regular teenager. I would think of a regular person. I think of someone that is in style.

Q. What about someone from the islands?

A. Jamaicans. They dress with neon colors. Most of the girls wear gold and stuff like that.

Some of the young people told us that they saw little if any difference between the ethnic blacks and the American blacks. Many stressed the Caribbeanization of black New York and described how all the Americans were interested in being Caribbean now:

It use to be Jamaicans and American blacks did not get along because everyone was afraid of Jamaicans. But now I guess we are closer now. You tell an American that you are Jamaican and it is no big deal. Americans are acting more like Jamaicans. Jamaicans are acting like Americans.

Q. What do you mean by acting like each other?

A. Sure there are a lot of Americans out there speaking patois. And then all the Jamaicans are coming over here and they are like "Yo, what's up" and they are like that. Pretty soon you can't really tell who is Jamaican and who is American.

However, the parents of the American-identified teens have expressed to their children the same negative impressions of American blacks that the ethnic-identified teens reported. These teenagers report many negative appraisals of American blacks by their parents:

They always say Haiti is better in this way or in that way. They say the kids here have no respect. The kids here are brought up without any supervision. My father is always talking about they [American blacks] be hanging out on the corner. And he says you won't find Haitians doing that. My mom always says you will marry a Haitian. Why are you talking to those American boys?

This young Haitian American teen tries to disagree with her mother and to temper her mother's interpretations of American blacks:

Q. Are there any characteristics or traits that come to mind about Haitian Americans?

A. Not really. I don't really—cause most people are Haitian American if they are born here. . . . Like me, I don't know if I act like a Haitian or do I have Haitian characteristics, but I'm mostly—like everything I do or like is American. My parents, they do not like American blacks, but they feel that they are lazy. They don't want to work and stuff like that from what they see. And I feel that, um, I feel that way too, but sometimes it won't be that person's fault, so I try to stick up for them. And my mother is like, yeah, you're just too American.

In marked contrast to the ethnic-identified teens, though, the American-identified teens disagreed with their parents' statements about American blacks, reluctantly agreed with some of it but provided qualifications, or perhaps, most disturbingly, accepted the appraisals as true of American blacks in general and themselves as American blacks. This young Trinidadian American swallows her parents' stereotypes and applies them directly to herself:

Q. How close do you feel in your ideas about things to West Indians?

A. Not very close. My feelings are more like blacks than theirs. I am lazy. I am really lazy and my parents are always making comments and things about how I am lazy. They are always like, in Trinidad you could not be this lazy. In Trinidad you would have to keep on working.

The fact that the teens are identifying as American and that their parents have such negative opinions of Americans causes some conflict. The teens either adopt a negative opinion of themselves or disagree with their parents' assessments of American blacks. But it is not just their parents who criticize black Americans. These youngsters are very aware of the generalized negative view of blacks in the wider culture. In answer to the question "Do whites have an image of blacks?" all of them responded that whites have a negative view of blacks, seeing them as criminal, lazy, violent, and uncaring about family. Many of the teenagers prefaced their remarks by saying that they did not know any whites but that they knew this is what whites thought through the mass media and through the behaviors of whites they encountered in buses, trains, and stores. This mostly involved incidents such as whites protecting their handbags when the teenagers arrived or store clerks following them and expecting them to shoplift. This knowledge that the society in which they live devalues them because of their skin color and their identity affected these teens deeply.

Immigrant-Identified Teens

The more recently arrived young people who still identify as immigrant differed from both the ethnic- and the American-identified youth. They did not feel as much pressure to "choose" between identifying with or distancing from black Americans as did either the American or the ethnic teens. Strong in their national-origin identities, they were neutral toward American distinctions between ethnics and black Americans. They tended to stress their nationality or their birthplace as defining their identity. They also pointed to their experiences growing up and attending school in a different country. This young man had dreadlocks and a strong Jamaican accent. He stresses his African roots and lets his Jamaican origin speak for itself:

Q. What is your ethnicity? For example, when forms or surveys ask what your ethnic group or ancestry is what do you put?

A. African.

Q. Do you ever put Jamaican or anything?

A. No, not really. Only where Jamaican comes up is if someone asks where you're from. I'll say I am from Jamaica.

Q. What do people usually think you are?

A. They say I am Jamaican.

Q. They know that immediately?

A. Yeah.

Q. How do they know?

A. I change my voice. I don't have to tell them. I think it's also because of my locks sometimes and the way I carry myself, the way I dress.

While an ethnic-identified Jamaican American is aware that she might be seen by others as American and thus actively chooses to present herself as Jamaican, an immigrant-identified Jamaican could not conceive of herself as having a choice, nor could she conceive of being perceived by others as American. While an ethnic-identified teen might describe herself as Jamaican American, for the immigrant teen Jamaican would be all the label needed. Most teens in this category were recent immigrants. The few U.S.-born teens classified as immigrant identified had strong family roots on the islands, were frequent visitors to the islands, and had plans to return to live there as adults. A crucial factor that allows these youngsters to maintain this identity is that their accents and styles of clothing and behavior clearly signaled to others that they were foreign born.

Q. How important is it to you that your friends think of you in terms of your ethnicity?

A. Oh, very important. You know, I try hard not to lose my roots, you know, when I come to the United States. A lot of people who come here try to lose their accent, you know. Even in the workplace, you know, because they fear what other people might think of them. Even in the workplace. Me, I never try to change, you know, the way I am. I always try to, you know, stay with them, the way of my culture.

Q. So it's something you want people to recognize?

A. Yeah, definitely, definitely, absolutely.

Q. Why?

A. Why? I'm proud of who I am, you know. I'm proud of where I'm from and I'm not going to change because somebody might not like the way I walk, talk or dress, you know.

The importance of birthplace was stressed repeatedly by the immigrant identified as they stressed their difference from American-born coethnics:

Q. What would you put on a form or survey that asked about your ethnicity?

A. I'll say I'm Jamaican. You gotta say where you come from.

Q. And do you think of yourself more as a Jamaican or more as an American?

A. I think of more of a Jamaican 'cause it's, I wasn't born here. I was born in Jamaica and was there for fourteen years.

Q. And what about kids who are born in America, but their parents were born in Jamaica?

A. Well, you see that is the problem. You see, kids whose parents are Jamaican, they think that, well, they are Jamaican. They need to recheck that they're Americans 'cause they was born in the country and they wasn't born outside the country. So I think they should, you know, know more about American than Jamaican.

Some who adopt this strong identity with the immigrant country were born in the United States, but the combination of strong family roots on the island, frequent visits, and plans to go live there when they are older allows them to think of themselves as not really American at all. This is especially easy to do in the public high schools where there are large numbers of freshly arrived youngsters from the islands.

Q. What do you think your race is?

A. Well, I'm black. I consider myself black. I don't consider myself black American, Afro-American and stuff like that because it's hard to determine, you know, for a person as an individual to determine himself to be Afro-American. . . . I'll be more a Guyanese person because certain things and traditions that I am accustomed to back home, it's still within the roots of me. And those things have not changed for a long period of time, even though you have to adapt to the system over here in order to get ahead and cope with what is going on around you.

While the ethnics tended to describe people as treating them better when they described their ethnic origins, and the Americans tended to stress the antiblack experiences they have had and the lack of difference between the foreign born and the American, the immigrant teens spoke about anti-immigrant feelings and discrimination and responded with pride in their national origins.

Contrasting Identities

In some sense one can see each of these identities as an embrace of one identity and an opposition to another. The American-identified youth are assimilating, in fact, to the American black subculture in the neighborhood. They are adapting to American black cultural forms, and they do so in distinction to their parents' ethnic identities and the wider mainstream white identities. These students adopt some of the "oppositional" poses that American black teenagers show toward academic achievement: the idea of America, the idea of opportunity, and the wider society (Fordham, 1988; Ogbu, 1990; Portes and Zhou, 1993). They also are opposed to their parents' outlooks and ideas, stressing that what worked as a life strategy and a child-raising technique in the islands does not work in the United States. These teens tend to adopt a peer culture of racial solidarity and opposition to school authorities. What is clear from the interviews is that this stance is in part a socialized response to a peer culture, but the vast majority of it comes about as a reaction to their life experiences. Most specifically, the teens respond to their experiences with racial discrimination and their perceptions of blocked social mobility. The lives of these youngsters basically lead them to reject their parents' immigrant dream of individual social mobility and to accept their peers' analysis of the United States as a place with blocked social mobility where they will not move far.

The American-identified teens do not seem aware of the scholarly literature and the perceptions among ethnic- and immigrant-identified youngsters that the foreign born are of higher social status than the American born. In the peer culture of the neighborhood and the school, these teenagers describe a situation in which being American offers higher social status than being ethnic. For instance, several youngsters described "passing" as black American in order not to be ridiculed or picked on in school:

> I used to be scared to tell people that I was Haitian. Like when I was in eighth grade there were lots of Haitians in the ESL classes, and people used to beat them up. They used to pick on them. I said to myself I am going to quiet down, say I am American.

When asked about the images others held of being from the islands, most of the teens described neutral attributes, such as styles of dress. However, many who identified as Americans also described negative associations with the immigrants' identities. The Jamaicans said most people thought of drug dealers when they thought of Jamaicans. A few of the teens also intimated that people from the islands were backward in not knowing how to live in a big city, both in appreciating the wonders of the city and being street smart to avoid crime and hassles with other people. In terms of the former attribute, the teens described people from the islands who were not accustomed to shopping in big malls or having access to a wide variety of consumer goods.

Not one of the American-identified teens voiced the opinion of the overwhelming majority of the ethnic teens that whites were more likely to like the foreign born. In part, this reflected the differences the groups had in their contact with whites. Most of the inner-city ethnic-identified teens had almost no contact with whites, except for teachers. They also are in schools where the vast majority of the students are foreign born or second generation. The larger number of middle-class teens who were ethnic-identified were more likely to have white classmates in citywide magnet high schools, in parochial schools, or in suburban schools or workplaces.

The inner-city American-identified teens also voiced more positive appraisals of black Americans than did the immigrant or the ethnic-identified teens. Their descriptions reflect the reality of living in neighborhoods where there is crime and violence. A majority of the American-identified teens said that a good trait of black Americans is that they work hard and they struggle. These are the very same children whose parents describe black Americans primarily as lazy and unwilling to take advantage of the opportunities available to them. The children seem to be perceiving a reality that the parents cannot or will not.

Many of these teens live in neighborhoods that are all black and also attend schools that are all black. So, aside from teachers, these young people have almost no contact with white Americans. This does not stop them from absorbing the fact that whites have negative stereotypic views of blacks. But unlike the middle-class blacks who come in contact with whites who tell them that they are "good blacks," these youths live in the urban areas associated with crime, they dress like the typical black urban youth, and they talk with Brooklyn accents and black American slang. When they do encounter whites in public places, the whites do not ask about their parents' backgrounds.

Q. Have you ever experienced any discrimination or hostility in New York?

A. From being Trinidadian no. But because of being black, you know, everybody stereotypes. And they say "blacks, they tend to steal, and stuff like that." So, like, if I am walking down the street and a white lady go by and they smile and I smile. They put their bag on the other side.

The parents of these teens grew up in situations where blacks were the majority. The parents do not want their children to be "racial" in the United States. They define "being racial" as being overly concerned with race and with using race as an excuse or explanation for lack of success at school or on the job. The first generation tends to believe that, while racism exists in the United States, it can be overcome or circumvented through hard work, perseverance, and the right values and attitudes. The second generation experiences racism and discrimination constantly and develops perceptions of the overwhelming influence of race on their lives. These teens experience being hassled by police and store owners, not being given jobs, even being attacked on the streets if they venture into white neighborhoods. The boys adopt black American culture in their schools, wearing flattops, baggy pants, and certain types of jewelry. This contributes to the projection of the "cool pose," which in turn causes whites to be afraid of them. This makes them angry and resentful. The media also tells these youngsters that blacks are disvalued by American society. While parents tell their children to strive for upward mobility and to work harder in the face of discrimination, the American-identified teens think the rewards for doing so will be very slim.

This causes a wide gulf between the parents and their children. These parents are absolutely terrified of their children becoming Americans. For the children, to be American is to have freedom from the strict parental controls of the immigrant parents. This is an old story in the immigrant saga, one visible in novels and movies about conflicts between Jewish and Italian immigrants and their children. But the added dimension here is that these parents are afraid of the downward social mobility that becoming an American black represents to them. And this idea is reinforced constantly to these parents by whites who tell them that they are better than American blacks.

One question about how things had changed since the civil rights movement shows the different perceptions of the teens about race in American society. The ethnically identified gave answers I suspect most white Americans would give. They said that things are much better for blacks now. They state that blacks now can ride at the front of the bus and go to school with whites. The irony, of course, is that I was sitting in an all-black school when they told this story. The vast majority of the American-identified teens state that things are not better since the civil rights movement; the change is that discrimination now is "on the down low," covered up, more crafty. Some pointed out that we were in an all-black school. The result of these different world views is that the parents' view of an opportunity structure that is open to hard work is systematically undermined by their children's peer culture and, more important, by the actual experiences of these teens.

On the other hand, the ethnic-identified teens, whose parents are more likely to be middle class and doing well or who attend parochial or magnet schools, see clearer opportunities and rewards ahead, despite the existence of racism and discrimination. Their parents' message that hard work and perseverance can circumvent racial barriers does not fall on unreceptive ears. The ethnic-identified youngsters embrace an identity derived directly from their parents' immigrant identity. Such an identity is in opposition to their peers' identities and in solidarity with their parents' identities. These youngsters stress that they are Jamaican Americans and that, while they may be proud of their racial identity as black, they see strong differences between themselves and black Americans. They specifically see their ethnic identities as keys to upward social mobility, stressing, for instance, that their parents' values of hard work and strict discipline help them to succeed in the United States when black Americans fail. This ethnic identity is very much an American-based identity—it is in the context of American social life that these youngsters base their assumptions of what it means to be Jamaican or Trinidadian. In fact, the pan-ethnic identities of Caribbean or West Indian often are the most salient label for these youngsters, as they see little differences among the groups and it is more important to differentiate themselves as second-generation Americans. The distancing that these teens show from black Americans often leads them to accept many negative stereotypes of black Americans. These youngsters tend to have ethnic friends from a West Indian background, white American friends, and very few, if any, black American friends.

The immigrant-identified teens are different from either of the other two, because of how they think about who they are not as well as how they think about who they are. These teens have a strong identity as Jamaican or Trinidadian, but this identity tends to be related to their interactions with other Jamaicans or Trinidadians rather than their interactions with black or white Americans. These youngsters identify with their homelands or their parents' homelands, but not in opposition to black Americans or in opposition to white Americans. They tend to be immersed in the immigrant community, to have friends who are all the same ethnicity or from other islands. They tend to be more recent arrivals. Unlike the ethnically identified, however, they do not distance themselves from American blacks, and they have neutral or positive attitudes and relations with them. At the same time, they see themselves as different from, but not opposed to, black Americans.

These identities are fluid and change over time and in different social contexts. We found cases of people who describe identifying very strongly as black American when they were younger and who became more immigrant identified when they reached high school and found a large immigrant community. Most new arrivals to the United States start out as immigrant identified, and the longer they stay in the United States, the more they begin to think of themselves in terms of American categories. The kind of social milieu the child faces, especially the school environment, has a strong influence on the outcome. A school with many black Americans creates pressure to identify racially; likewise a neighborhood and school with many immigrants makes it possible to avoid thinking much about American categories. In the face of much pressure not to follow the rules and not to succeed academically, youngsters who are doing well in school and do value education increasingly come to stress their ethnic backgrounds as an explanation for their ambition and success.

The American racial classification system that pushes toward an either/or—"black or white"—designation of people makes the immigrant option harder to hold onto. When others constantly identify the individual as black and refuse to make distinctions based on black ethnicity, pressure builds for the individual to adapt his or her identity to that outside identification—either to say "Yes, I am black," and to accept categorization with black Americans or to resent the characterization and strongly make an ethnic identification as Trinidadian American. The American myopia about ethnic differences within the black community makes the middle-ground immigrant identity unstable. Because every young person is aware of the negative images held by whites and the wider society of black Americans, the acceptance of an American black identity also means the acceptance of the oppositional character of that identity. Oppositional identities, as Ogbu (1990) clearly argues, are self- and group-affirming identities for stigmatized groups—defining as good and worthy those traits and characteristics that are the opposite of those valued by the majority group. This tends to draw the aspirations of the teens downward.

Implications of the Patterns

Some of the distancing shown by the ethnic-identified teens vis-à-vis underclass black identity is the same as that exhibited by middle-class black Americans. Elijah Anderson (1990) has noted that middle-class blacks in a gentrifying neighborhood in Philadelphia use various verbal and nonverbal strategies to convey to others that they are not from the ghetto and that they disapprove of the ghetto-specific behaviors of the blacks who live there. Being an ethnic black in interactions with whites seems to be a shorthand way of conveying distance from the ghetto blacks. Thus, the second generation reserves their ethnic status for use as an identity device to stress their distance from poor blacks and to stress their cultural values, which are consistent with American middle-class values. This same use of an ethnic identity is present among first-generation immigrants of all social classes, even those in racially segregated poor neighborhoods in New York.

The second generation in the segregated neighborhoods, with little chance for social mobility, seems to be unaware that status as a black ethnic conveys higher social status among whites, in part because they have not had much contact with whites. The mass media conveys to them the negative image of American blacks held by whites but does not convey to them the image among intellectuals, middle-class whites, and conservative scholars, such as Thomas Sowell, that they have cultural capital by virtue of their immigrant status. They do get the message that blacks are stereotyped by whites in negative ways, that the all-black neighborhoods they live in are violent and dangerous, and that the neighborhoods of whites are relatively safe. They also encounter a peer culture that values black American cultural forms. The immigrant culture of struggle, hard work, and educational success that their parents try to enforce is experienced in negative ways by these youngsters. They see their parents denying them privileges that their American peers enjoy and, unlike the middle-class youth, they do not automatically associate hard work, lack of dating and partying, and stress on scholastic achievement with social mobility. In the peer culture of the school, immigrant and ethnic-identified teens tend to be the best students. In the neighborhood inner-city schools, newly arrived immigrants who have attended better schools in the islands tend to outperform the students who have spent their lives in substandard New York City public schools. This tends to reinforce the association between ethnicity and school success—and the more American-identified teens adopt an adversarial stance toward school.

Warner and Srole (1945), in their study of Yankee City in the 1930s, report that it is the socially mobile white ethnics whose ties to the ethnic group and the ethnic identity decline. In their work, those individuals stuck in the lower classes turned to their ethnic identities and groups as a sort of consolation prize:

> Our class system functions for a large proportion of ethnics to destroy the ethnic subsystems and to increase assimilation. The mobile ethnic is much more likely to be assimilated than the non-mobile one. The latter retains many of the social characteristics of his homeland. . . . Some of the unsuccessfully mobile turn hostile to the host culture, develop increasing feelings of loyalty to their ethnic traditions, become active in maintaining their ethnic subsystems, and prevent others from becoming assimilated. But, generally speaking, our class order disunites ethnic groups and accelerates their assimilation. (p. 284)

It could be that the process will be exactly the opposite for black immigrants and black ethnics. In this case, the more socially mobile cling to ethnic identity as a hedge against their racial identity. The less mobile blacks see little advantage to stressing an ethnic identity in the social worlds in which they travel, which are shared mostly with black Americans. Stressing an ethnic identity in that context risks being described as "acting white," being seen as rejecting the race and accepting the white stereotypes, which they know through their everyday lives are not true.

The changes in race relations in the United States since the 1960s are very complicated and most surely involve a mixing of class and race. Some white Americans are trying to see the difference between ghetto inner-city blacks, whom they fear and do not like, and middle-class blacks, whom they do not fear and with whom they would like to have contact, if only to prove to themselves that they are not racist or, in a more formal sense, to meet their affirmative goals.

Middle-class blacks realize this and try to convey their class status in subtle and not so subtle ways (Feagin, 1991). The immigrants also utilize the fact that New Yorkers tend to use foreign-born status as a proxy for the class information they are seeking. The white New Yorkers we interviewed do notice differences among blacks, and they use ethnic differences as clues for class differences. If the association found here between social class and ethnic identity is widespread, this perception could become a self-fulfilling prophesy. It could be that the children of poor parents will not keep an ethnic identity and the children whose parents achieve social mobility will keep the ethnic identity. This will reinforce the image in the minds of whites that the "island people" are "good blacks," thus giving the edge in employment decisions and the like to ethnic blacks over American blacks.

On the other hand, it remains to be seen how long the ethnic-identified second generation will continue to identify with their ethnic backgrounds. This also is related to the fact that whites tend to make racial judgments about identity when it comes to blacks. The second generation does not have an accent or other clues that immediately telegraph their ethnic status to others. They are aware that, unless they are active in conveying their identities, they are seen as black Americans, and that often in encounters with whites, the status of their black race is all that matters. It could be that by the time they have children, they will have decided that the quest not to be seen as a black American will be a futile one.

Notes

1. The families of the teens were from twelve different countries including Jamaica (31 percent); Trinidad (21 percent); Guyana (16 percent); Barbados (10 percent); Haiti (10 percent); Grenada (5 percent); and a few each from the smaller islands of Montserrat, Saint Thomas, Anguilla, Saint Lucia, Dominica, and Nevis.

2. While there are many Spanish-speaking immigrants from the Caribbean who also define themselves or are defined by others as racially black, the identity choices for these people are quite different from those for English-speaking immigrants. The first-generation respondents in this study were restricted to English-speaking immigrants.

3. Rumbaut and Ima (1988) and Rumbaut (1991) have suggested using the term generation 1.5 for youngsters born abroad but educated in whole or part in the United States. Others have used second generation to include both children of immigrants and the immigrants who came as children (Jensen, 1990; Portes and Zhou, 1993). Circular migration makes these categories even more difficult to define, as some youngsters who were born in the United States may have spent more time in their parents' native country (having returned there often to live for short periods) than other youngsters who were born abroad but do not return often to their native country.

4. Middle class was defined as having at least one parent with a college degree or a professional or business position. Working class was defined as a parent with a low-skill job; poor were students whose parents were not currently employed.

9

Social Capital and the Adaptation of the Second Generation: The Case of Vietnamese Youth in New Orleans

MIN ZHOU AND CARL L. BANKSTON III

Elizabeth Nguyen, sixteen, was born in the Versailles neighborhood of eastern New Orleans two years after her parents arrived in the United States from Vietnam. Her father is a former South Vietnamese military officer who now works as a fisherman. She is a straight-A student, as are her two older sisters. She meets every day after school with a study group of four friends. "My parents know pretty much all the kids in the neighborhood," she says, "because we all go to the same church. Everybody here knows everybody else. It's hard to get away with much."

Hai Nguyen, seventeen, arrived in the Versailles neighborhood with his family in 1984, at the age of eleven, from a refugee camp in Malaysia. They settled in eastern New Orleans because his mother, who was born and raised in the Vietnamese village of Vung Tau, had a brother in the neighborhood. Hai is a high school junior now and he is planning to attend college after another year. He

The authors gratefully acknowledge the assistance of Stephen J. Caldas in the Louisiana State Department of Education, Holly Flood at New Orleans Accountability, and the principal and his staff of the public high school under study. We are thankful to Alejandro Portes and two anonymous International Migration Review referees for their suggestions on the earlier version of this chapter.

says he wants to go to Tulane or Loyola because he has friends from the neigh-
borhood at both institutions and he expects they will help him with any prob-
lems he may have.

Cuong Dang, seventeen, left Vietnam by boat in 1983 with his mother and his
stepfather. His stepfather is a fisherman, who is frequently away from home for
weeks at a time, on his boat in the Gulf of Mexico. His mother works as a check-
out clerk at a grocery store. Cuong is still in school and intends to graduate,
but he has no intention of going on to college. He says that all of his friends are
Vietnamese but says that none of them are interested in Vietnam or things
Vietnamese. "All that, that's all old stuff," he says. Asked whether he consid-
ers himself Vietnamese or American, he simply shrugs.

G ROWING up in the United States can be a difficult and confusing process for immigrant children, who frequently are caught between pressures to assimilate into American society and pressures to preserve their own cultures of origin. This process presents additional hardships for refugee children since they must confront the loss of loved ones, the loss of social status, and the loss of homeland, and must work through the myriad problems of uprooting and sociocultural disruption (Eisenbruch, 1988). This chapter examines how aspects of an immigrant, refugee culture can serve as sources of social capital to offset the adaptational difficulties of immigrant offspring. Specifically, it focuses on how Vietnamese culture assists the adaptation of youth in a New Orleans community by influencing orientation toward schoolwork and academic achievement.

Immigrant Cultural Orientations and Social Capital

Immigrant culture often is referred to as the "original" culture of a group, consisting of an entire way of life: languages, ideas, beliefs, values, behavioral patterns, and all that immigrants bring with them when they arrive in their new country. There are sharply contrasting views on its effects: One view sees adherence to the old ways as hindering the progress of the immigrant, while the other sees the maintenance of the original culture as facilitating adaptation.

The first view, which stems from the classic assimilationist perspective, posits that immigrants must divest themselves of their previous cultural patterns, including their ethnic identification and languages, and adopt those of the host society to become assimilated as full members of their new country. This bipolar process is usually painful and lengthy, as first-generation immigrants are trapped in a "marginal-man" situation where they are pulled in the direction of the mainstream culture but drawn back by cultures of their own (Park, 1928; Stonequist, 1937). In the assimilationist perspective, distinctive ethnic traits, such as language, religion, and skin color, are disadvantages that negatively affect assimilation (Warner and Srole, 1945). Although, as Milton M. Gordon (1964) has suggested, complete acculturation to the dominant American culture may not ensure full social participation in the society, immigrants must free themselves from their old cultures in order to rise up from marginal positions. Over the course of generations, ethnic traits gradually disappear, ethnic boundaries break down, and the descendants of immigrants become "American."

In *Italian or American? The Second Generation in Conflict*, Irving L. Child (1943) develops a typology of different ways in which immigrant children respond to the conflicting cultural values or goals of their own ethnic groups and those of the larger society. Based on the experience of Italian youth, Child classifies reactions to cultural conflict among the second generation into three possible patterns: rebellion, in-group conformity, and apathy. Rebellion involves the abandonment of ethnic membership for the sake of new affiliations, namely becoming "American." In-group conformity refers to adherence to group membership in the ethnic community. Apathy occurs when young people give up on both rebellion and in-group conformity and instead resort to escapism.

Child argues that these different patterns of adaptation are primarily results of individual attributes, such as temperament, personal experiences with the ethnic group and the larger society, and the individual's evaluation of the rewards and punishments of a particular reaction. Child does acknowledge the importance of the general public's level of acceptance of an ethnic group's "Americanization" in determining which of these three patterns of response will be chosen by the group's young. Implicitly, Child suggests that rebels are best adjusted because of their readiness to abandon old cultural patterns and embrace new ones. In-groupers and escapists, on the other hand, are underadjusted or unadjusted because of ties to ethnicity or because of conscious withdrawal from the larger society.

While the assimilationist perspective has gained credibility from research on European immigrant groups such as Italian Americans (Gans, 1979; Alba, 1985), its application to the more recent non-European immigrant groups, who have been arriving in large numbers since 1965, has met with challenges. Published evidence has suggested that immigrant adaptation is not necessarily a bipolar process but a segmented one. For the second generation, growing up with two cultures can be a matter of smooth acceptance or traumatic confrontation, and it can lead to various outcomes. One outcome may be acculturation into the mainstream culture; another may be permanent poverty and underclass membership; still a third may be rapid economic advancement with deliberate preservation of the immigrant community's values and solidarity (Portes and Zhou, 1993).

Studies of Haitian children in Miami have found that adult immigrants' pride of culture and hopes for mobility on the basis of ethnic solidarity have been shattered by the rapid assimilation of their offspring into the subculture of the impoverished black inner city (Portes and Stepick, 1993). By contrast, research on Southeast Asian refugee children has shown that, despite close proximity to urban ghettos and attendance at often troubled urban schools, many of these children have been able to succeed in school through the use of the material and social resources that their families and ethnic communities make available (Caplan, Choy, and Whitmore, 1992).

A growing body of scholarship suggests that immigrant groups may adjust their original cultural orientations to fit the current struggle for incorporation into American society and that these adjusted orientations may serve as potential resources rather than disadvantages. A number of studies have found that ethnic group membership and retention of original cultural patterns can create sources of adaptive advantages (Light, 1972; Matute-Bianchi, 1986; Gibson, 1989; Caplan, Choy, and Whitmore, 1992; Gold, 1992; Portes and Zhou, 1992; Zhou, 1992). This perspective on immigrant adaptation provides insight into how ethnicity may be utilized as a distinct form of social capital, built up from cultural endowments, such as obligations and expectations, information channels, and social norms (Coleman, 1988).

Social capital is defined as closed systems of social networks inherent in the structure of relations among persons within a collectivity (Coleman, 1990; Portes and Sensenbrenner, 1993). On the issue of education, Coleman cites evidence from Asian families that parental interest in children's learning can promote academic achievement even when the parents have little human capital. Moreover, Coleman finds that the stability and the strength of a community's social structure plays a vital role in supporting the growth of social capital in the family. Social capital in a community, in turn, allows parents " . . . to establish norms and reinforce each other's sanctioning of the children" (Coleman, 1990: 318). Conformity to the expectations of the family and the ethnic community endows individuals with support and direction.

Recent research on non-European immigrant children has indicated that social capital within the family and the community can help generate human capital in the second generation. Matute-Bianchi attributes the scholastic success of Mexican American students to a strong Mexican identity (1986: 236–240). Gibson (1989) finds that Punjabi students in California surpass the performance of their native white peers through the influence of their ethnic community by avoiding "becoming American." Similarly, studies on Indochinese refugees have found that aspects of Indochinese culture, family, and community have promoted academic achievement of Indochinese children and that they succeed in school precisely because their parents pass on cultural values that encourage achievement (Caplan, Choy, and Whitmore, 1989; 1992; Gold, 1992).

The social capital thesis is a near relative of one of the older sociological theories, Durkheim's theory of social integration. Durkheim (1951) maintains that individual behavior should be seen as the product of how integrated into their society the individuals are. The greater the integration into a social group, the greater the control of the group over the individual. In the context of immigrant adaptation, children who are more highly integrated into their ethnic group are likely to follow the forms of behavior prescribed by the group, such as studying or working hard, and to avoid the forms of behavior proscribed by the group.

If ethnic communities are interpreted in terms of social capital, it becomes possible to suggest a mechanism by which the adherence to community-based support systems and positive cultural orientations can provide an adaptive advantage for immigrants and their offspring. However, this mechanism is never stagnant; it constantly accommodates changes in the process of immigration. Social capital thus should be treated as "a process," rather than a concrete object, that facilitates access to the benefits and resources (Fernández Kelly, 1995) best suiting the goals of specific immigrant groups.

The effect of ethnicity depends on the microsocial structures on which ethnicity is based as well as on the macrosocial structures of the larger society. Ultimately, whether immigrant cultures confer disadvantages or advantages can be considered in terms of whether these original cultures frustrate or enable upward mobility on the part of the second generation. In the following analysis, we attempt to show that the "dense set of associations" (Coleman, 1990: 316) provided by the immigrant community can offer a system of supports and constraints that promote advantageous action. We stress that the community is not simply the sum of individual family units but is contained within a set of structural parameters maintained inside the group as well as imposed from outside. Thus, an explanation of differential patterns of adaptation must take into account the normative qualities of immigrant families and the patterns of social relations surrounding these families.

Data and Methods

The study is based on a case study of a Vietnamese community in New Orleans. We selected the Vietnamese as our focal group because of considerations that bear directly on the theoretical arguments just outlined. First, unlike other contemporary immigrants from Asia, the Vietnamese were mostly forced out of their homeland by the threat of political persecution. They left hastily, without adequate preparation and without much control over their final destination. Regardless of socioeconomic status before immigration, many Vietnamese started their American lives in poverty. In 1980, about a third of Vietnamese were poor, and almost all of them were on some form of government assistance (Montero, 1979; O'Hare and Felt, 1991). As a group the Vietnamese started from low levels of human and financial capital and therefore offer a good basis for studying the contribution of social capital.

Second, almost all Vietnamese immigrants arrived in the United States in the late 1970s. They have become a numerically important and highly visible segment of the American population in a remarkably short period of time. This recency of arrival and the fact that they arrived en masse mean that their life in America offers an important and unique opportunity to test theoretical explanations of immigrant adaptation.

Third, upon arrival in the United States, the Vietnamese lacked pre-existing ethnic community networks, and their resettlement was largely decided and overseen by government agencies or by voluntary agencies working with the government, such as Catholic Charities, which initially aimed at dispersing them around the country (Montero, 1979; Finnan, 1982; Starr and Roberts, 1982; Starr and Jones, 1985: 2; Duiker, 1989; Tollefson, 1989). However, after a short period of transition, the immigrants tended to cluster and rebuild their communities, mostly in declining urban neighborhoods. This residential pattern means that many Vietnamese children grow up in close proximity to urban ghettos and in the often disruptive environment of urban public schools.

The initial disadvantaged status, the recency of arrival, and their residential patterns provide a basis to expect that successful adaptation on the part of the younger generation may be accounted for either by their cultural backgrounds and ethnic solidarity or by the abandonment of these original cultural patterns. We consider adaptation as the capacity for upward social mobility. For young people, one important indication of adapting to a society is educational attainment, which we conceptualize as grades and aspirations for future education. We maintain that immigrant children, especially those in poor communities, adapt and will continue to adapt to normative structures of American society largely depending on the values they have held, the work habits they have developed, and their involvement in the ethnic community.

In the following sections, we investigate three interrelated issues: (1) What components of immigrant culture are characteristic of the Vietnamese American community under study? (2) Can we speak of a coherent complex of Vietnamese American cultural orientations? If so, what exactly is it? (3) If such a complex exists, how does it affect the academic orientation of Vietnamese youth? We first provide a description of the Vietnamese community in New Orleans to highlight certain cultural patterns unique to immigrant communities. We then conduct empirical analyses to examine how immigrant cultural patterns are related to the adaptation of the second generation.

We rely on census data, newspaper reports, and interviews with members of the community to describe the setting. Our empirical tool is a survey of Vietnamese youth attending a neighborhood public school situated in the Versailles area of eastern New Orleans, where the largest Vietnamese community in Louisiana is located. The school is a typical urban public school, overwhelmingly attended by minority students, with a unique biracial makeup: 77 percent black and 20 percent Asian. (Almost all of the Asians are Vietnamese.) About half of the Vietnamese youth residing in the Versailles area are enrolled in this school. We surveyed the entire Vietnamese student population present on the day of the survey in May 1993 (N = 198).[1]

Vietnamese Community of Eastern New Orleans

The Vietnamese community of eastern New Orleans began in 1975, after the fall of Saigon, when about one thousand refugees were settled in the Versailles area on the eastern edge of New Orleans by Associated Catholic Charities.[2] These initial one thousand residents provided the end link in a system of chain migration. In 1976, another two thousand Vietnamese arrived on their own. While Associated Catholic Charities has continued to settle Vietnamese in this area, many of the residents have been drawn by ties to friends, relatives, and former neighbors. According to Sister Ann Devaney, head of refugee social services for Catholic Charities, three-fifths of those who have settled in the community have been secondary migrants from other states. The late Reverend Michael Viet-Anh, a priest who lived in the Versailles area, estimated that "about 60 percent of the Vietnamese in the Versailles community once lived in Bui Chi province in North Vietnam and later moved to Vung Tau (a coastal town in former South Vietnam)" (Ashton, 1985: a12). Another 30 percent of the inhabitants are from two other northern villages that moved south en masse in the 1954 division of Vietnam. This reconstruction of Vietnamese villages on the bayous has resulted from channeling by ethnic networks rather than from official resettlement policy. "Despite the appearances, no villages were resettled . . . in New Orleans by Associated Catholic Charities. The villagers apparently regrouped on their own."[3]

Unlike earlier immigrant enclaves, which often were found in close proximity to central business districts of old industrial cities, the Vietnamese community was established on the fringe of New Orleans as a result of the cheap housing left vacant by a trend of "white flight" since the 1970s. Census data show that the racial composition of the Versailles area has changed from 99 percent white and 1 percent black in 1970 to 10 percent white, 46 percent black, 43 percent Vietnamese, and 1 percent other races in 1990 (U.S. Bureau of the Census, 1991). Generally, the area is characteristic of a rapidly deteriorating working-class suburb.

Table 9.1 provides some detailed demographic information on the Vietnamese community compared with Orleans Parish as a whole and the State of Louisiana. Block Group 3, which contains 70 percent of the Vietnamese in the Versailles area (Tract 17.29), is an extremely poor and essentially biracial neighborhood. Many of the people in the neighborhood are struggling economically; the median household income was only $12,790, much lower than that of Tract 17.29, the parish, and the state. About 23 percent of the households depended on public assistance, contrasted with 18 percent in the Versailles area as a whole, 15 percent in the parish, and 12 percent in the state. Nearly half of the households were below the poverty level, a much higher proportion than other areas. Moreover, Block Group 3 is made up of a higher proportion of female-headed households, except among the Vietnamese. (Over 95 percent of Asians in Block Group 3 and Tract 17.29 are Vietnamese.) These figures indicate that the Vietnamese are clustered in the poorest part of a poor area in a poor city in a poor state.

While in many respects the Vietnamese display characteristics of poverty, there is one major exception to this pattern: family structure. The overwhelming majority (81 percent) of Vietnamese families in the Versailles area were married-couple families. In Tract 17.29, female-headed families accounted for only 6 percent of the Vietnamese family households, compared with 42 percent of black families and 17 percent of white. In the most disadvantaged part of this census tract (Block Group 3), less than 7 percent of Vietnamese families were headed by females, compared with 55 percent of black families and 18 percent of white families.

Table 9.1 Comparison of Block Group 3, Tract 17.29, Orleans Parish, and Louisiana: 1990

	Block Group 3	Tract 17.29	Orleans Parish	Louisiana State
Total population	6,399	10,607	496,938	4,219,973
Percent Vietnamese	49.3	10.0	1.3	0.04
Percent black	42.0	45.8	62.1	67.3
Percent white	7.0	30.5	34.7	30.8
Percent other	1.7	1.2	1.9	1.9
Median household income (in dollars)	12,790	17,044	18,477	21,949
Percent on public assistance	23.0	18.0	15.0	12.0
Percent below poverty	48.6	37.1	31.6	23.6
Percent female-headed households	31.7	25.5	24.1	20.9
Asian	6.8	6.0	10.6	10.1
Black	55.3	41.8	50.9	45.2
White	18.3	17.3	15.7	11.5
Percent high school graduates	50.6	60.0	68.1	68.3
Asian	28.5	36.5	59.3	68.1
Black	74.6	76.2	58.4	53.1
White	67.3	73.5	81.4	74.2
Percent high school dropouts[a]	13.2	10.2	13.1	12.6
Asian	10.0	3.2	3.4	4.9
Black	18.9	14.4	15.4	14.9
White	50.0	46.0	8.1	11.3
Percent college graduates	9.4	14.4	22.4	16.1
Asian	3.6	4.0	24.0	31.4
Black	15.6	19.3	11.6	9.1
White	13.9	26.9	36.6	18.7

SOURCE: U.S. Census Bureau (1991).
[a]Defined as those aged sixteen to nineteen who were not enrolled in school and were not high school graduates.

Most of the Vietnamese are from modest socioeconomic backgrounds. As shown in table 9.1, the Vietnamese in Block Group 3 have exceptionally low levels of education; less than a third had finished high school. The limited educational level of the Vietnamese is reflected in our survey of Vietnamese youth. Among those who were able to respond to the questions about their parents' education, 80 percent said that their fathers had completed no higher level than high school education and 81 percent said that their mothers had gone no further than high school. Even these figures, however, may inflate the educational background of parents in this community, since 53 percent of the respondents were unable to report fathers' education and 59 percent of the respondents were unable to report their mothers' education. Despite the low educational level of adult Vietnamese, Vietnamese aged sixteen to nineteen had a much lower dropout rate than their American counterparts.

The Vietnamese of eastern New Orleans also have fairly low occupational status. A 1979 task force appointed by the mayor of New Orleans described them as "agriculturalists and fishermen" in their native country (Indochinese Resettlement Task Force, 1979: 10–11). The 1990 5-percent Public Use Microdata Sample of the U.S. Census of Population and Housing indicates that Vietnamese in the New Orleans metropolitan area work in relatively low-paying, blue-collar occupations. Although the Vietnamese are not concentrated in any one occupational area, the general tenor of their employment is suggested by the few jobs in which more than 3 percent of them are employed: cashiers (4 percent), waiters and waitresses (3 percent), cooks (3 percent), fishermen (3 percent), and textile sewing machine operators (5 percent) (U.S. Census Bureau, 1992).

These demographic and socioeconomic characteristics of the Vietnamese in eastern New Orleans coincide with those of the Vietnamese in the United States in general. However, this particular community is also typical of other poor immigrant communities settled in deteriorating metropolitan urban areas. If Vietnamese children of this community can advance in society, they cannot do so on the basis of the human or financial capital of their families since these are so limited, an important exception being the social capital provided by their intact families. We argue that children in this community are not supported by their families alone, however, but by the entire community, which forms the social context in which individual families function.

The most conspicuous characteristic of the Vietnamese community is the high level of normative integration of families. Vietnamese families are usually large and extended, including minor children, unmarried grown children, married children, and grandchildren. Parents and children are instilled with the idea that "the family always goes first." They honor mutual, collective obligations to one another and their relatives in order to attain respect, cooperation, and harmony within the family (Caplan, Choy, and Whitmore, 1992: 39; Gold, 1992).

Although intact families are important in the Vietnamese community, they do not function in isolation. Rather, they are contained in a web of social and kinship relations. While young people are certainly members of a social group as individuals, much of their involvement in the group is mediated by their families. Strong normative integration of families is accompanied by a high degree of consensus over values and behavioral standards, which supports goal attainment in the community. The main goal in the Vietnamese community is to incorporate into the mainstream American middle class. The Vietnamese have come to believe that education is the chief means for their children to achieve this goal, and they have adjusted their cultural patterns to orient the younger generation toward educational and occupational attainment. The interlocking family networks in the Vietnamese community reiterate and reinforce community goals and behavioral standards.

The degree of integration into the group is reflected in the behavioral patterns of group members. Just as families promote values consensus among their younger members, these families also promote behavioral conformity. Because the norms of individual families stem from the ethnic community and are supported by it, the behavior expected by parents and by others around the children are essentially the same, suggesting that young people receive little competition from other desiderata when their social world is restricted to the closed and highly interconnected circles of the ethnic group. What is considered bad or good is clearly specified and closely monitored by these networks. The community is watchful and ever-vigilant (Nash, 1992), providing effective social control over individual families and the younger generation. Both parents and children are constantly observed and judged by others under "a Vietnamese microscope" (Nash, 1992). If a child flunks out or drops out of school, or if a boy falls into a gang or a girl becomes pregnant without getting married, he or she brings shame not only to himself or herself but also to the family. On the contrary, if a child makes good grades or wins awards in school, the community honors both the individual and the family. As one parent remarked, "My children know that if they become doctor or become engineer, I share it with them, and our friends and neighbors share it. But if they fail, we all fail."

Vietnamese parents and students whom we interviewed consistently reported that their families emphasized obedience, industriousness, and helping others but discouraged egoistic values of independent thinking and popularity, which are most commonly associated with contemporary American society. Children are constantly reminded of their duty to respect their elders, to take care of younger siblings, to work hard, and to make decisions upon approval of parents. Moreover, they are pressured to avoid hanging out too much with non-Vietnamese children in the neighborhood, dating non-Vietnamese, and becoming too "American." These Vietnamese family values constitute a source of direction to guide children in their adaptation to American society.

Associated with normative integration of families is also a high level of involvement in the ethnic community. Members of this community know each other and are aware of what is going on within their community, such as what each family is doing, who has just opened up a store, who has bought a new house, who is getting married, who has died, whose child has won a scholarship, and whose child has been involved in a gang or a shameful activity. They also frequently do things together. Funerals and weddings are big family events, where people go not so much to participate in the occasion as to show off the recent accomplishments of their families, to see how others are doing, and to exchange gossip and rumors.

The high level of involvement of Vietnamese families is also seen in their close ties to the Catholic Church. More than 80 percent of Vietnamese in the Versailles area are Catholics, and the Mary Queen of Vietnam Church has served not only as a place of worship but also as the focal point of secular community activities. After-school classes for young people take place in a building behind the church. Community meetings to discuss problems and goals are held at the church at irregular intervals. Every Saturday morning, the church grounds are turned into an open-air market, where all Vietnamese in the Versailles neighborhood can sell their goods.

As some members of the community have achieved a measure of material success, and as self-employment has increased (from virtual nonexistence in 1980 to over 8 percent in 1990), a system of formal civic organizations has been established, the most important of which are the Vietnamese-American Voters' Association, the Vietnamese Educational Association, and the Vietnamese Parent-Teacher Association. Successful fishermen or owners of small businesses have become involved in these civic organizations not simply by making monetary contributions but also by taking up leadership positions. These organizations have interlocking memberships, and although their members are not precisely the same individuals at any given time, the same group of people tends to provide members for each of them. All of these civic organizations have close ties to the church, use church facilities, and work through the church in pursuing their secular goals. For example, the Vietnamese Educational Association uses the church to hold annual awards ceremonies for outstanding Vietnamese students.

Overall, this is a society in which individual members of families are integrated into a densely knit system of relations with the church as a physical and social center. Through frequent involvement in the ethnic community, Vietnamese children tend to develop and employ ethnic communication skills, to have a strong ethnic identity, and to conform to the values, behavioral standards, and expectations specified by the community. In order to understand the process of adaptation of younger members of this community, it is essential to consider these young people as members of this system of social relations rooted in Vietnamese American culture.

Adaptation of Vietnamese Youth: An Empirical Example

To what extent does this Vietnamese American community channel its children into productive directions? What are the main components of the immigrant culture under study? How may the culture furnish social support and control? Results from our high school survey provide insight into some of the important issues these questions raise about the adaptation of Vietnamese children.

We emphasize that immigrant culture is dynamic, constantly changing to fit the newly established goals in the process of immigrant adaptation. Therefore, the cultural patterns of one particular immigrant group can be quite similar to those of other immigrant groups. However, the consequences may vary depending on the ability of a group to utilize the resources already available and to generate resources on its own, and on how it is received and treated by the larger society (Portes and Rumbaut, 1990).

We first examine value orientations within the Vietnamese family. Our interviewees consistently reported that they regarded obedience, industriousness, and helping others as traditional Vietnamese family values, and they contrasted these with the independence of thinking and concern with individual social prestige (which we call "egoistic values") that they saw as characteristic of American or "Americanized" families. We asked Vietnamese students to consider whether obedience, working hard, helping others, thinking for oneself, or popularity were the most important values of their families.

Table 9.2 presents a pattern of Vietnamese family-value orientations from the perspective of young people. An overwhelming majority of the Vietnamese students who participated in the survey strongly agreed that obedience and working hard were important values in their families; less than 5 percent of them disagreed or strongly disagreed. Although responses to the item indicating the perceived im-

Table 9.2 Percentage Distribution of Family Value Orientations Among 198 Vietnamese Youth

	Strongly Agree	Agree a Little	Disagree or Strongly Disagree
Traditional family values			
My family views "to obey" as the most important value for a child to learn to prepare for life.	80.3	15.2	4.5
My family views "to work and study hard" as the most important value for a child to learn to prepare for life.	81.3	15.2	3.5
My family views "to help others whenever they need help" as the most important value for a child to learn to prepare for life.	43.4	49.0	7.6
Egoistic family values			
My family views "to think for oneself" as the most important value for a child to learn to prepare for life.	30.8	44.4	24.8
My family views "to be popular" as the most important value for a child to learn to prepare for life.	39.9	41.4	18.7

portance of helping others as a family value were not as emphatic as the responses to the other two items, the pattern remained the same: 43 percent strongly agreed while less than 8 percent disagreed or strongly disagreed with the statement that helping others was an important value in their families. In contrast, positive responses to survey items indicating the perceived importance of thinking for oneself and popularity dropped to under 40 percent while negative responses increased by more than half compared with responses to the other three statements.

Families tend to display the values of the ethnic group, and their children tend to identify with these values to the extent that they are bound up in the web of ethnic associations. The findings in table 9.2 offer quantitative support for our interviewees' perception of two distinct value orientations as representative of "traditional" Vietnamese families and "Americanized" Vietnamese families.

Next, we look at the work orientations among Vietnamese youth. We asked students to respond to two survey items: frequency of help-

Table 9.3 Percentage Distribution of Work Orientations Among 198 Vietnamese Youth By Gender

	Male	Female	Total
How often do you help with housework?			
Always	15.2	45.5	30.3
Often	23.2	25.3	24.2
Sometimes	49.5	23.2	36.4
Never	12.1	6.1	9.1
How many hours do you usually spend on homework each day?			
More than two	23.2	23.2	23.2
One to two	22.2	24.2	23.2
One-half to one	25.3	34.2	29.8
Less than one-half[a]	29.3	18.2	23.7

[a]Includes those who answered, "do not do homework." Among those who reported that they spend less than 30 minutes, about a third of them reported they did not do homework when they came home after school each day.

ing with housework and time spent on homework. These items indicate work habits and are related to two of the adolescents' most important institutional environments: home and school. In table 9.3, over half of the students reported that they always, or often, helped with housework, and only 9 percent (mostly boys) reported that they rarely did. There is a significant gender difference with regard to time spent on housework because household chores are the responsibility of girls in the Vietnamese family. But this gap narrowed in terms of time spent on homework daily. Almost half of the students (both boys and girls) reported that they spent at least an hour each day on homework. About 30 percent spent half to one hour, and less than a quarter spent under 30 minutes or did not do homework.

We next explore the extent to which Vietnamese youth are involved in their community. We construct five indicators to suggest some core aspects of ethnic involvement: languages spoken at home, Vietnamese literacy, self-identification, ethnicity of close friends, and the likelihood of endogamy. These characteristics are rooted in integration into the immigrant group and contribute to this integration. For instance, literacy is a sophisticated communication skill. The ability to speak the native language enhances communication between immigrant parents and children and between the community and its younger members. Further, acquiring the ability to read and write a language requires considerable expenditure of time and effort. When children achieve this ability, it is because parents and the community see it as important and provide encouragement and means of direction. Identifying

**Table 9.4 Percentage Distribution of Ethnic Involvement Among
198 Vietnamese Youth**

Language spoken at home	
Vietnamese	91.9
English	8.1
Ability to read and write	
Vietnamese	
Quite well	54.5
A little	33.3
Not at all	12.1
Self-identification	
Vietnamese	51.0
Vietnamese American	27.3
Other[a]	21.7
Ethnicity of Close Friends	
Vietnamese	80.3
Other	19.7
Commitment to endogamy	
Likely	59.0
Uncertain	34.4
Unlikely	6.5

[a] This category includes 15.6 percent of the students who identified as "Asian American," 6.1 percent as "other." No students identified themselves as "American."

with the ethnic group tends to make the ethnic community the primary reference group of young people. Similarly, having a preponderance of friends and associates who belong to this community means that those who encourage and validate particular attitudes and forms of behavior will share similar perspectives. The importance a young person attributes to his or her own ethnicity is reflected in the commitment to in-group marriage, and this commitment, in turn, intensifies the individual's dedication to the community and increases the community's control over the individual.

As shown in table 9.4, Vietnamese students display high levels of ethnic involvement on all of our indicators. Over 90 percent spoke Vietnamese at home; 55 percent of them reported that they were able to read and write Vietnamese well; over half of them unequivocally identified as Vietnamese rather than Vietnamese American or American; 80 percent reported that their close friends were mostly Vietnamese; and 60 percent said that they were likely to marry someone of Vietnamese origin.

Our results so far have indicated that adherence to these traditional Vietnamese family values and behavioral orientations combines with

**Table 9.5 Factor Analysis of Selected Characteristics of
198 Vietnamese Youth**

Selected Characteristic	Factor 1	Factor 2	Factor 3	Factor 4
Eigen value	2.409	1.775	1.399	1.134
Factor loadings of selected characteristics				
To obey			0.524	
To work hard			0.773	
To help others			0.718	
To be popular		0.785		
To think for oneself		0.690		
To help with housework				0.731
Time spent on homework daily				0.715
Language spoken at home	0.741			
Ability to read and write Vietnamese	0.559			
Self-identification	0.619			
Ethnicity of friends	0.639			
Commitment to endogamy	0.556			
Correlation matrix				
Factor 1 (ethnic involvement)	1.000			
Factor 2 (egoistic family values)	−0.002	1.000		
Factor 3 (traditional family values)	0.055	0.019	1.000	
Factor 4 (commitment to a work ethic)	0.125	−0.071	0.143	1.000

a high level of ethnic involvement to form a coherent complex of immigrant culture. But can we speak of a coherent complex of associated
Vietnamese American cultural orientations among Vietnamese youth?
A factor analysis has provided a positive answer. As shown in table
9.5, all variables under consideration are clearly loaded on four factors,
which we term traditional family values (to obey, to work hard, and to
help others), egoistic family values (to think for oneself and to be popular), commitment to a work ethic (time spent on housework and
homework), and ethnic involvement (language spoken at home, Vietnamese literacy, self-identification, ethnicity of friends, and the likelihood of endogamy). By creating scales of these four indicators, we can
see that while traditional family values, commitment to a work ethic,
and ethnic involvement are positively related to one another, they are
all negatively related to egoistic value orientations.[4] Therefore, we can

identify the complex of Vietnamese cultural orientations as having a strong adherence to traditional family values, a strong commitment to a work ethic, a high level of ethnic involvement, and a weak adherence to egoistic family values.

If this complex of cultural orientations exists among Vietnamese youth, how does it affect their adaptation to American society? As mentioned earlier, the Vietnamese in eastern New Orleans live in a very poor neighborhood, and the younger members of this immigrant community are vulnerable to disruptive social factors typical of urban ghettos, such as low levels of educational attainment, high dropout rates, drug abuse, and disruptive behavioral problems. For example, in 1992, only 13 percent of the students of the high school we studied equaled or exceeded the fiftieth percentile of the California Achievement Test, while over half (53 percent) of them equaled or fell below the twenty-fifth percentile (New Orleans School Board, 1993). A school supervisor whom we interviewed described the school as "serving mostly students from low-income families, with a lot of disciplinary problems." Over the past seven years, the school has had four principals. One teacher, who wished to remain anonymous, candidly attributed this turnover to the search for a principal who can keep order. Teachers at the school reported high levels of drug use and drug dealing among students, although it is difficult to quantify the prevalence of substance abuse in order to compare it with other schools. Several of the teachers reported seeing students smoke marijuana on the athletic field almost every day. Armed guards patrol the halls. "There are fights in this school every day," remarked a teacher who maintained that teachers had been targets of attacks by students.

However, there is a consensus among teachers that the Vietnamese tend to work hard, to be well disciplined, and to outperform their native minority counterparts and that, despite language difficulties for some, they are well adapted to school. The 1990 census shows that the dropout rate for the Vietnamese in the Versailles neighborhood as well as in the parish and the state was significantly lower than that for other racial groups. (See table 9.1.) Vietnamese students have consistently made up a disproportionate number of academic award recipients. In the spring of 1994, nine graduating seniors were awarded Louisiana Honors Scholarships based on academic excellence; seven of them were Vietnamese. We perceive the academic achievement of Vietnamese students as a direct result of the social capital provided by the ethnic community. We hypothesize that the coherent complex of Vietnamese American cultural orientations increases the likelihood that a student will do well in school.

Table 9.6 presents a set of bivariate relations between Vietnamese cultural orientations and academic orientation. Academic orientation is

Table 9.6 Tabulations of Self-Reported Grades, College Plans, and Academic Orientation by Selected Ethnic Characteristics of 198 Vietnamese Youth

	Most Frequently Received Grades (Percent A's and B's)	Plans to Go to College (Percent)	Number
Traditional family values			
Weak	33.3	50.0	6
Average	69.8	60.5	43
Strong	78.5	78.5	149
p	.080	.051	
Egoistic family values			
Weak	76.0	80.0	75
Average	72.7	70.5	88
Strong	80.0	68.6	35
p	.523	.640	
Commitment to a work ethic			
Weak	61.1	63.9	36
Average	76.3	72.2	114
Strong	83.3	89.6	48
p	.100	.053	
Ethnic involvement			
Weak	38.9	50.0	18
Average	75.9	72.2	79
Strong	81.2	79.2	101
p	.006	.054	

measured by current academic performance and plans for future education. To measure current academic performance, we asked respondents to report the grades that they received most often. Possible answers ranged from A or B, C, D, to F. To measure plans for future education, we asked respondents if they planned to attend college. Possible answers ranged from a definite no, uncertain, to a definite yes.

As displayed in table 9.6, almost all of the bivariate relationships between traditional family values, commitment to a work ethic, and ethnic involvement with each of the academic orientation measures were significant (one-tailed level). Specifically, students having strong traditional family values, commitment to a work ethic, and ethnic involvement disproportionately tend to receive A's and B's and to have definite college plans. As expected, egoistic family values had no significant effect on academic orientation. These results imply that immigrant cultural orientations, by promoting positive outcomes, help Vietnamese young people avoid many of the perils of their environment.

In order to examine the independent effect of each of the variables and to detail the apparent system of causal relations at work, we used a regression model controlling for sex, age upon arrival, number of siblings, living arrangement, work status of parents, and father's education. Our dependent variable, academic orientation, is a composite variable created from the sum of most frequently received grades and plans to go to college (r = .405). The values of this variable range from a high of 6 for strong academic orientation, indicating that the student received mostly A's and had definite plans to attend college, and a low of 0 for weak academic orientation indicating that the student received mostly D's and F's and had no plans for college.[5] Table 9.7 shows the means, standard deviations, range of values, and regression coefficients of major variables predicting academic orientation.

When all other effects are taken into account, adherence to traditional family values, commitment to a work ethic, and ethnic involvement all have significant effects on academic orientation, supporting the view that the involvement in an ethnic community can lead to desirable outcomes in schoolwork. Our controlled variables, which do not show significant influence, represent possible explanations of the behavior and performance of this group of Vietnamese students. It is often suggested that some young people do better than others because they have the support of unbroken, that is, two-parent, families. Similarly, it may be argued that children who have two working parents ("latch-key" children) lack support and direction and therefore have problems in developing constructive habits and in school performance. Our results support neither of these explanations at the level of the individual family. Neither having two working parents nor living in a two-parent family has a significant effect. Since many of our informants have described "broken" families as a characteristic of "Americanized" Vietnamese, this would appear to support the argument that those who are well integrated into the Vietnamese community tend to live in two-parent families and that two-parent families are more likely to subscribe to the traditional values of the ethnic community. Moreover, father's education has no significant effect on any of the endogenous variables under consideration, which contrasts with the general belief that children's school performance is due to the levels of parents' educational attainment. This finding may be a consequence of the limited range in this predictor because parental education in this sample is uniformly low. Nonetheless, it suggests that, in

Table 9.7 OLS Regression Results for Major Variables Predicting Academic Orientation of 198 Vietnamese Youth

	Mean	Standard Deviation	Minimum	Maximum	Regression Coefficient[a]
Dependent variable					
Academic orientation	4.525	1.191	0	6	n.a.
Predictors					
Traditional family values	10.869	1.268	0	12	.181** (.070)
Egoistic family values	3.929	1.559	0	8	−.026 (.056)
Commitment to a work ethic	4.126	1.768	0	7	.111* (.053)
Ethnic involvement	11.303	3.165	0	15	.063* (.028)
Control variables					
Sex (male)	.500	.501	0	1	−.102 (.173)
Age upon arrival (over 12 years)	.424	.495	0	1	−.255 (.195)
Number of siblings	3.167	2.447	0	12	.001 (.037)
Living with both parents	.747	.436	0	1	−.119 (.209)
Having both parents working	.232	.423	0	1	.005 (.204)
Father's education	.288	.454	0	1	.162 (.186)
Intercept					.686*
R^2					.129
Number of cases					198

[a]Standard error in parentheses. Statistical significance: * = $p \le .05$ (two-tailed); ** = $p \le .01$ (two-tailed).

this particular ethnic community, the social capital made available to children is more important than the human capital and other individual characteristics of parents in determining the adaptation of immigrant children.

Discussion and Conclusions

This chapter has investigated some of the ways in which Vietnamese cultural orientations can serve as a form of social capital that facilitates the adaptation of Vietnamese children to American schools and society. Our results suggest the existence of a coherent complex of immigrant cultural orientations and the significant positive influence of this cultural complex on the adaptation of Vietnamese youth. We believe that these results provide a deeper insight into the sociological literature about immigrant adaptation.

In our view, immigrant cultural orientations not only are rooted in the social structure of the immigrant community but also are responsive to the social environment surrounding the community. In disadvantaged neighborhoods where difficult conditions and disruptive elements often are found, immigrant families may have to preserve traditional values consciously by means of ethnic solidarity to prevent the next generation from assimilating into the underprivileged segments of American society in which their community is located. This ethnic solidarity may be seen as social integration into a particular ethnic community. As we have suggested in the discussion of social capital, ethnic social integration creates a form of capital that enables an immigrant family to receive ongoing support and direction from other families and from the religious and social associations of the ethnic group. Consequently, community standards are established and reinforced among group members, especially among younger members who may otherwise assimilate into an underclass subculture. We thus conclude that social capital is crucial and, under certain conditions, more important than traditional human capital for the successful adaptation of younger-generation immigrants.

This conclusion is supported by anecdotal evidence. Monsignor Dominic Luong, pastor of the Vietnamese church, has observed that the youths who spend their time idling on street corners or using drugs are those who are alienated from the society of their adult coethnics. Dr. Joseph Vuong, a Vietnamese counselor at a New Orleans junior high school, refers to the youth on the margins of the local Vietnamese culture as "overadapted" to American society. "They have become Americans in their own eyes, but they do not have the advantages of white Americans. So, they lose the direction that their Vietnamese culture can give them. Since they do not know where they are going, they just drift." The "adapted" Vietnamese youth, according to Vuong, receive direction from the ethnic networks that surround them, and, as a result, they pursue well-established goals with energy and intensity. Apparently, ideas about adaptation among members of the Vietnamese community are quite different from Child's typology, where the best adjusted are those who are most acculturated by abandoning their group membership. In the eyes of the Vietnamese, these so-called best-adjusted rebels are most likely to be the ones who are rapidly assimilated into the local underclass.

We believe that this community study provides insight into the workings of a specific Vietnamese community and offers a point of departure for studying the Vietnamese in America as a whole. At a higher level of abstraction, the conceptual links among ethnicity, social integration, and social capital that we have begun to outline can help to provide a means of understanding how patterns of social relations within ethnic groups may affect adaptation to a host society.

The issue of social context also demonstrates how different dynamics may be at work for different sets of immigrants. Above all, our results illustrate one of the paths—the least conventional—possible under the concept of segmented assimilation (Portes and Zhou, 1993). Those who have sufficient human capital or financial capital may find immediate assimilation to the host country advantageous. If immigrants possess earning power in American society, it may be desirable to move into a middle-class American suburb and adopt the outward traits and characteristics of neighbors. However, when immigrants lack individual resources, they tend to find themselves in relatively undesirable neighborhoods. In such a situation, ethnicity itself can be a resource; indeed, it may be the only resource available.

In looking at ethnicity as a resource, within a specific social context, we have suggested that social integration, one of the classic ideas in sociology, offers a way of conceptualizing how ethnicity can provide social capital. In providing children with the habits and skills for socioeconomic advancement, families do not exist in isolation; they are directed by the entire community, and they rely on the community's reinforcement.

The theoretical issues that we have raised will require more elaboration and refinement. It will be necessary, also, to delve into how and under what circumstances our findings may be generalized to other situations. Therefore, additional research is needed to examine the ways in which families are connected to one another by ethnic communities. Follow-up research on how Vietnamese young people and young people of other ethnic groups fit into the socioeconomic structures of the larger society after they leave the ethnic concentration also will yield useful insights. Finally, comparisons of the Vietnamese to other Asian and non-Asian immigrant groups, in terms of the degrees of social integration within the groups, will help to shed light on how ethnicity functions in the process of the social adaptation of immigrants.

Notes

1. The sample contains about 70 percent of all students identified as Asian in the school register. The absentees include non-Vietnamese Asians and Vietnamese students who had transferred to other schools (but whose names remained in the register), students who were sick, and those who were truants. It is plausible to suggest that the truants included a disproportionate number of low achievers. However, we do not believe that this presents a serious problem of selection. Of the minority who did not take the survey, only a portion were missing because of truancy. School officials present at the survey also felt that the large majority of students included were representative of the Vietnamese in the school. While we cannot entirely dismiss the possibility that, due to truancy, there may have been a very slight overselection of better students, the only influence on our results of missing a few of the poorest students (who would be difficult to include by any method) would be to limit variation at the bottom end of academic achievement.

2. The Associated Catholic Charities was one of the major volunteer agencies in charge of refugee resettlement in the United States. The agency has offices in major cities of Louisiana, such as New Orleans and Baton Rouge.

3. Quoted in the *Times Picayune* from an interview with the former head of Associated Catholic Charities Michael Haddad, cited in Ashton (1985).

4. A strong adherence to traditional family values indicates that the respondent strongly agreed with each of the three statements, while a weak adherence indicates that he or she strongly disagreed with the statements. Adherence to egoistic family values is scaled the same way as adherence to traditional family values. A strong commitment to a work ethic indicates that the respondent reported spending an hour or more on homework each day and always or often helped with housework, while a weak commitment indicates that he or she spent less than thirty minutes on homework each day and rarely helped with housework. A high level of ethnic involvement indicates that the respondent reported speaking Vietnamese at home, could read and write Vietnamese well, identified himself or herself unequivocally as Vietnamese, had mostly Vietnamese friends, and was committed to endogamy.

5. Except for number of siblings, all the control variables are dummy variables: sex coded 1 as male; age upon arrival coded 1 as arriving at or after age twelve; living with both parents coded 1 as yes; having both parents working coded 1 as yes; and father's education coded as 1 as completed high school education or more.

References

Abramson, H. J. 1980. "Assimilation and Pluralism." In *Harvard Encyclopedia of American Ethnic Groups*, ed. by S. Thernstrom. Cambridge, MA: Harvard University Press.

Adams, J. 1856. *Life and Works*. Boston: Little, Brown. [Originally published 1780.]

Alba, R. D. 1985. *Italian Americans: Into the Twilight of Ethnicity*. Englewood Cliffs, NJ: Prentice-Hall.

————. 1990. *Ethnic Identity: The Transformation of White America*. New Haven, CT: Yale University Press.

Anderson, E. 1990. *Streetwise: Race, Class and Change in an Urban Community*. Chicago: University of Chicago Press.

Antin, M. 1912. *The Promised Land*. New York: Houghton Mifflin.

Aschenbrenner, J. 1978. "Continuities and Variations in Black Family Structure." In *The Extended Family in Black Societies*, ed. by D. Shimkin and others. The Hague: Mouton.

Ashton, G. 1985. "Carving a Slice of American Dream." *Times Picayune*, April 1, p. A1.

Bach, R. L. 1978. "Mexican Immigration and the American State," *International Migration Review*, 12(Winter): 536–558.

Baker, R., and W. Dodd, eds. 1926. *Public Papers of Woodrow Wilson*. New York: Harper.

Baron, D. 1990. *The English-Only Question*. New Haven, CT: Yale University Press.

Barrera, M. 1980. *Race and Class in the Southwest: A Theory of Racial Inequality*. Notre Dame, IN: Notre Dame University Press.

Bean, F. D., and M. Tienda. 1987. *The Hispanic Population of the United States*. New York: Russell Sage Foundation.

Bean, F. D., B. Edmonston, and J. S. Passel, eds. 1990. *Undocumented Migration to the United States*. Washington, DC: Urban Institute.

221

Bellah, R. N., and others. 1985. *Habits of the Heart: Individualism and Commitment in American Life.* Berkeley: University of California Press.

Bernal, M. E., and G. P. Knight, eds. 1993. *Ethnic Identity: Formation and Transmission Among Hispanics and Other Minorities.* New York: State University of New York Press.

Billingsley, A. 1968. *Black Families in White America.* Englewood Cliffs, NJ: Prentice-Hall.

Boissevain, J. 1974. "Network Analysis: A Reappraisal," *Current Anthropology,* 20: 392–394.

Bonacich, E., and J. Modell. 1980. *The Economic Basis of Ethnic Solidarity: Small Business in the Japanese American Community.* Berkeley: University of California Press.

Borjas, G. J. 1985. "Assimilation, Changes in Cohort Quality, and the Earnings of Immigrants," *Journal of Labor Economics,* 3(4): 463–489.

——. 1990. *Friends or Strangers: The Impact of Immigrants on the U.S. Economy.* New York: Basic Books.

Borjas, G. J., and M. Tienda. 1987. "The Economic Consequences of Immigration," *Science,* 235: 645–651.

Borjas, G. J., and S. J. Trejo. 1991. "Immigrant Participation in the Welfare System," *Industrial and Labor Relations Review,* 44(2): 195–211.

Boswell, T. D., and J. R. Curtis. 1984. *The Cuban-American Experience.* Totowa, NJ: Rowman & Allanheld.

Bouvier, L. F., and R. W. Gardner. 1986. "Immigration to the United States: The Unfinished Story," *Population Bulletin,* 32(4): 1–44.

Briggs, V. 1984. *Immigration Policy and the American Labor Force.* Baltimore, MD: The Johns Hopkins University Press.

Bryce-Laporte, R. 1972. "Black Immigrants: The Experience of Invisibility and Inequality," *Journal of Black Studies,* 3: 29–56.

——. 1987. "New York City and the New Caribbean Immigration: A Contextual Statement." In *Caribbean Life in New York City: Sociocultural Dimensions,* ed. by C. R. Sutton and E. M. Chaney. New York: Center for Migration Studies.

Caplan, N., M. H. Choy, and J. K. Whitmore. 1989. *The Boat People and Achievement in America: A Study of Family Life, Hard Work, and Cultural Values.* Ann Arbor: University of Michigan Press.

——. 1991. *Children of the Boat People: A Study of Educational Success.* Ann Arbor: University of Michigan Press.

——. 1992. "Indochinese Refugee Families and Academic Achievement," *Scientific American,* (February): 36–42.

Carpenter, N. 1927. *Immigrants and Their Children, 1920: A Study Based on Census Statistics Relative to the Foreign-Born and the Native White of Foreign or Mixed Parentage.* Washington, DC: Government Printing Office. Reprinted in New York by Arno Press, 1960.

Child, I. L. 1943. *Italian or American? The Second Generation in Conflict.* New Haven, CT: Yale University Press.

Chiswick, B. R. 1978. "The Effect of Americanization on the Earnings of Foreign-Born Men," *Journal of Political Economy,* 86: 897–921.

————. 1979. "The Economic Progress of Immigrants: Some Apparently Universal Patterns." In *Contemporary Economic Problems*, ed. by W. Felner. Washington, DC: American Enterprise Institute.

Coleman, J. 1988. "Social Capital in the Creation of Human Capital," *American Journal of Sociology* (Supplement), S95–121.

————. 1990. *Foundations of Social Theory*. Cambridge, MA: The Belknap Press of Harvard University Press.

Cropley, A. J. 1983. *Education of Immigrant Children: A Social-Psychological Introduction*. London: Croom Helm.

Cummins, J. 1981. "Empirical and Theoretical Underpinnings of Bilingual Education," *Journal of Education*, 163(Winter): 16–29.

Daniels, R. 1990. *Coming to America: A History of Immigration and Ethnicity in American Life*. New York: HarperCollins.

De Jong, G. F. 1990. "The Changing Occupational Characteristics of Immigrants." Paper presented at the annual meeting of the American Sociological Association, Washington, DC.

De Vos, G. A., and M. M. Suárez-Orozco. 1990. *Status Inequality: The Self in Culture*. Newbury Park, CA: Sage.

Dillard, J. L. 1985. *Toward a Social History of American English*. New York: Mouton.

Dinnerstein, L., and D. M. Reimers. 1982. *Ethnic Americans: A History of Immigration and Assimilation*. Cambridge, MA: Harper & Row.

Duiker, W. J. 1989. *Vietnam Since the Fall of Saigon*. Athens, OH: Center for International Studies, Ohio University.

Duncan, B., and O. D. Duncan. 1968. "Minorities and the Process of Stratification," *American Sociological Review*, 33: 356–364.

Durkheim, E. 1951. *Suicide: A Study in Sociology*, trans. J. A. Spaulding and G. Simpson and ed. by G. Simpson. New York: The Free Press. [Originally published in 1897.]

Eisenbruch, M. 1988. "The Mental Health of Refugee Children and Their Cultural Development," *International Migration Review*, 22(2): 282–300.

Erikson, E. H. 1950. *Childhood and Society*. New York: W. W. Norton.

————. 1968. *Identity: Youth and Crisis*. New York: W. W. Norton.

Espiritu, Y. L. 1992. *Asian American Panethnicity: Bridging Institutions and Identities*. Philadelphia, PA: Temple University Press.

Farley, R. 1991. "The New Census Question about Ancestry: What Did It Tell Us?" *Demography*, 28: 411–430.

Faunce, W. A. 1984. "School Achievement, Social Status, and Self-Esteem," *Social Psychology Quarterly*, 47(1): 3–14.

Feagin, J. R. 1991. "The Continuing Significance of Race—Antiblack Discrimination in Public Places," *American Sociological Review*, 56(1): 101–116.

Fernández Kelly, M. P. 1994. "Towanda's Triumph: Social and Cultural Capital in the Transition to Adulthood in the Urban Ghetto," *International Journal of Urban and Regional Research*, 18(1): 89–111.

————. 1995. "Social Capital and Cultural Capital in the Urban Ghetto: Implications for the Economic Sociology and Immigration." In *Economic Sociology*, ed. by A. Portes. New York: Russell Sage Foundation.

Fernandez, R. M., and F. Nielsen. 1986. "Bilingualism and Hispanic Scholastic Achievement: Some Baseline Results," *Social Science Research*, 15: 43–70.

Figueroa, R. A., and E. Garcia. 1994. "Issues in Testing Students from Culturally and Linguistically Diverse Backgrounds," *Multicultural Education*, 2(Fall): 10–23.

Finnan, C. 1982. "Community Influences on the Occupational Adaptation of Vietnamese Refugees," *Anthropological Quarterly*, 55: 161–169.

Fishman, J. A. 1969. "A Sociolinguistic Census of a Bilingual Neighborhood," *American Journal of Sociology*, 75: 323–339.

Fishman, J. A., and C. Terry. 1969. "The Validity of Census Data on Bilingualism in a Puerto Rican Neighborhood," *American Sociological Review*, 34: 636–650.

Foner, N. 1987. "The Jamaicans: Race and Ethnicity Among Migrants in New York City." In *New Immigrants in New York*, ed. by N. Foner. New York: Columbia University Press.

Fordham, S. 1988. "Racelessness as a Factor in Black Students' School Success: Pragmatic Strategy or Pyrrhic Victory," *Harvard Education Review*, 58(1)(February).

Fordham, S., and J. U. Ogbu. 1987 "Black Students' School Success: Coping With the Burden of 'Acting White,' " *Urban Review*, 18(3): 176–206.

Franklin, B. 1959. *The Papers of Benjamin Franklin*, ed. by Leonard W. Labarre. New Haven, CT: Yale University Press.

Fuchs, L. H. 1990. *The American Kaleidoscope: Race, Ethnicity and the Civic Culture*. Hanover, NH: University Press of New England.

Gans, H. J. 1979. "Symbolic Ethnicity: The Future of Ethnic Groups and Cultures in America," *Ethnic and Racial Studies*, 2(1): 1–20.

———. 1990. "Deconstructing the Underclass," *APA Journal*, 56(Summer): 1–7.

———. 1992. "Second Generation Decline: Scenarios for the Economic and Ethnic Futures of Post-1965 American Immigrants," *Ethnic and Racial Studies*, 15(April): 173–192. .

Gibson, M. A. 1989. *Accommodation Without Assimilation: Sikh Immigrants in an American High School*. Ithaca, NY: Cornell University Press.

———. 1995. "Additive Acculturation as a Strategy for School Improvement." In *California's Immigrant Children: Theory, Research, and Implications for Educational Policy*, ed. by R. G. Rumbaut and W. A. Cornelius. La Jolla, CA: Center for U.S.-Mexican Studies, University of California, San Diego.

Glazer, N. 1954. "Ethnic Groups in America." In *Freedom and Control in Modern Society*, ed. by M. Berger, T. Abel, and C. Page. New York: Van Nostrand.

———. 1993. "Is Assimilation Dead?" *Annals of the American Academy of Political and Social Science*, 530: 122-136.

Gleason, P. 1980. "American Identity and Americanization." In *Harvard Encyclopedia of American Ethnic Groups*, ed. by S. Thernstrom. Cambridge, MA: Harvard University Press.

Gold, S. J. 1992. *Refugee Communities: A Comparative Field Study*. Newbury Park, CA: Sage Publications.

Gordon, M. M. 1964. *Assimilation in American Life: The Role of Race, Religion, and National Origins*. New York: Oxford University Press.

Granovetter, M. 1985. "Economic Action and Social Structure: The Problem of Embeddedness," *American Journal of Sociology*, 91: 481–510.

———. 1990. "The Old and New Economic Sociology: A History and an Agenda." In *Beyond the Marketplace*, ed. by R. Friedland and A. F. Robertson. Hawthorne, NY: Aldine de Gruyter.

Haller, A. O., and A. Portes. 1973. "Status Attainment Processes," *Sociology of Education*, 46(Winter): 51–91.

Handlin, O. 1973. *The Uprooted: The Epic Story of the Great Migrations That Made the American People*, 2nd edition, 1951. Boston: Little, Brown.

Hatcher, R., and B. Troyna. 1993. "Racialization and Children." In *Race, Identity, and Representation in Education*, ed. by C. McCarthy and W. Crichlow. New York: Routledge.

Hays, W. C., and C. H. Mindel. 1973. "Extended Kinship Relations in Black and White Families," *Journal of Marriage and the Family*, 35: 51–57.

Hill, R. B. 1971. *The Strengths of Black Families*. New York: Emerson Hall.

Hirschman, C. 1994. "The Meaning of Race and Ethnic Population Projections." Paper presented at 13th Albany Conference on American Diversity, State University of New York at Albany, April 15–16.

Hirschman, C., and E. P. Kraly. 1988. "Racial and Ethnic Inequality in the United States: 1940 and 1950," *Ethnic and Racial Studies*, 11: 332–365.

———. 1990. "Immigrants, Minorities, and Earnings in the United States: 1950," *International Migration Review*, 24: 4–33.

Hurtado, A., P. Gurin, and T. Peng. 1994. "Social Identities—A Framework for Studying the Adaptations of Immigrants and Ethnics: The Adaptation of Mexicans in the United States," *Social Problems*, 41(1): 129–151.

Hutchinson, E. P. 1956. *Immigrants and Their Children, 1850–1950*. New York: John Wiley and Sons.

Indochinese Resettlement Task Force. 1979. *Impact Analysis of Indochinese Resettlement in the New Orleans Metropolitan Area: A Task Force Study*. New Orleans, LA: Mayor's Office of Policy Planning.

Jasso, G., and M. R. Rosenzweig. 1990. *The New Chosen People: Immigrants to the United States*. New York: Russell Sage Foundation.

Jencks, C. 1992. *Rethinking Social Policy: Race, Poverty, and the Underclass*. Cambridge, MA: Harvard University Press.

Jensen, L. 1988. "Patterns of Immigration and Public Assistance Utilization, 1970–1980," *International Migration Review*, 22(1): 51–83.

———. 1989. *The New Immigration: Implications for Poverty and Public Assistance Utilization*. New York: Greenwood Press.

———. 1990. "Children of the New Immigration: A Comparative Analysis of Today's Second Generation." Working Paper No. 1990–32, Institute for Policy Research and Evaluation, Pennsylvania State University.

Kasinitz, P. 1992. *Caribbean New York: Black Immigrants and the Politics of Race*. Ithaca, NY: Cornell University Press.

Kasinitz, P., and J. Rosenberg. 1994. "Missing the Connection: Social Isolation and Employment on the Brooklyn Waterfront." Working Paper, Michael Harrington Center for Democratic Values and Social Change, Queens College of the City University of New York.

Keely, C. B. 1975. "Effects of U.S. Immigration Law on Manpower Characteristics of Immigrants," *Demography*, 12(2): 179–190.

Kerckhoff, A. C., and R. T. Campbell. 1977. "Black-White Differences in the Educational Attainment Process," *Sociology of Education*, 50(January): 15–27.

Kitano, H. 1976. *Japanese Americans: The Evolution of a Subculture*, 2nd edition. Englewood Cliffs, NJ: Prentice-Hall.

Kitano, H., and R. Daniels. 1988. *Asian Americans: Emerging Minorities*. Englewood Cliffs, NJ: Prentice-Hall.

Lambert, W. E., and G. R. Tucker. 1972. *Bilingual Education of Children: The St. Lambert Experiment*. Rowley, MA: Newbury House.

Lamm, R. D., and G. Imhoff. 1985. *The Immigration Time Bomb: The Fragmenting of America*. New York: E. P. Dutton.

Laosa, L. M. 1990. "Psychosocial Stress, Coping, and Development of Hispanic Immigrant Children." In *Mental Health of Ethnic Minorities*, ed. by F. C. Serafica and others. New York: Praeger.

Levine, D. B., K. Hill, and R. Warren, eds. 1985. *Immigration Statistics: A Story of Neglect*. Washington, DC: National Academy Press.

Levitan, S. A. 1990. *Programs in Aid of the Poor*, 6th edition. Baltimore: The Johns Hopkins University Press.

Lieberson, S. 1980. *A Piece of the Pie: Blacks and White Immigrants since 1880*. Berkeley: University of California Press.

Lieberson, S., G. Dalto, and M. E. Johnston. 1975. "The Course of Mother Tongue Diversity in Nations," *American Journal of Sociology*, 81(July): 34–61.

Light, I. 1972. *Ethnic Enterprise in America: Business Welfare among Chinese, Japanese and Blacks*. Berkeley: University of California Press.

MacLeod, J. 1995. *Ain't No Making It: Leveled Aspirations in a Low-Income Neighborhood*, 2nd edition. Boulder, CO: Westview Press.

Marckwardt, A. H. 1980. *American English*. New York: Oxford University Press.

Margolis, M. 1994. *Little Brazil, An Ethnography of Brazilian Immigrants in New York City*. Princeton, NJ: Princeton University Press.

Massey, D. 1990. "American Apartheid: Segregation and the Making of the Underclass," *American Journal of Sociology*, 96(2)(September): 329–357.

———. 1993. "Latinos, Poverty, and the Underclass: A New Agenda for Research," *Hispanic Journal of Behavioral Science*, 15(November): 449–475.

Massey, D., L. Goldring, and J. Durand. 1986. "Ethnic Identities and Patterns of School Success and Failure among Mexican-Descent and Japanese-American Students in a California High School: An Ethnographic Analysis," *American Journal of Education*, 95(1): 233–255.

———.1994. "Continuities in Transnational Migration: An Analysis of Nineteen Mexican Communities," *American Journal of Sociology*, 99(May): 1492–1533.

Matute-Bianchi, M. E. 1991. "Situational Ethnicity and Patterns of School Performance Among Immigrant and Nonimmigrant Mexican-Descent Students." In *Minority Status and Schooling: A Comparative Study of Immigrant and Involuntary Minorities*, ed. by M. Gibson and J. U. Ogbu. New York: Garland.

McKenney, N. R., and A. R. Cresce. 1993. "Measurement of Ethnicity in the United States: Experiences of the U.S. Bureau of the Census." In *Challenges of Measuring an Ethnic World: Science, Politics, and Reality: Proceedings of the Joint Canada-United States Conference on the Measurement of Ethnicity, April 1–3, 1992.* Washington, DC: Government Printing Office.

Michael, S. 1990. "Children of the New Wave Immigration." In *Emerging Perspectives on the Black Diaspora,* ed. by A. V. Bonnett and G. L. Watson. Lanham, MD: University Press of America.

Min, P. G., ed. 1995. *Asian Americans: Contemporary Trends and Issues.* Thousand Oaks, CA: SAGE Publications.

Montero, D. 1979. *Vietnamese Americans: Patterns of Resettlement and Socioeconomic Adaptation in the United States.* Boulder, CO: Westview Press.

———. 1980. *Japanese Americans: Changing Patterns of Ethnic Affiliation over Three Generations.* Boulder, CO: Westview Press.

Moynihan, D. P. 1969. *Maximum Feasible Misunderstanding.* New York: Random House.

Nash, J. W. 1992. *Vietnamese Catholicism.* Harvey, LA: Art Review Press.

Neidert, L. J., and R. Farley. 1985. "Assimilation in the United States: An Analysis of Ethnic and Generation Differences in Status and Achievement," *American Sociological Review,* 50: 840–850.

New Orleans School Board. 1993. *Norm-Reference Test Result of the New Orleans Public Schools: A Comprehensive Report on Their Relationship to Major Student Characteristics.* Prepared by the Department of Educational Accountability, Division of Educational Programs. New Orleans, LA.

Ogbu, J. U. 1990. "Minority Status and Literacy in Comparative Perspective," *Daedalus,* 119(2)(Spring): 141–168.

———. 1991. "Immigrant and Involuntary Minorities in Comparative Perspective." In *Minority Status and Schooling: A Comparative Study of Immigrant and Involuntary Minorities,* ed. by M. A. Gibson and J. U. Ogbu. New York: Garland.

O'Hare, W. P., and J. C. Felt. 1991. *Asian Americans: America's Fastest Growing Minority Group.* Report by Population Reference Bureau, Inc.

Olsen, L. 1988. *Crossing the Schoolhouse Border: Immigrant Students and the California Public Schools.* San Francisco: California Tomorrow.

Owens, T. J. 1994. "Two Dimensions of Self-Esteem: Reciprocal Effects of Positive Self-Worth and Self-Deprecation on Adolescent Problems," *American Sociological Review,* 59(3): 391–407.

Papademetriou, D. G., and others. 1989. *The Effects of Immigration on the U.S. Economy and Labor Market.* Immigration Policy and Research Report 1. Washington, DC: U.S. Department of Labor.

Park, R. 1928. "Human Migration and the Marginal Man," *American Journal of Sociology,* 33: 881–893.

Passel, J. S., and B. Edmonston. 1992. "Immigration and Race: Recent Trends in Immigration to the United States." Paper No. PRIP-UI-22. Washington, DC: The Urban Institute.

———. 1994. "Immigration and Race: Recent Trends in Immigration to the United States." In *Immigration and Ethnicity: The Integration of America's*

Newest Arrivals, ed. by B. Edmonston and J. S. Passel. Washington, DC: The Urban Institute Press.

Peal, E., and W. E. Lambert. 1962. "The Relation of Bilingualism to Intelligence," *Psychological Monograph* 76(27): 1–23.

Pérez, L. 1986a. "Cubans in the United States," *Annals of the American Academy of Political and Social Science,* 487(September): 126–137.

———. 1986b. "Immigrant Economic Adjustment and Family Organization: The Cuban Success Story Reexamined," *International Migration Review,* 20(1)(Spring): 4–20.

Persons, S. 1987. *Ethnic Studies at Chicago 1905–45.* Urbana: University of Illinois Press.

Phinney, J. S. 1990. "Ethnic Identity in Adolescents and Adults: Review of Research," *Psychological Bulletin,* 108(3): 499–514.

——— 1991. "Ethnic Identity and Self-Esteem: A Review and Integration," *Hispanic Journal of Behavioral Sciences,* 13(2): 193–208.

Piore, M. 1979. *Birds of Passage.* New York: Cambridge University Press.

Porter, J. R., and R. E. Washington. 1993. "Minority Identity and Self-Esteem," *Annual Review of Sociology,* 19: 139–161.

Portes, A. 1978. "Migration and Underdevelopment," *Politics and Society,* 8: 1–48.

———. 1984. "The Rise of Ethnicity: Determinants of Ethnic Perceptions among Cuban Exiles in Miami," *American Sociological Review,* 49(3): 383–397.

———. 1993. "The Longest Migration," *The New Republic,* 26(April): 38–42.

Portes, A., and R. G. Rumbaut. 1990. *Immigrant America: A Portrait.* Berkeley: University of California Press.

Portes, A., and J. Sensenbrenner. 1993. "Embeddedness and Immigration: Notes on the Social Determinants of Economic Action," *American Journal of Sociology,* 98(May): 1320–1350.

Portes, A., and A. Stepick. 1993. *City on the Edge: The Transformation of Miami.* Berkeley: University of California Press.

Portes, A., and C. Truelove. 1987. "Making Sense of Diversity: Recent Research on Hispanic Minorities in the United States," *Annual Review of Sociology,* 13: 359–385.

Portes, A., and M. Zhou. 1992. "Gaining the Upper Hand: Economic Mobility among Immigrant and Domestic Minorities," *Ethnic and Racial Studies,* 15: 491–522.

———. 1993. "The New Second Generation: Segmented Assimilation and Its Variants," *Annals of the American Academy of Political and Social Sciences,* 530(November): 74–96.

Reimers, D. M. 1992. *Still the Golden Door: The Third World Comes to America,* 2nd edition. New York: Columbia University Press.

Rieff, D. 1987. *Going to Miami: Exiles, Tourists, and Refugees in the New America.* Boston: Little, Brown.

Roberts, B. 1995. "The Effect of Socially Expected Durations on Mexican Migration." In *The Economic Sociology of Immigration: Essays on Networks, Ethnicity, and Entrepreneurship,* ed. by A. Portes. New York: Russell Sage Foundation.

Rosenberg, M. 1965. *Society and the Adolescent Self-Image*. Princeton, NJ: Princeton University Press.

———. 1979. *Conceiving the Self*. New York: Basic Books.

Rosenberg, M., C. Schooler, and C. Schoenbach. 1989. "Self-Esteem and Adolescent Problems: Modeling Reciprocal Effects," *American Sociological Review*, 54: 1004–1018.

Rosenblum, G. 1973. *Immigrant Workers: Their Impact on American Radicalism*. New York: Basic Books.

Rothman, E. S., and T. J. Espenshade. 1992. "Fiscal Impacts of Immigration to the United States," *Population Index*, 58: 381–415.

Ruggles, P. 1990. *Drawing the Line: Alternative Poverty Measures and Their Implications for Public Policy*. Washington, DC: Urban Institute Press.

Rumbaut, R. D., and R. G. Rumbaut. 1976. "The Family in Exile: Cuban Expatriates in the United States," *American Journal of Psychiatry*, 133(4): 395–399.

Rumbaut, R. G. 1990. *Immigrant Students in California Public Schools: A Summary of Current Knowledge*. CDS Report No. 11. Baltimore, MD: Center for Research on Effective Schooling for Disadvantaged Students, Johns Hopkins University.

———. 1991. "The Agony of Exile: A Study of Indochinese Refugee Adults and Children." In *Refugee Children: Theory, Research, and Services*, ed. by F. L. Ahearn, Jr. and J. L. Athey. Baltimore, MD: Johns Hopkins University Press.

———. 1994. "Origins and Destinies: Immigration to the United States Since World War II," *Sociological Forum*, 9(4): 583–621.

———. 1995. "The New Californians: Comparative Research Findings on the Educational Progress of Immigrant Children." In *California's Immigrant Children: Theory, Research and Implications for Educational Policy*, ed. by R. G. Rumbaut and W. A. Cornelius. La Jolla, CA: Center for U.S.-Mexican Studies, University of California, San Diego.

———. Forthcoming. "Ties That Bind: Immigration and Immigrant Families in the United States." In *Immigration and the Family*, ed. by A. Booth, A. C. Crouter, and N. S. Landale. Hillsdale, NJ: Lawrence Erlbaum Associates.

Rumbaut, R. G., and K. Ima. 1988. "Determinants of Educational Attainment among Indochinese Refugees and Other Immigrant Students." Paper presented at the annual meeting of the American Sociological Association, Atlanta. August.

———. 1988. *The Adaptation of Southeast Asian Refugee Youth: A Comparative Study*. Washington, DC: U.S. Office of Refugee Resettlement.

Sánchez, G. J. 1993. *Becoming Mexican American: Ethnicity, Culture and Identity in Chicano Los Angeles, 1900-1945*. New York: Oxford University Press.

Sanjek, R. 1974. "What Is Network Analysis and What Is It Good For?" *Reviews in Anthropology*, 1: 588–597.

Sassen, S. 1988. *The Mobility of Labor and Capital: A Study in International Investment and Labor Flow*. New York: Cambridge University Press.

———. 1995. "Immigration and Local Labor Markets." In *The Economic Sociology of Immigration: Essays on Networks, Ethnicity, and Entrepreneurship*, ed. by A. Portes. New York: Russell Sage Foundation.

Sewell, W. H., and R. M. Hauser. 1972. "Causes and Consequences of Higher Education: Models of the Status Attainment Process," *American Journal of Agricultural Economics*, 54(December): 651–661.

Simon, J. 1984. "Immigrants, Taxes and Welfare in the United States," *Population and Development Review*, 10(1): 55–69.

Smith, R. C. 1992. *"Los ausentes siempre presentes:* The Imagining, Making, and Politics of a Transnational Community between New York City and Ticuani, Puebla." Manuscript. Institute for Latin American and Iberian Studies, Columbia University, New York, October.

Sowell, T. 1981. *Ethnic America: A History.* New York: Basic Books.

Stafford, S. B. 1987. "Language and Identity: Haitians in New York City." In *Caribbean Life in New York City: Sociocultural Dimensions*, ed. by C. R. Sutton and E. M. Chaney. New York: Center for Migration Studies.

Starr, P. D., and W. Jones, Jr. 1985. *Indochinese Refugees in America: Problems of Adaptation and Assimilation.* Durham, NC: Duke University Press.

Starr, P. D., and A. E. Roberts. 1982. "Occupational Adaptation of Refugees in the United States," *International Migration Review*, 13: 25–45.

Stepick, A., and C. Dutton-Stepick. 1994. "Preliminary Haitian Needs Assessment." Report to the City of Miami. June.

Stewart, S. A. 1993. "New Page in English-only Debate," *USA Today*, June 25, 1993, p. 8A.

Stonequist, E. V. 1937. *The Marginal Man.* New York: Charles Scribner's Sons.

Suárez-Orozco, M. M. 1989. *Central American Refugees and U.S. High Schools: A Psychosocial Study of Motivation and Achievement.* Palo Alto, CA: Stanford University Press.

———. 1991. "Immigrant Adaptation to Schooling: A Hispanic Case." In *Minority Status and Schooling: A Comparative Study of Immigrant and Involuntary Minorities*, ed. by M. A. Gibson and J. U. Ogbu. New York: Garland.

Suárez-Orozco, M. M., and C. Suárez-Orozco. 1995. "The Cultural Patterning of Achievement Motivation: A Comparative Study of Mexican, Mexican Immigrant, and Non-Latino White American Youths in Schools." In *California's Immigrant Children: Theory, Research, and Implications for Educational Policy*, ed. by R. G. Rumbaut and W. A. Cornelius. La Jolla, CA: Center for U.S.-Mexican Studies, University of California, San Diego.

Sung, B. L. 1987. *The Adjustment Experience of Chinese Immigrant Children in New York City.* Staten Island, NY: Center for Migration Studies.

Sutton, C. R., and S. P. Makiesky. 1975. "Migration and West Indian Racial and Ethnic Consciousness." In *Migration and Development: Implications for Ethnic Identity and Political Conflict*, ed. by H. I. Safa and B. M. Du Toit. Paris: Mouton and Co.

Tajfel, H. 1981. *Human Groups and Social Categories.* London: Cambridge University Press.

Taylor, R. L. 1994. "Black American Families." In *Minority Families in the United States: A Multicultural Perspective*, ed. by R. L. Taylor. Englewood Cliffs, NJ: Prentice-Hall.

Thernstrom, S., ed. 1980. *Harvard Encyclopedia of American Ethnic Groups.* Cambridge, MA: Harvard University Press.

Thomas, W. I., and F. Znaniecki. 1958. *The Polish Peasant in Europe and America*, Vol. 2. New York: Dover. [Originally published in five volumes, 1918–1920.]

Tollefson, J. 1989. *Alien Winds: The Reeducation of America's Indochinese Refugees*. New York: Praeger.

U.S. Bureau of the Census. 1991. *Census of Population and Housing, 1990: Summary Tape File 3* (Louisiana) [machine producer and distributor]. Washington, DC: Department of Labor.

———. 1992a. *Census of Population and Housing, 1990: Public Use Microdata Samples U.S.* [Machine-readable data files]. Washington, DC: Bureau of the Census.

———. 1992b. *Census of Population and Housing, 1990: Public Use Microdata Sample U.S. Technical Documentation*. Washington, DC: Bureau of the Census.

———. 1992c. *Census of Population, 1990: General Population Characteristics, United States*. Washington, DC: U.S. Government Printing Office.

———. 1993a. *Census of Population: The Foreign-Born Population in the United States, 1990 CP-3–1*. Washington, DC: Government Printing Office.

———. 1993b. *1990 Census of Population: The Asians and Pacific Islanders in the United States, 1990 CP-3–5*. Washington, DC: Government Printing Office.

———. 1993c. *1990 Census of Population: Persons of Hispanic Origin in the United States, 1990 CP-3–3*. Washington, DC: Government Printing Office.

U.S. Department of Labor, Bureau of International Labor Affairs. 1989. *The Effects of Immigration on the U.S. Labor Economy and Labor Market*. Immigration Policy and Research, Report No. 1. Washington, DC: U.S. Department of Labor.

U.S. Immigration and Naturalization Service. 1991. *Statistical Yearbook of the Immigration and Naturalization Service, 1990*. Washington, DC: U.S. Government Printing Office.

Vega, W. A., and R. G. Rumbaut. 1991. "Ethnic Minorities and Mental Health," *Annual Review of Sociology*, 17: 351–383.

Vega, W. A., R. L. Hough, and A. Romero. 1983. "Family Life Patterns of Mexican-Americans." In *The Psychological Development of Minority Group Children*, ed. by G. J. Powell. New York: Bruner/Mazel.

Vigil, J. D. 1988. *Barrio Gangs: Street Life and Identity in Southern California*. Austin: University of Texas Press.

Waldinger, R. 1992. "The Making of an Immigrant Niche." Manuscript. University of California–Los Angeles.

Warner, W. L., and L. Srole. 1945. *The Social Systems of American Ethnic Groups*. New Haven, CT: Yale University Press.

Waters, M. C. 1990. *Ethnic Options: Choosing Identities in America*. Berkeley: University of California Press.

———. Forthcoming. "The Intersection of Gender, Race and Ethnicity in Identity Development of Caribbean American Teens." In *Urban Adolescent Girls: Resisting Stereotypes*, ed. by B. Leadbeater and N. Way. New York: New York University Press.

Whyte, W. F. 1955. *Street Corner Society: The Social Structure of an Italian Slum*, 2d ed. Chicago: University of Chicago Press.

Wilson, W. J. 1987. *The Truly Disadvantaged: The Inner-City, the Underclass, and Public Policy*. Chicago: University of Chicago Press.

————. 1991. "Studying Inner-City Social Dislocations: The Challenge of Public Agenda Research," *American Sociological Review*, 56(1): 1–14.

Woldemikael, T. M. 1989. *Becoming Black American: Haitian and American Institutions in Evanston, Illinois*. New York: AMS Press.

Yinger, J. M. 1981. "Toward a Theory of Assimilation and Dissimilation," *Ethnic and Racial Studies*, 4(3): 249–264.

————. 1994. *Ethnicity: A Source of Strength? Source of Conflict?* Albany, NY: State University of New York Press.

Zhou, M. 1992. *Chinatown: The Socioeconomic Potential of an Urban Enclave.* Philadelphia: Temple University Press.

————. 1992. *New York's Chinatown: The Socioeconomic Potential of an Urban Enclave.* Philadelphia: Temple University Press.

Index